John Barnard Byles

Sophisms of Free-Trade and Popular Political Economy Examined

John Barnard Byles

Sophisms of Free-Trade and Popular Political Economy Examined

ISBN/EAN: 9783744735254

Printed in Europe, USA, Canada, Australia, Japan

Cover: Foto ©Suzi / pixelio.de

More available books at **www.hansebooks.com**

SOPHISMS OF FREE-TRADE

AND

POPULAR POLITICAL ECONOMY

EXAMINED.

BY A BARRISTER.

(SIR JOHN BARNARD BYLES, JUDGE OF COMMON PLEAS.)

"A nation, whether it consume its own productions, or with them purchase from abroad, can have no more to spend than it produces. Therefore, the supreme policy of every nation is to develop its own producing forces."

FIRST AMERICAN, FROM THE NINTH ENGLISH EDITION,

AS PUBLISHED BY THE MANCHESTER RECIPROCITY ASSOCIATION.

MANCHESTER:
JOHN HEYWOOD, 141 AND 143 DEANSGATE.
LONDON: SIMPKIN, MARSHALL & CO.

PHILADELPHIA:
HENRY CAREY BAIRD,
INDUSTRIAL PUBLISHER,
406 WALNUT STREET.
1872.

PREFACE TO THE AMERICAN EDITION

'SOPHISMS OF FREE TRADE," now for the first time presented to the American public through the medium of an American edition, is a volume which has long been famous in England, and deserves a widely extended circulation in this country, especially at the present time, when the questions here brought under review are attracting so great a degree of public attention. The first English edition appeared in 1849, the ninth in 1870. Almost from the first hour of its appearance it took rank as one of the most acute and vigorous treatises within the entire range of economic literature, and it is not asserting too much to say that it holds that position at this moment. Neither have its arguments been successfully answered.

The author, the HON. SIR JOHN BARNARD BYLES, KNT. BACHL., is a man who would occupy an eminent position in any country. Born at Stowmarket, Suffolk, 1801, he was called to the bar at the Inner Temple, 1831; went the Norfolk circuit; was appointed recorder of Buckingham, 1840; serjeant at law, 1843;

i

was made Queen's serjeant, 1857; and judge of the
Common Pleas, 1858, an important post, which he still
continues to fill and to adorn. Upon occasion of being
called to the bench, he received the honor of knight-
hood. Besides the present, he is the author of a
volume "On the Usury Laws" and a "Treatise on
Bills of Exchange." The last-named is well known
to the bench and bar of Great Britain, the United
States, and all English-speaking countries, as a work of
the very highest merit and authority. The "Sophisms"
will now, it is believed, make his name and fame
familiar to a large body of thoughtful Americans beyond these limits, who are ardently and earnestly
working for the wealth, prosperity and happiness of
their country, and believe that these results are to be
arrived at only by building up and sustaining throughout our broad land, and among its ingenious and
enterprising people, a thoroughly diversified industry.

H. C. B.

PHILADELPHIA,
Feb. 22, 1872.

PREFACE TO THE FIRST EDITION.

———•◦•◦•———

Whoever contemplates, on the one hand, the enormous powers of production in the United Kingdom, and on the other, the misery which nevertheless grinds down masses of the population, will necessarily conclude that the circumstances which ensure or promote the creation and due distribution of wealth, are yet unknown or mistaken. He will see the science which assumes to teach these things, discredited, helpless, and utterly at fault. There must be something fearfully wrong or essentially deficient in the prevailing system: there must necessarily be some *error in theory*. No adequate practical measures of relief can be devised till it is discovered.

The following sheets are not written to aid a party, but to assist, if possible, in reaching the truth on a very complex and difficult subject. Protectionists will find no defence of a high price of subsistence, and free-traders no acquiescence in their recommendation of unlimited and indiscriminate imports.

If any who profess the doctrines of modern English political economy, should condescend to cast their eye on these pages, they will, no doubt, dissent from nearly all that is said on free-trade, population, pauperism, wages and currency.   But among political economists,* as well as among their opponents, in England, France, Germany, and America, are to be found those who cherish the true spirit of scientific inquiry.   That spirit is a simple devotion to THE TRUTH, whatever it shall turn out to be, and an entire indifference to the results of inquiry, so that they be but TRUE.†   Criticism and correction by such are not deprecated—they are respectfully and earnestly invited.

The vulgar, however, on both sides are incapable of independent judgment, take their opinions on trust, and mix up abstract and scientific truth with strong party feelings and predilections.   They begin to read with a secret but irresistible wish before-hand that a particular doctrine should prove true.   The discovery of truth is not given to such a disposition.   On complex and really disputable subjects, what a man earnestly wishes to be true, he will find true.   Reading and enquiry only serve to entrench him in his notions. Whether those notions be truth or error is the result, not of really free and unprejudiced inquiry, but of previous accident.

---

* Mr. Mill is an example.

† "To be indifferent which of two opinions is true, is the right temper of the mind that preserves it from being imposed on, and disposes it to examine.   This is the only direct and safe way to TRUTH."—Locke.

An apology is due from a lawyer who presumes to meddle with subjects out of his own profession. He is, it is said, a man of narrow mind, and necessarily limited information. It is not for him to say (perhaps he could not say) that the imputation is unjust. But, by way of compensation, he has, on a subject of this nature, some advantages over others. That narrow and microscopic vision with which he is charged, does not altogether unfit him for the minute and steady examination of the abstract *theories* of political economy. He has no interest, except in the general welfare; and living, as a mere lawyer does, retired from the world and general politics, he has a chance of being in a measure exempt from the prejudices of party, and from that fanaticism, which in politics and political economy, as well as in other things, sometimes, like an epidemic seizes the people, high and low.

In France, Germany, Holland, and the United States, the general opinion of educated men on these subjects is very different from that which yet reigns here. Indeed, until lately, no Englishman, who should have ventured to dispute the passionate persuasion of the public, could have hoped for a fair and candid hearing. It was necessary to wait. As a brilliant Frenchman once said of fanaticism of a different sort, "Il faut attendre que l'air soit purifié."

No one is more conscious of the defects to be found in these pages, than the writer. He is sensible that a more popular tone has been adopted than is perhaps quite appropriate to the severity of such inquiries. But it was necessary.   A mere dry dissertation, in the better style of political economists, about yards of cloth and quarters of corn, would never have had even a chance of being read.   He trusts, however, that he has not been betrayed into any disrespectful or uncandid language towards those who think differently, and who are perhaps better informed.

London   October 31, 1849.

CONTENTS.

POSITIONS EXAMINED.

1*   vii

CHAPTER V.

CHAPTER VI.

CHAPTER VII.

CHAPTER VIII.

CHAPTER IX.

CHAPTER X.

CHAPTER XI.

CHAPTER XIX.

CHAPTER XXVI.

CHAPTER XXVII.

CHAPTER XXVIII.

CHAPTER XXIX.

CHAPTER XXX.

CHAPTER XXXI.

CHAPTER XXXII.

SOPHISMS OF FREE-TRADE

AND

POPULAR POLITICAL ECONOMY EXAMINED.

CHAPTER I.

"Political economy is a science."

THE fallacy seems to lie in using the present tense, instead of the future tense. Political economy *will be* a science. The political economy of Munn and Gee in 1750 was very different from the political economy of M'Culloch and Mill* in 1850. But, perhaps, it was not more different than the political economy of M'Culloch and Mill now is, from what will be the political economy of 1950.

If by a science be meant a collection of truths ascertained by experiment, and on which all well-informed men are agreed, then political economy is manifestly not yet a science.

If by a science be meant a subject on which some little has gradually become known, but the great body of solid knowledge yet remains to be discovered by experience, observation, and patient thought, then, indeed, in this lower sense, political economy is a science.

------

* I desire to speak of Mr. Mill with the utmost respect, and the more so because on other recondite subjects, where he thinks himself to have been in error, he has the candor to say so.

13

But if political economy claim to be a science at all, she must abate much of her pretensions, much of her dogmatism, descend to a lower rank, and adopt a more modest and inquiring tone; she must learn to tolerate doubt, to endure contradiction. If she aspire to learn in the book of experience, she must expect as she turns over the leaves to meet with problems wholly unexpected, and ultimate solutions at variance with all preconceived notions; she must make up her mind to see theory after theory supported by great names, and confidently propounded, yet after all rebuked and exposed by experiment; she must remember that there are twenty wrong courses of public policy to one right one, and that all the erroneous ones are often tried before the right one can be demonstrated by experience to be right.

A slow, painful, humiliating road to knowledge—but the only true one. Other paths may lead to conjecture or opinion more or less plausible; this alone to certain and demonstrable knowledge. But what we want is, not to conjecture, but to *know;* in the forcible language of the father of experimental philosophy, "haud belle et probabiliter opinari, sed certo et ostensive scire."

What experimental science is there in which the whole truth was discovered at once, or in the course of a few years? Much less are we to suppose that we have been favored with sudden and preternatural illumination on a subject so complex and difficult as political economy.

If we would form a just estimate of our modern English notions on this matter, we must look backwards, look around us, and look forward; or we shall resemble the rustic, whose history and geography are circumscribed by his own life in his own parish.

We must look backwards into times past.

When modern political economists are spoken of as

if nobody knew anything before them, and as if nobody will discover anything of moment after them, we may be sure that we hear the language of empiricism, not of science. "Vixere fortes ante Agamemnona." There are many writers before Adam Smith, of whom posterity will form an estimate more favorable than is now entertained. Bacon, Montesquieu, Fénélon, Petty, Swift, and Voltaire will not hereafter be less esteemed because they did not use the parade of scientific terms, and were not embarrassed by modern and doubtful theories.

The need of a political economy, very different from the inert and barren system now in fashion, is but too apparent to any one who looks around him. Modern society presents to the serious observer, as the consequences of past and present systems of political economy, practical results by no means flattering. The immense progress of physical science has multiplied a thousandfold the means of producing wealth. There is in the overflowing and exhaustless bounty of · nature, not only enough, but a superfluity for every one of the children of men. Yet some mysterious and invisible but impassable barrier impedes its distribution, and shuts out the masses from the promised land. Portentous and gigantic social evils, present and approaching, mock the wisdom of the wise.

Political economists! Look at England's boundless wealth and hopeless poverty; at Ireland's dearest children escaping for their lives, like Lot from the cities of the plain! at the periodical alternations of manufacturing prosperity and manufacturing depression and starvation! at the expanse of untilled or half-cultivated lands, spread abroad amidst a starving, idle, and congested population! at your own differences and disagreements about rent, population, currency, wages, profits! at the theories opposed to yours (not only in fashion and in power) in France, Germany, Russia, and

America, but supported by the most original thinkers and greatest writers. Some of these writers have been unjust to you. They affirm that instead of a science, solid and practical, you are but the authors of a literature, unsatisfactory, obscure, presumptuous, and which would be dangerous, were it not eminently tedious.*

But we must also look forward with courage and confidence. The imperfect and rudimentary condition of the science of political economy, while it accounts for present evils, is for that very reason the sure ground of hope for the future. It is manifest that we have not yet hit on the true theory. But in the meantime, the tools and implements with which the new and true political economy is destined to work, are beginning to multiply around us. The Steam-engine, Steam-navigation, Railways, Mechanical Inventions, the Electric Telegraph, Modern Chemistry, have not appeared for nothing. A science of political economy will yet dawn that shall perform as well as promise—a science that will rain the riches of nature into the laps of the starving poor. Men do not even yet dream of the prosperity which is in store for all orders of the people.

As in other sciences, so in political economy, each accession of knowledge will not only be a step to further, but to greater acquisitions. True and solid knowledge will not only advance, but advance in a continually increasing ratio. The world now presents a variety of communities far advanced in civilisation; the field of experience is enlarged and diversified. But, besides ordinary experience, there is an artificial experience, which is called *experiment*. At this moment the anxious and vigilant attention of theoretical and practical men is invited to vast *experiments* now in progress. It were to be wished that some other community, and not the noble British Empire, had been selected as the *vile*

---

* M. Thiers.

corpus of experiment. We shall suffer much, and what is worse, the innocent will be the sufferers. We shall probably lose a large portion of our possessions. But we shall be wiser. We shall finally adopt the true policy, and after much tribulation enter a better state of things.

Is it more correct to say that political economy *is already* a science. or that it *will be* one?

CHAPTER II.

" Legislate on sound principles."

WHICH, being interpreted, means, "SURRENDER
YOURSELF TO THE SPIRIT OF SYSTEM"—"CARRY OUT
YOUR THEORIES."

The SPIRIT OF SYSTEM, a fertile source of error, fertile in most sciences, is peculiarly so in political economy.
It is a foe to solid knowledge; the more insidious and
fatal because it usually ·accompanies superior mental
capacity, being very nearly allied to that love and relish
of truth which distinguishes minds of a superior order.*
The spirit of system consists in a tendency to reduce all
phenomena to a few general rules, and to find a greater
degree of order, symmetry, and simplicity in the natural,
moral, or political world than really exists, or can exist.
Instead of expanding the mind to the rich and endless

---

* History shews that it is not the learned only whom the spirit
of system fascinates and misleads : it is sometimes an epidemic
passion, or fever, maddening all ranks down to the very popu-
lace.

Republican government has the charm of simplicity. The
English and French nations have accordingly been seized, each
in their turn, with a fanaticism for it. Straightway the blessings
of prescriptive and stable government were sacrificed, and blood
poured out like water, for an impracticable political theory.

So, a few years ago, England was fascinated with the specious
and simple theory of free-trade. The agricultural interest, the
colonies, the shipping interest, the whole kingdom of. Ireland
were dust in the balance ; the manufacturing towns, who were
the most clamorous for the change, little dreaming that they
would be the first and greatest sufferers. The enthusiasm is beginning to evaporate, and men will soon marvel how they ever
came to be under its influence.

variety and subtilty * of nature or art, it would contract that variety to the narrow limits of the human understanding. It finds ready acceptance with all men; for it flatters both the pride and the indolence of human nature. It is much easier to comprehend and apply a few general rules than to understand the complicated structure and regulations of human society. Any man may make a parade of knowledge by dogmatising about imaginary general principles, but to master facts, details, and the results of experience, is a long, toilsome, and humbling occupation.

Men are not often undeceived who worship a few general principles, however erroneous. When a man has grown grey in the honest assertion of doctrines which he believed to be right, has spent in the endeavor to disseminate them his best years, depends on them for his reputation and self-approval, what a cruel fate to be undeceived—to discover that they are not only erroneous, but mischievous! Besides there is no longer vigor of mind left to straighten the erroneous bent of early life. Accordingly, we find that erroneous general principles last for a generation; that to expect an inveterate theorist to abandon his theories is as reasonable as to expect him to slay his children. The seed of truth must be sown in the fresh and grateful soil of a new generation.

Lord Bacon† warns us of this tendency of the human

---

* Subtilitas naturæ subtilitatem sensûs et intellectûs multis partibus superat.—*Nov. Org.*

† The following observations of Professor Playfair seem especially to deserve the attention of political economists:

"The idols of the *tribe*, or of the race, are causes of error founded on human nature in general, or on principles common to all mankind. 'The mind,' Lord Bacon observes, 'is not like a plain mirror which reflects the image of things exactly as they are: it is like a mirror of uneven surface, which combines its own figure with the figures of the object it represents.'

"Among the idols of this class we may reckon the propensity which there is in all men to find in nature a greater degree of

mind to expect a greater degree of order, regularity, and conformity with general rules than really exists.* He calls it, in his poetical but most appropriate language, an idol, and charges mankind in general, and philosophers especially, with gross idolatry at its shrine. Without saying of modern political economy, as of the city of old, that it is wholly given to idolatry, it may, without any breach of charity, be doubted, whether the worship of idols is anywhere more prevalent, or the sacrifices more costly.

Reader! will you accompany me on a pilgrimage to the shrines? Let us essay to visit them, not on the one hand as blind devotees, nor on the other as reckless

---

order, simplicity, and regularity, than is actually indicated by observation. Thus, as soon as men perceived the orbits of the planets to return into themselves, they immediately supposed them to be perfect circles, and the motion in those circles to be uniform; and to these hypotheses, so rashly and gratuitously assumed, the astronomers and mathematicians of all antiquity labored incessantly to reconcile their observations.

"The propensity which Bacon has here characterised so well, is the same that has been, since his time, known by the name of the *spirit of system*. The prediction that the sources of error would return, and were likely to infest science in its most flourishing condition, has been fully verified, with respect to this illusion, in the case of sciences which had no existence at the time when Bacon wrote. When it was ascertained by observation that a considerable part of the earth's surface consists of minerals disposed in horizontal strata, it was immediately concluded that the whole exterior crust of the earth is composed, or has been composed, of such strata continued all round without interruption; and on this, as on a certain and general fact, entire theories of the earth have been constructed.

"There is no greater enemy which science has to struggle with than this propensity of the mind; and it is a struggle from which science is never likely to be entirely relieved—because, unfortunately, the illusion is founded on the same principle from which our love of knowledge takes its rise."

* Intellectus humanus ex proprietate sûa facile supponit majorem ordinem et æqualitatem in rebus quàm invenit. Et cum multa sint in naturâ monodica, et plena imparitatis, tamen affingit parallela, et correspondentia, et relativa, quæ non sunt.— *Nov. Org.*

scoffers and iconoclasts, but as unprejudiced and candid inquirers.

As in all such cases, we shall be overwhelmed with obloquy. Our understanding and our motives will both be called in question. If we should be tempted to recriminate we will endeavor to resist the temptation.

CHAPTER III.

" Let things alone—Laissez faire, laissez passer."

ONE of the most common and invincible fallacies is this—that things are good by nature and spoiled by art. So said Rousseau of man as an individual; so many still say of human society. It is a common error; most young men fall into it, and are only undeceived by bitter experience. It is invincible, for, having its root deep in human nature, it springs again with every fresh generation.

But it is nevertheless an error. Everything may be improved by culture. Nothing is so natural as art. The indigenous sloes and crabs and weeds of England, when cultivated and improved in orchards, and gardens, are plums and apples and flowers. Man without artificial culture, without intellectual, moral, religious education, is a stupid, sensual, ferocious, and disgusting savage. Such is natural, uncultivated man, not as poets paint him, or philosophers imagine him, but as travellers actually see him. The same human creature, subjected to early culture, instructed, disciplined, Christianised, is but a little lower than the angels.

Nor is artificial regulation less necessary to man in the aggregate than to man individually. Life, personal liberty and inviolability, family, property, reputation, are guarded by laws, complex and artificial, in proportion to the advanced stage of society. Personal injuries, if not entirely prevented, are nearly extirpated, by an artificial system of penal sanctions, and further diminished in number and intensity by the compensation which in most cases the injured party is entitled to exact from the aggressor. The jealous and despotic supervision and enforcement of the marriage contract by the state * is the artificial source of the endearing and humanising relationships of father and child, brother and sister, of family duties, family education, family restraints. Withdraw the interference of the law, leave things alone, and families no longer exist, society relapses into barbarism. The institution of property, the spring of all industry and improvement, leans entirely on an artificial system of laws, civil and criminal, defining its limits, protecting its enjoyment, and securing its peaceable and certain transmission.

The vulgar eye, surveying the surface and admiring the achievements of modern society, penetrates not to its anatomy—to its secret but complex mechanism. Much that is due to art is attributed to nature.

But a still deeper and steadier insight into the constitution of society will disclose not only artificial political arrangements, but commercial and fiscal ones, tending to the virtue, the happiness, the wealth, the power, the grandeur, and the duration of states. The possibility of such artificial regulations is agreeable to analogy and conformable to experience. But both analogy and experience forbid the expectation, that increase of wealth and its fair and equitable distribution, by the full, various, and permanent employment of the people, will flow from the *let-alone* system. On the contrary, there is too much reason to apprehend that the natural course of things will here, as elsewhere, be a vicious one; that the sum of national wealth will not increase, as it might be made to increase; that its distribution will be imperfect; that land will be but half cultivated; that employment will be precarious and wages scanty; that the bulk of the people will not be

---

* Unhappily relaxed since these observations were written.

2

clothed, fed, and housed as they ought to be and might be.

Let us incline ourselves before the teachings of history.

What triumphs has the *let-alone* system to show since the world began? On the other hand, history is full of the marvellous achievements of industry forced into artificial channels by the foresight and power of wise governments.

Ancient and modern history each presents examples of an artificial direction of industry, not only assailing and subduing the apparently invincible infecundity of the soil, but compelling it ever after to feed successive generations, and sustain the power of mighty kingdoms.

What was Egypt by nature?—a sterile and moving sand. It has been well observed that its noble river, full of black mud, too filthy to slake the thirst or wash the person, was once of little use, except to the rats, the insects, and the hideous reptiles.

Immense labors at length achieved a dominion over it. Canals, reservoirs, and multiform contrivances for irrigation, led it at length to every door—the minister of health, cleanliness, and fertility. Now there was, and ever since has been, corn in Egypt. Ever since, in spite of bad government under the Pharaohs, the Persians, the Ptolemys, the Romans, the Caliphs, the Mamelukes, and the Pachas, it has been the land of plenty. What would Egypt have been all this while, if, three thousand years ago, our modern theories had been in fashion there?

The cry of our wise men would have been, "Don't attempt to force labor and capital into artificial channels, and at such an expense to bring into cultivation sterile lands. Buy at a cheaper rate from your neighbors, the Arabs, the Numidians, the Carthaginians, the

Syrians, the Sicilians. As for your means of purchase, let them take care of themselves. *Laissez faire, laissez aller;* in other words, remain as you are."

Ancient Egypt's parallel and antitype is modern Holland.

In Holland, below the level of the sea, and the surface of adjacent rivers and canals, have been created by human art, fat pastures teeming with flocks and herds, rich artificial garden land, nourishing the industrious and thriving population of innumerable cities, towns, and villages. The very coast is an artificial fortification against the ocean, the ancient and natural monarch of the country. Here he is defied by leagues of artificial sea banks,—there by miles of granite masonry. Rivers and canals are made to run many feet above the level of the country. Armies of indefatigable windmills are perpetually pumping and draining. Amsterdam and Rotterdam, populous, opulent, and splendid cities, rest but on piles driven into the mud. This concentration of native industry and art on the most unpromising of soils, resulted not only in agricultural, but commercial prosperity. The seventeenth century saw Holland the greatest of maritime and commercial powers, under the most enlightened of governments. When religious bigotry disgraced and depopulated alike Catholic France and Protestant England, Holland became the sanctuary of religious liberty. From Holland English Puritans set sail for North America, and founded a yet greater state, where the same industrial maxims prevail, and as everywhere else, with the same results. From Holland came the power which sustained in England itself, not only civil liberty and the Reformation, but a highly artificial commercial policy, enduring for a hundred and fifty years, and leading to the grandest consequences. At this day, therefore, even we ourselves, and our children beyond the Atlantic, are debtors to what would now be deemed to be the unscientific and misdirected industry of the Seven United Provinces.

Compare this artificial legislation in ancient Egypt, and modern Holland, with the *let-alone* system in Ireland—the most fertile country under heaven.

Well may a living French writer and statesman of incontestable ability and experience, for he has been Prime Minister of France, M. Thiers, exclaim of the let-alone system (that system which would always and everywhere leave labor and capital to their own course), in stronger language than literary courtesy will justify us in using, that it is "a system of indifference, inaction, impotence, and folly."

But, in truth, the natural course of commercial affairs uninfluenced by legislation is impossible. You must have a revenue; you must have customs and excise duties. Your fiscal regulations may destroy or may create—will decisively harm or help a hundred sorts of industry. Will the least harm and the most good surely spring from the least possible care? It has been well observed that you might as well say, "Shoot without taking aim, and you will be sure to hit the mark."

CHAPTER IV.

" *Foreign commodities are always paid for by British com-*
*modities. THEREFORE, the purchase of foreign
commodities encourages British industry as much as the
purchase of British commodities.*" *

UNHAPPILY the first proposition is untrue, as we now
too well know.

Nevertheless, let us here assume the premises to be
true; yet the conclusion does not follow.

Supposing every foreign commodity imported to be
paid for in British commodities, it may still be for the
interest of THE NATION to buy British commodities in
preference to foreign. In other words, home trade is
more advantageous than foreign trade.

On this text, hear the apostle of free-trade himself,
Adam Smith :—

"The capital which is employed in purchasing in
one part of the country in order to sell in another the
produce of the industry of that country, generally
replaces by such operation two distinct capitals that had
both been employed in the agriculture or manufacture
of that country, and thereby enables them to continue
that employment. . . . . . When *both* are the
produce of domestic industry, it necessarily replaces, by
every such operation, *two distinct capitals*, which had
both been employed in supporting productive labor, and
thereby enables them to continue that support. The

* See M'Culloch's *Principles of Political Economy*, p. 152.

capital which sends Scotch manufactures to London, and brings back English manufactures and corn to Edinburgh, necessarily replaces, by every such operation, *two British capitals*, which had *both* been employed in the agriculture or manufactures of *Great Britain*.

"The capital employed in purchasing foreign goods for home consumption, when this purchase is made with the produce of domestic industry, replaces, too, by every such operation, two distinct capitals, but *one of them only* is employed in supporting domestic industry. The capital which sends British goods to Portugal, and brings back Portuguese goods to Great Britain, replaces by every such operation *only one British* capital. The other is a Portuguese one. Though the returns, therefore, of the foreign trade of consumption should be as quick as those of the home trade, the capital employed in it will give but ONE-HALF THE ENCOURAGEMENT TO THE INDUSTRY OR PRODUCTIVE LABOR OF THE COUNTRY. . . .

"A capital, therefore, employed in the home trade, will sometimes make twelve operations, or be sent out and returned twelve times, before a capital employed in the Foreign trade of consumption has made one. IF THE CAPITALS ARE EQUAL, THEREFORE, THE ONE WILL GIVE FOUR-AND-TWENTY TIMES MORE ENCOURAGEMENT AND SUPPORT TO THE INDUSTRY OF THE COUNTRY THAN THE OTHER." *

What does Adam Smith mean by the expression— "*replace capital?*" It is an expression not to be passed over in haste, but well deserving to be attentively considered and analysed.

He means, that the whole value of a commodity is spent in its production, and yet reappears in the shape of the new product. That in its production there is an expenditure not of the profit merely, but of the *entire value*,† and that *the whole of* that expenditure not only

---

* Adam Smith's *Wealth of Nations*, book ii. chap. 5.
† Say asserts the same thing, as we shall presently see.

maintains landlords, tenants, tradesmen and workpeople, but furnishes an effective demand and market for other productions. He means *that the clear gain, the spendable revenue, the net income of the producing nation, is increased by the amount of the entire value of the domestic product, and that the nation is so much the richer; for while producing, it spends the entire gross value, and, nevertheless, after it has produced, it yet has the entire gross value left in another shape.*

He then goes on and says, that if with British commodities you purchase British commodities, you replace two British capitals; but if with British commodities you purchase foreign commodities you replace only one British capital.* That is to say, you *might have had the entire gross value of two industries to spend, and thereby also to create and sustain markets; but you are content to have the value and the market of one industry only.*

These observations of Adam Smith, though demonstrably true, derive additional weight from the quarter from which they come. They are the admissions of the founder of the existing school of political economists, on a point of vital importance, so vital that it affects the entire theory of free-trade.

At the risk, therefore, of being charged with prolixity and repetition, I venture to invite the candid and serious attention of the reader to a further consideration of this problem.

The entire price or gross value of every *home-made* article constitutes net gain, net revenue,† net income

---

* Say maintains the same position. " Le commerce intérieur est le plus avantageux. Les envois et les retours de ce commerce sont nécessairement les produits du pays. IL PROVOQUE UNE DOUBLE PRODUCTION." Liv. i. chap. 9, vol. 2, p. 6, 4th edition.

† Say concurs in this view. See *Traité d'Economie Politique*, liv. ii. chap. 5, vol. 2, p. 69, 4th edition. He analyses the price of a watch, and shows how the whole of it is distributed as net

to British subjects. Not a portion of the value, but *the whole value*, is resolvable into net gain, income, or revenue maintaining British families, and creating or sustaining British markets. Purchase British articles with British articles, and you create *two* such aggregate values, and two such markets for British industry.

Change your policy—purchase foreign articles with British articles, and you now create only *one* value for your own benefit instead of creating *two*, and only *one* market for British industry instead of *two*. You lose by the change of policy the power of spending the entire value of one industry which you might have had, as well as the other, and you lose a market for British industry to the full extent of the expenditure of that superseded industry.

A small difference in price may cause the loss, but will not compensate the nation for that loss. For example, suppose England can produce an article for £100, and can import it for £99. By importing it instead of producing it, she gains £1 ; but, though she pay for it with her own manufactures, she loses (not, indeed, by the exchange itself, but by the collapse of the suspended industry) £100 of wealth which she might have had to spend by creating the value at home; that is to say, on the balance, she loses £99 which she might have had in addition, by producing both commodities at home.

---

income or revenue among those who have contributed to its production. He then observes, " C'est de cette manière que la valeur entière des produits se distribue dans la société. *Je dis leur valeur* TOUTE ENTIERE." He then gives another illustration, by tracing the distribution of the value of cloth, and adds, "On ne peut concevoir AUCUNE PORTION de la valeur de ce drap, qui n'ait servi à payer UN REVENU. Sa valeur toute entière y a été employée." And subjoins in a note, "Même la portion de cette valeur qui a servi au rétablissement du capital du fabricant. Il a usé ses metiers par supposition. Il les a fait reparer par un mécanicien : le prix de cette reparation fait partie du revenu du mécanicien."

Nor can it be said that what the producer loses the consumer gains. The producer loses £100, the consumer gains £1. The nation, moreover, loses the markets which that superseded industry supported.

Let us examine a little more in detail the position, that the *entire price* or *gross value* of every home-made commodity constitutes *net national gain or revenue*,— net income to British subjects, such revenue as a man may spend with his tradesmen, and maintain his family upon, and yet the nation grow no poorer.*

Take a quarter of English wheat. Suppose the price to be 50s. The whole of this 50s. is resolvable into net income. A portion, say 5s., goes as rent to the English landlord, and is to him net income, which he may spend with his tradesmen in maintaining his family. Next 30s. go for wages. Those wages are the net income of the English laborer. Then 10s. go for rates, tithe, rent-charge, and taxes. The first contribute to the net income of the poor; the second to the net income of the English clergyman, or impropriator; the third to the net income of the government. Then 2s. 6d. go for implements of husbandry, the whole of which 2s. 6d. is also, as we shall presently see, resolvable into net income to some person or other. The residue, being 2s. 6d., we will suppose is the net profit of the farmer, and would be net income to him, but that half of it, viz. 1s. 3d., goes as interest to a friend who has lent him money. This last 1s. 3d. is, however, net income—not, indeed, of the farmer, but of his creditor. Trace home, with stubborn attention, every penny of the price, and you

---

* The attention of the reader is particularly invited to this part of the inquiry. He will observe that the expression " *net income* " comprehends the spendable revenue of the whole community, from whatever source derived. The net profits of trade are but a part, and a very small part, of the net income of the nation. The wages of the laborer are his net income. The rent of the landlord, and the interest of the mortgagee, are also net income.

2*

will find that every penny at last assumes the shape of net income. The whole 50s., therefore, it is manifest, is an addition to the net spendable income of the country. The whole 50s. answers two purposes : first, it maintains the ultimate recipients and their families ; and, secondly, by means of their expenditure it creates a home market to the extent of the entire gross value or price of the quarter of wheat.

But is the sum of 2s. 6d., which we have just supposed to be spent for agricultural implements, also resolvable into net income or revenue?

It is! And though we should be still more guilty of repetition, let us patiently inquire how.

Suppose the 2s. 6d. spent for a spade. It may be that the money is laid out with the retail ironmonger in the next market-town. Sixpence, we will suppose, is the ironmonger's profit. A second sixpence is the cost of a wooden handle. That second sixpence is expended in this way :— One-fourth of it, or three halfpence, goes as rent to the owner of the copse from which the rough wood comes; threepence goes as wages to the laborers who cut or fashion the wood; and the remaining three halfpence goes as profit to the dealer in wooden spade handles. One shilling out of the 2s. 6d., the entire price of the spade, is thus traced back, and found to be net income.

The remainder of the price of the spade, viz. 1s. 6d., goes for the iron part of it, and has been paid by the retail dealer in spades to the wholesale dealer in the iron part of spades. Part of this 1s. 6d. is the retail dealer's profit, part goes to the manufacturer. The manufacturer's portion, when analysed, is again resolved into his profit—his payments for implements or machinery (also resolvable into net income)—his rent—and the cost price of the iron. The cost price of iron is, lastly, paid to the iron-master, and by him distributed to himself as profit, to his workmen as wages, to his landlord as rent.

The whole price and value of the spade is thus net gain or income to some person or other, available, like all the rest of the price of a quarter of English wheat, first, to the maintenance of British families, next, through their expenditure, to the creation or maintenance of British markets for cotton, linen, woollen, and hardware, bread, beef, beer, tea, soap, candles, buildings, and furniture.

Take any article you please, agricultural or manufactured, patiently analyse the ultimate distribution of its price, and you will find that the whole gross value denotes the creation of so much wealth in the nation in which it is entirely produced, enabling that nation to spend * and enjoy an equivalent to that whole gross value, without being the poorer for the consumption, and conferring on that nation the further advantage of a home market, equivalent to that expenditure.

To express the same truth in a formula, intelligible and familiar to political economists, the whole gross price of any article is ultimately resolvable into rent, profit, or wages: rent, profit, and wages are respectively national net income, and create markets where they are spent.

Now, suppose a nation which had produced both the exchanged values at home, or, to use Adam Smith's expression, had replaced two domestic capitals, should alter its policy, and should thenceforth import one of those values from abroad, giving for it the other value as before (which we will suppose the foreign nation

---

* *La valeur toute entière* des produits sert de cette manière à payer les gains des producteurs. CE N'EST PAS LE PRODUIT NET SEULEMENT, QUI SATISFAIT AUX BESOINS DES HOMMES. C'EST LE PRODUIT BRUT, LA TOTALITÉ DES VALEURS CRÉES—SAY. *Traité d'Economie Politique*, liv. i. chap. 2, vol. i. p. 18, 4th edition. The careful attention of the reader is solicited to this passage. Though it be true and accurately expressed, yet it must in candor be admitted, that Say, like Smith, is in other parts of his book inconsistent with himself

ready to take), that alteration of policy would entail
on the country adopting it a loss of national net income equivalent to the entire value of the commodity
formerly produced at home, and now produced abroad,
and the sacrifice of a home market to the same amount.

But, to descend from the abstract to the concrete, let
us illustrate this by an example.

Suppose stockings to the value of £500,000 a year
are made in Leicester, and exchanged annually for
gloves to the amount of £500,000 a year made in
Dover, the landlords and tradesmen, and workmen of
Leicester and Dover enjoy together an annual English
net income of a million. Suppose now, that for some
real or supposed advantage in price or quality, the
Leicester people, instead of exchanging their stockings
for gloves from Dover, exchange them for gloves from
the other side of the straits, say from Calais, thus de-
priving the Dover people of their Leicester market.
What is the consequence? It is this, that Dover loses
what Calais gets; that England loses and France gains
half a million a year by the new locality of the glove
manufacture—by its transference from England to
France. Englishmen have half a million a year less
to spend: Frenchmen have half a million a year more
to spend. English markets, of which Dover used to be
one, fall off to the extent of half a million a year:
French markets, of which Calais is one, are argmented
by half a million a year.

The English glove manufacture, with its half million of national net income, is gone from England,
where it used to maintain Englishmen and English
Markets—to France, where it now maintains Frenchmen and French Markets.

Nor does the mischief end here. On the Dover
glove-makers were dependent bakers, millers, grocers,
butchers, tailors, shoemakers, with their servants and
families. The migration of the glove trade from Dover

to Calais ruins all. They are destroyed like a hive of bees.

The illustration of Dover, which is on the confines of a neighboring State, has been chosen to make the case still clearer. Suppose, now, instead of the glove trade being transferred from Englishmen to Frenchmen, the Dover tradesmen and workmen crossed the straits along with their manufacture to Calais, and there carried it on; then nobody can doubt that England would lose half a million a year, and France gain it.

Indeed this latter supposition of the people themselves migrating, along with their industry, though setting the loss in the clearest light, would, of the two cases supposed, probably be the most advantageous for England; for if the trade migrated without the people, a nest of paupers would be left behind.

It is said that the Dover people if left in England could turn their hands and their capital to some new employment.* Alas! this is one of the things easier said than done. To find productive employment for the people is just the very thing which is so supremely difficult, as to be often pronounced impossible. It is the problem remaining for the true political economist to resolve. Its solution will be an event not less brilliant and far more important to mankind than the discovery of the solar system.

Now, under a system of free-trade, if the Leicester people can buy their gloves one per cent., or a minute

---

* Mr. M'Culloch has here fallen into a transparent error. He says, in his *Principles of Political Economy*, p. 151, that the displaced artificers would be employed in the production of the articles that must be sent as equivalents to the foreigner. But that is not so. It is the Leicester stocking-makers who are employed in producing the equivalents; but they were employed before. They used to deal with Dover, now they deal with Calais.

fraction per cent., cheaper from abroad, they will do
so. By so doing English glove consumers may gain
£5000 a year; but the nation hands over its glove
trade to the French, and will lose half a million a
year, minus five thousand pounds (that is, £495,000
a year of national net income), by the half million
worth of gloves being now produced in France, instead
of being produced as formerly, in England. England,
for a small percentage, sacrifices a principal sum. The
English nation also loses a home market equivalent to
its loss of national net income. What England loses
by the migration of the glove manufacture, France
gains. All this may happen even under a system of
reciprocity, so far as one industry is concerned, without
any disturbance of the currency.

The Leicester people gain no new market by sending their goods to France : they had a market to the
same extent before in England. There is no improvement in the condition of the Leicester people to compensate for the ruin of the Dover people. Reciprocity
itself, therefore, in the particular exchange, is no compensation to the English people at large.

Do the English consumers gain what the English
producers lose? No. The producers lose ninety-nine
per cent., and the consumers gain one per cent.

What, then, would be a compensation for the invasion of the English market by foreign goods?

Nothing short of a corresponding invasion of the
foreign market by English goods. When the French
invade our markets and displace our industry, even
though they should take our goods in payment to the
full amount of their importation, that alone (as we
have seen) is no compensation at all. They must,
over and above all this, allow and enable us to invade
their markets, and displace some other industry of
theirs to the same extent, and on the same terms.
The Frenchman must not only provide for the Leices-

ter people a new foreign market equivalent to their
former home market at Dover, but he, or some one
else, must also provide for the Dover people a new
found foreign market as a substitute for their lost home
market at Leicester. There must be not only reciprocity, but complete reciprocation. *

Nothing short of a NEW DOUBLE foreign market—a
foreign market for both the domestic industries that
used to interchange their products—will suffice. This
is admitted by Mr. Ricardo; † and it is the truth, as a
little consideration will evince.

---

* This can seldom be had except under the same government.

† Mr. Ricardo, in combating Adam Smith's position, that a capital
employed in the home trade gives twice as much encouragement to
the industry and productive labor of the country as a capital
employed in the foreign trade—the trade with Portugal for example—makes these observations:—

"This argument appears to be fallacious; for though two
capitals, one Portuguese and one English, be employed, as Dr.
Smith supposes, still a capital *will* be employed in the foreign
trade DOUBLE *of what would be employed in the home trade.*

"Suppose that Scotland employs always a capital of a thousand pounds in making linen, which she exchanges for the produce of a similar capital employed in making silks in England,
two thousand pounds, and a proportional quantity of labor, will
be employed in the two countries. Suppose, now, that England
discovers that she can import more linen from Germany for the
silks which she before exported to Scotland, and that Scotland
discovers that she can obtain more silks from France in return
for her linen, than she before obtained from England, will not
England and Scotland immediately cease trading with each
other, and will not the home trade of consumption be changed for
a foreign trade of consumption? But although two additional
capitals will enter into this trade—the capital of Germany and
that of France—will not the same amount of Scotch and English
capital continue to be employed? and will it not give motion to
the same amount of industry as when it was engaged in the
home trade?"—*Principles of Political Economy,* chap. 26.

It will be observed that Mr. Ricardo admits, or, more properly speaking, assumes, that if Scotch industry loses its English market because England buys from abroad, the Island of
Great Britain is not compensated by the foreign trade unless a
DOUBLE foreign market can be found; unless Scotland can find

When two domestic producers mutually exchange their products, each creates a value equivalent to the gross price of the product, and, moreover, each makes a market for the other. But if one, instead of buying as heretofore at home, now buys abroad, and finds in return a foreign market abroad to exactly the same extent as his former domestic market, that one is compensated. But what has become of the other? The other has lost his home market, and does not find a foreign one. To be compensated by foreign trade there must be a double reciprocity, this other also must find a new and co-extensive foreign market.

---

a foreign market for her linen, as well as England a foreign market for her silk.

The case may be illustrated by a diagram. The original state of things, when Scotland sent linen to England, and England sent in return silk to Scotland, will be thus represented:

{ SCOTLAND.
{   linen £1000.

{ silk £1000.
{ ENGLAND.

Great Britain has to spend as rent, profits, and wages, £2000.

Now, suppose England, instead of purchasing with its silk linen from Scotland, purchases (but still with its silk) linen from Germany; then the state of things will be thus represented:

{ SCOTLAND.   none.
{   .
       .
       .
{   silk £1000. ——— linen £1000. }
{ ENGLAND.   GERMANY.   }

SCOTLAND will have lost its market for linen, and thereby its power of production and consumption to the extent of £1000. Great Britain will have lost this £1000. Germany will have gained the £1000 which Great Britain will have lost.

The opening of the German market to English silk is no compensation to *Great Britain*, for the loss of its Scotch linen manufacture.

Great Britain has now to spend as rent, profits, and wages, but £1000 in the place of £2000.

The only adequate compensation to Great Britain for the loss

So that if you lay out ten millions a year abroad, which you used to lay out at home, you are not compensated by a foreign market to the extent of those ten millions a year; you must, in order to compensation by the foreign market, find in the aggregate a new foreign market to the extent of TWENTY millions a year. So says Adam Smith, and such is the truth.

To illustrate this by the former example. You lay out half a million a year with Calais which you used to lay out with Dover, but Calais takes your Leicester stockings in payment. Leicester, which used to send its stockings to Dover, is now compensated for the loss of its home trade with Dover, by its new foreign trade with Calais. But this new foreign trade does not com-

---

of the Scotch trade is a DOUBLE foreign market. Another foreign market, over and above the foreign market for English silk, must be found for Scotch linen. Then, indeed, the state of things would be thus represented :

$$\left\{ \begin{array}{ll} \text{SCOTLAND.} & \text{FRANCE.} \\ \text{linen £1000} & \text{silk £1000.} \end{array} \right\}$$

$$\left\{ \begin{array}{ll} \text{silk £1000.} & \text{linen £1000.} \\ \text{ENGLAND.} & \text{GERMANY.} \end{array} \right\}$$

Thus it appears, that perfect reciprocity itself, in the case of the superseded industry only, is no compensation to the nation for dealing abroad instead of at home. There must also be reciprocity in the other industry which is deprived of its customer. A DOUBLE foreign market must be found.

In other words, when you are about to take away one home market, you must open two foreign ones. You must find a double equivalent.

Mr. Ricardo says that this will be done—that two foreign markets *will* be found. But that is to assume (what is contrary to experience) that the foreign market is always as large as we require it to be. We cannot even find the *single* foreign market.

Mr. Ricardo's *illustration* involves another fallacy. Why should France buy Scotch linen when, according to the supposition, German linen is cheaper? Why should Germany buy English silk when, according to the supposition, French silk is cheaper?

pensate Dover. There is reciprocity for Calais, but where is the reciprocity for Dover? Dover, too, must find another new foreign trade to the extent of half a million a year more before Dover is compensated. But the NATION is not compensated by the foreign trade unless both Leicester and Dover are compensated. When, therefore, the nation lays out half a million a year in foreign gloves, which half million it used to lay out in English gloves, the nation is not compensated by a new foreign market of half a million a year. To be compensated by the foreign market, the nation must find a new foreign market of a MILLION a year in the whole.

It is obvious, no doubt, that one town does not exclusively deal with another in the way we have supposed in order to simplify a problem of extreme complexity.

It may be objected that, according to us, this incomplete reciprocity may injure both nations at one time by a displacement of industry in each, so that both may complain. And so it may. And so two nations do complain at this moment.

The result is, whenever you import instead of producing, you may be losers by the change till your additional exports double the value of the new import. *

What, therefore, we set out with venturing to submit, seems to be correct, viz., that even if the premises contained in the axiom at the head of these observations be true, the consequence does not follow.

The truth is this :—

The gross value of every product of industry is national net income.

When one product is exchanged for another, if you

---

* This loss will, as we have seen, be less by the percentage by which the foreign article is cheaper than the domestic one.

have produced both products, you have created two such national net incomes. If you now change your policy, and produce one only, and leave the foreigner to produce the other, though he should fairly exchange with you, you create *but one* national net income and *sacrifice the other.* You, even in that case, sacrifice the principal on the part of the producer to gain a percentage in favor of the consumer.

But if these things be done in the green tree, what shall be done in the dry? So far from being able to find a new DOUBLE foreign market, we cannot even find a new SINGLE one commensurate to the enormous increase of our imports. If such may be the consequences where there is reciprocity, what will be the consequences of that sort of free-trade which does not compensate either industry, but tends to supersede both?

The public at present entertain very inadequate conceptions of the devastating consequences. *

---

* This last sentence was written more than twenty years ago. The public are now better able to judge, notwithstanding that in the meantime vast discoveries of the precious metals, the expenditure of 500 millions on railways, and the reckless operations of the new joint stock companies, created in the meantime a temporary and deceitful prosperity.

CHAPTER V.

"Buy in the cheapest market."

A RECOMMENDATION perfectly sound, provided you are sure that every one will be as fully and profitably employed in producing the means of purchase as he was before. In that event, to buy in the cheapest market, though it should be a foreign one, is the manifest pecuniary advantage of each individual and of the whole community.*

But if the foreign market for exports be (as it always is) limited, so that the preparation of exports will not employ the whole industry that was before employed, then the case is at once changed. To buy in a cheaper foreign market will still be the *immediate* interest of individuals, but it ceases to be even the pecuniary interest of the community as a whole.†

Capital employed in production is spent, yet reproduces itself. It feeds, lodges, and clothes the industrious workman with his family, and pays the employer and the landlord. It constitutes the spendable income of the nation. Yet, having done all this, after being entirely consumed, like the phœnix, it rises again imme-

---

* That is to say, regarding immediate *pecuniary* considerations only, and disregarding considerations of more moment, such as the variety, the constancy and security, the salubrity, the moral and political tendency of the employments of the people.

† We are perfectly aware that it is a doctrine of political economists that the pecuniary interest of individuals and the pecuniary interests of society coincide—a maxim wherein it is proposed to examine carefully hereafter.

diately from its ashes in the shape of the new finished product. We behold, in the place of the spent capital, a new and reproduced but equal capital.

This is the true explanation of the phenomenon that meets one constantly wherever a new and successful manufacture is established. We see that wealth springs up suddenly, as by magic, not from paltry savings, but in huge masses. The truth is, that a new income is at once created for everybody concerned in it, which income they may every year freely spend, and by that expenditure create markets for other people. Yet the nation is no poorer for this expenditure, for there still remains the finished product, which is an exact equivalent for what has been spent :—the price of it remains if it have been sold, or the value of it if it have not, provided there be a market for it.

And where the markets are not only good but close at hand (which is a great advantage in many other ways), the capital may be turned over several times in a year, and this spendable income created, and these hungry markets supplied afresh every time.

Wherever, therefore, a commodity is produced by the aid of capital, TWO CAPITALS or values are to be regarded. There is, first, the capital or value spent and consumed in production; and there is, secondly, the capital or value reproduced.

It is the capital SPENT that remunerates the laborer, the landlord, and the dealer—that pays wages, rent, and profits. It is, moreover, this spent capital that creates MARKETS. For it confers on the laborer, the landlord, and the dealer, the revenue they severally have to spend.

Every act of domestic production by the aid of capital, enables a nation to expend safely the whole value or price of the finished article among laborers, landlords, and dealers, in the shape of wages, rent, or profit. This expenditure further creates a body of consumers

with money in their hands—in other words, an entirely
NEW MARKET to the extent of the WHOLE PRICE.
Yet the nation is no poorer for the expenditure; for it
still has the new-made article of the same value.

The nation or empire, therefore, that has the privilege of producing at both ends of the exchange, has the
benefit of spending two consumable capitals instead of
one. It pays a double set of laborers, dealers, and
landlords. It gets a double amount of rent, profits,
and wages to spend. It doubles its net income. It
doubles its home markets for all other commodities.

We must, at the risk of repetition, remind our readers
that in strictness, FOUR CAPITALS have been engaged
where an exchange of the products of industry takes
place.

TWO CAPITALS are to be considered in production.
First, the capital *spent* in producing, next the new capital *produced*. It is capital SPENT which forms the income of the producers. This is the capital that pays
rent, profit and wages. This capital creates markets.
The new capital produced enables you to spend the
other without loss. The new capital also, as well as the
consumed capital, creates markets.

When, therefore, two productions are mutually exchanged, FOUR CAPITALS are engaged. Two spent capitals, one consumed on each side, paying rent, profit, and
wages, and creating markets. Two new reproduced
capitals, enabling the two other capitals to be entirely
spent without loss, and also themselves mutually creating markets for each other.

When, therefore, the exchange of two domestic productions takes place, two sums together equivalent to
the gross value of the products on both sides are
national net income. Two home markets are opened
by the expenditure of those two capitals in rent, profit,
and wages, together equivalent to the gross value of
both. Two other new home markets are also opened

by the two new reproduced capitals. Each forms a home market for the other. You create by this process two national net incomes, and you open four home markets.

Now, if you interpose an obstacle to the mutual exchange of the two new reproduced capitals, you may thereby destroy the market which those two new reproduced capitals used mutually to provide for each other, and stop production on both sides. The nation then loses the opportunity of consuming, without loss, as national net income, both the capitals that otherwise would have been spent, and it moreover loses both the markets, or, rather, both the series of markets which those two consumable capitals, if spent, would have created.

The expression *series of markets* may invite reflection, and lead to some difficult and recondite inquiries; for the acquisition or loss of a market is a benefit or injury not stopping with itself, but extending to an indefinite and incalculable extent.

Part of the capital spent in production pays wages. This payment makes a market for labor. A portion of the wages so received, buys, we will suppose, a bedstead. The very same value which has just found a market for labor, now finds a market for the upholsterer. The upholsterer spends part of the self-same sum with the butcher, and so finds him a market. The butcher does the same for the baker; the baker for the brewer; the brewer for the blacksmith; and so on *ad infinitum*. Create one market, and you create others, and stimulate and nourish production in an infinite series.

So, on the other hand, the loss of a market is felt and propagated through a similar series. Market after market fails; production after production ceases. The whole structure of industry was a house of cards: touch one, and many fall.

The nation is now recklessly scattering that vast capital abroad. Well-grown and intelligent Englishmen are wandering about in the receipt of poor-rates, and other nations create and spend the riches.

Men will find, that for some mysterious and unaccountable reason, they cannot get a living; they will, with the present facilities of locomotion, be tempted to desert their native country; but it is the healthy, the industrious, the thrifty, the enterprising, that will go; the halt, the old, the debauched, the pauper, will be left behind, not to bear, but to swell, the national burthens, and ensure the national degradation.*

This sort of emigration reacts again on the national wealth, and still further diminishes it; for such emigrants take out not only their industry and skill, but their property. Ireland has already reached this point —having, indeed, taken no property, because she had none to take, but sending property back to encourage still further emigration; England and Scotland are approaching it.

And all this mischief and ruin are perpetrated while there exist in England, Scotland, Ireland, and the Colonies and dependencies, the neglected means of producing within the empire, if not supplies of food, yet raw materials of all kinds at a moderate rate, superabounding and all sufficient, not only for the existing population, but for an infinitely larger one; means not only ample to fill every mouth, but to employ every idle pair of hands in the most natural, healthy, virtuous, and contenting occupations; means not only of procuring plenty of cheap bread, but (what is much more important) of putting into every man's hand the wherewithal to buy it.

It is said that all the capital and labor displaced by the invasion of foreign industry will find other and more profitable employment.

---

* This passage was written in 1849.

Let us dissect this bold assertion, and compare each portion of it with the FACTS.

Take first the displaced capital. Unhappily the wretched condition of capital, seeking employment and finding none, is not only not uncommon in this country, but it is one of our notorious social miseries. The competition of capital for employment is here so intense that the profits of trade are already driven down below a living and honest standard. The manufacturer is driven to inferior workmanship or adulteration. The anxious father is afraid to place his son in trade; his experienced eye descries, through the low profits and the bad debts, the vista that conducts straight to bankruptcy. Want of employment for capital, and the consequent low rate of profit, necessarily next superinduce a low rate of interest. Accordingly we find capital lent on discounts at the rate of two per cent. per annum. Ever and anon the impatience of the capitalist, to find at least some employment for his idle capital, bursts through the restraints of prudence. Now you have loans (many of which turn out to be gifts) to foreign States; next you have joint-stock companies not only ruining their projectors, but engulfing the public and their property. Such is the want of employment that awaits any *circulating* capital displaced by the invasion of foreign industry. Much worse is the doom of *fixed* capital, such as mills and machinery, so superseded. Its value evaporates at once; or, if any value remain, it is eaten up by poor-rates.

Nay, the insuperable difficulty, the absolute impossibility of finding profitable employment for vast masses of capital, is so undeniable that it has driven some political economists into the paradox of asserting that there is too much capital in these lands. That is the same thing as saying that we possess too many valuable things; that there are, in the aggregate, too many houses and buildings—too much improved and culti-

3

vated land—too many docks, harbors, and ships—too many railways and locomotives—too many spades, ploughs, looms, and steam-engines—too much wheat, barley, oats, cotton, wool, iron, timber, leather, hemp, tea, coffee, sugar, specie, oxen, sheep, pigs, horses, and vehicles; for it is the aggregate of such visible and tangible things that constitutes the national capital. To say that we are distressed because we have too much capital, is to say that we are so poor because we are so rich. But to say that we have much more capital than we can (as things now are) productively employ, or, in other words, that vast masses of capital do not, and cannot find productive and remunerative employment, is, alas! too true.

Precisely what we have not got, and sorely want, yet cannot get, is this—sufficient employment for our capital, the power of bending it to reproductive uses. To tell us, therefore, that capital displaced will necessarily find not only employment, but more profitable employment than before, is to bandage our eyes with a theory. A glimpse of the real facts discloses the transparent emptiness of the assertion.

Why, if you act on the principle of always buying in the cheapest market, should this certain and more profitable employment of displaced English capital be to be found?

Where is it to be found?

How is it to be found?

When is it to be found? We have been looking for it for twenty years.

Will not displaced movable capital that can find no profitable employment in England, migrate?

Will not vast masses of capital be destroyed?

These are the searching interrogatories with which, in every case, the practical man, whose capital has been displaced, will cross-examine the political economist.

Learned professor! the industrious but displaced and starving artisan, also, humbly and respectfully implores an answer to these questions. He admits that he has now a breakfast-table free enough, but unfortunately it is free, not so much from taxes as from food. What you take away is an enormous aggregate value, and a certainty. Your compensation must not be a phantom.

But even this is not all. If space sufficed it would not be difficult to show that the injudicious displacement of any portion of the national capital is not only a wound that will not cure itself, but a gangrene and leprosy, threatening other portions of it.

So much for the first branch of the assertion, viz., that displaced *capital* will necessarily find other and more profitable employment.

Let us now look at the other branch, viz., that displaced *labor* will necessarily find other and more profitable employment.

The union workhouses and the poor-rates in England and Ireland afford but too solid an answer.

The Dorsetshire laborers, Bethnal Green, the Spitalfields weavers, and the Irish poor re-echo the refutation.

Nor is it labor of the lowest order only that vainly craves employment. Let a clerkship in a bank, or at a railway station, be vacant, straightway you have five hundred applicants.

The difficulty, amounting as yet to an impossibility, of finding employment for the population, is the plague not only of this country, but more or less of all old Europe.

To say, therefore, that labor which has been deprived of employment will necessarily not only find it, but find more or better than it lost, is to fly in the face of the best-established and universal facts ; it is to presume on the indolent credulity of the public.

Then it is said, if home trade will not necessarily employ displaced capital and labor, foreign trade will employ both.

But we have already shown that if you buy abroad what you formerly produced at home, you must, in order to compensation, find a DOUBLE foreign market. But the facts are, that so far from finding a DOUBLE foreign market, you cannot even find a SINGLE one.

In one sense, indeed, this objection is true, but capable of being retorted with damaging effect. Foreign trade will perhaps find employment for British capital and labor, but it will find it abroad, and not here. It is but too true that not only labor but capital which survives the shock, and can extricate itself from the spreading and universal ruin, will fly to some foreign country, where capital is cherished and protected.

It will next be said, that however it may be with particular nations, if all countries practised free-trade, the world at large would be a gainer.

But, first, that is not the question now before us. The question is, must *every* nation be a gainer, or must WE, therefore, as you say we must, NECESSARILY be gainers, should such an Utopia be found?

And, secondly, if it were the question whether the world at large would be a gainer by such a system, it must not be assumed that the true answer would be in the affirmative: some reasons, out of place here, will presently be adduced, tending to evince that the true answer would be in the negative.

But, lastly, when the world at large agrees to practise universal free-trade, it will be time enough to discuss what the effect on the policy of this country should be. The discussion may be postponed without much inconvenience for a thousand years.

Then it will be said—If protection be good for a

country, for the same reasons it must be good for a county, or a department.

By no means. Production to be good, cheap, and profitable, must be on a large scale—must require and remunerate expensive machinery, expensive processes, large capital—must feed on large markets. All these a large kingdom or empire with its colonies and dependencies can well supply, but a county or a department cannot. Yet it does not follow that the larger the area of mutual exchange the better, even if all countries practised free exchange, still less in the case now under consideration, when they do not.

The true and advantageous area of mutual international exchange is not a subject for dogmatism; it is a very complex problem, varying with circumstances—a problem for the great practical statesman to solve.

Lastly, it is objected, that according to these principles, England should grow wine in hot-houses, though it would cost thirty times as much as foreign wine.

Not at all. The moment the price of the domestic commodity exceeds by a very large proportion the price of the corresponding foreign one, the main reason for producing at home ceases.

Take the supposed case of wine. Assume that it would cost £100 to produce in England wine that would cost from abroad only £3. By importing instead of growing it, you must gain £97. You could lose but £3, at the outside, even supposing the whole of your wine-producing land, labor, and capital, utterly and for ever thrown out of employment. You can actually afford to throw away 97 per cent. of your former wine-growing capital; you are insured to that extent. Moreover, an article of luxury, superfluity, and partial consumption (like wine in England) could employ but a very small proportion of the capital of the country; so that the *whole* of what is set at liberty has a much better chance of employment. In a word, the gain is large and certain; the risk is small, and such as it is, it affects but a small value. Hence, luxuries and superfluities, for whose production the soil and climate of a country are unfit, are among the true and legitimate subjects of foreign trade.

If the views advocated in this and the last preceding chapter be correct, we may expect to see countries where the rule of buying in the cheapest market has not prevailed, rich and flourishing, and countries where it has prevailed, poor, stationary, or retrograding.

And this is exactly what we do behold: not that we who are blinded by theory will see it; for of us it may truly be said, "Eyes have they, but they see not."

CHAPTER VI.

*" If all countries practised free trade all countries would be
gainers."*

By dint of perpetual repetition, without contradiction, this assertion is almost universally believed. It is
even assumed without proof as an axiom, or self-evident
truth. But if the candid reader will suspend his judgment till he has pondered the evidence on the other
side, peradventure he may be induced to doubt it very
much. Nay, it is possible that he may arrive at the
opposite conclusion. He may be convinced that a
protective policy is not only eminently conducive, but
absolutely necessary to the diffusion of industry and
wealth over the surface of the globe, and that the
absence of artificial regulations tends to concentrate
both in a few favored spots, and to leave the greater
portion of the earth and the majority of mankind without either.

There are some few countries in the world which
enjoy peculiar facilities for the production of particular
commodities: such as the south of France, for wine;
Cuba, for sugar; some districts of England, for coals
and iron. But the immeasurably greater portion of the
surface of the habitable globe consists of countries
moderately—and but moderately—adapted for the production even of the necessaries and comforts of life, of
food, clothing, and lodging. These countries can, in
every single article that they produce, be surpassed and
undersold by some country or other.

Put the case of such a country, with *moderate* facilities for the production of most things, with *extraordinary* facilities for the production of nothing. It can grow wheat, but not so cheap as Poland; it can grow wine, but not so cheap as France or Spain; it can manufacture, but not so cheaply as England.

First, imagine that country under a system of protection, so strict as to be jealous, and, if you please, injudicious. The nation cultivates the land, and works up the produce. It creates wealth at both ends of the exchange. Its manufactures exchange with its agricultural products. Native industry can and does supply it with the necessaries and comforts of life. A numerous population may be employed, fed, clothed, and lodged. Industry and plenty reign. All this may be, and is, done under great natural disadvantages, both of soil and climate. Human art and industry triumph, nevertheless, over every obstacle, and can raise, as in the case of Holland, a great and powerful state in a morass. Foreign trade will in the end be introduced, supplying luxuries and carrying away superfluities.

Now, imagine that country under a universal system of free-trade and unrestricted imports. Except in a few favored spots, it cannot grow wheat; for Poland will be able to undersell it, not only in foreign markets, but in its own. It cannot manufacture; for in cottons, hardware, woollens, and other products of manufacturing industry, England can undersell it abroad and at home. It cannot grow wine; for France or Spain can everywhere undersell it. Neither can it continue to import its corn, its manufactures, or its wine from abroad; for, its own industry being superseded and smothered, it has nothing to give in exchange. It becomes, then, in this condition—it can neither grow nor make for itself, nor yet buy from abroad. It *goes without;* or, if not entirely without, it is scantily and wretch-

edly supplied.* A starving and ragged population
derive a wretched and precarious subsistence from half-
cultivated land. It has neither domestic industry nor
foreign trade.

Such is the natural capability of a very large proportion of the countries in the world. They enjoy moderate
facilities for the production of everything necessary for
the sustenance of a population; extraordinary facilities
for the production of little or nothing. With a gener-
ally-diffused system of judicious and discriminating protection, concentrating the industry of each country on its
own soil and indigenous materials, industry flourishes,
wealth increases, commerce follows, population multiplies, throughout the globe. But without such artificial
regulations, population, industry, and wealth have a
tendency to concentrate and confine themselves to certain favored spots: there, indeed, they may flourish,
but over the vast area of the world at large they have a
tendency to dwindle and decay; but Protection wisely
regulated, instead of being, as has been represented, a
blight on universal industry, is a system of universal irrigation, diffusing industry where industry would otherwise never have flowed, and making even the desert
rejoice.

Suppose France, at the close of the war, fifty years
ago, had repealed the laws protecting the manufactures of cotton and hardware, where would now have
been the industry of the banks of the Seine, of Rouen
and Elbœuf? What would have become of the thriving
population of Tourcoing and Roubaix, and Mulhausen
and St. Etienne? Manchester and Birmingham, and
Glasgow and Sheffield would have prostrated all, and
turned the banks of the Seine and half of the thriving

---

* Like Ireland, which for many years has had perfectly free-
trade with the greatest commercial country in the world.

3*

towns of France into a desert. But the loss to France
would have been so enormous that her power of purchasing would have been well-nigh destroyed. We should
eventually have gained little in comparison with the prodigious loss of France. Then England might have
flourished, but France, except in her wine districts,
would, so far as manufactures are concerned, have been
laid waste.

What France would not do, Ireland has done. The
Act of Union provided for the gradual and total ex-
tinction of the then existing protection to Irish manufactures against English ones. But France acted otherwise, and her manufacturing industry now rivals ours.

Mark the result!

Belfast is an exception. But that manufacture was
founded and nurtured by protection and government
grants for a long series of years.

According to received theories, it is immaterial,
though the cotton-grower live five thousand miles from
the cotton-spinner and weaver, and the farmer as far
from the miller, baker, or consumer.

But a careful examination will discover immense
advantages in the *mutual vicinity* of various producers.
Let the farmer, the flax-grower, the gardener, live close
by the miller, the woollen manufacturer, the linen manufacturer, and then the cultivator finds at his own door
a sure market, not only for his corn, hay, wool, cheese,
flax, hops, but for his more perishable articles, his beef,
mutton, and pork, not salted and half-spoilt, but fresh ;
for his poultry, eggs, fruit, and fresh butter. The
manufacturer finds all around and near him, not a speculative, but an explored and safe market for coats, shirts,
gowns, and stockings. Nay, the very filth and ordure
of the neighboring town create the fertility and beauty
of the adjacent country.

Agriculture, manufactures, and trade no longer
merely fringe the seashore and the rivers, but penetrate

into the interior, and add a solid and tenfold value to
the most retired and inaccessible glens.

But it is not merely every square inch of territory,
and the products of every industry down to its very
refuse, that are thus utilised by mutual vicinity. In
her human creatures, as well as in her other animals
and plants, great Nature everywhere luxuriates in
variety. In every place she presents you, not only with
the young, the old, the middle-aged, of both sexes, but
with every variety and combination of bodily and
mental capacity and inaptitude. The variety of the
occupations open to the people utilises all human gifts
and talents. Let agricultural and manufacturing industry flourish side by side, and you have everywhere
occupation fit for every body. There is appropriate
employment for stolid strength, for manual skill, and
dexterity, for inventive genius, for the active and the
sedentary, for chilhood as well as youth and mature
age, nay, even for caducity and decrepitude.

Everybody's industry, instead of superseding, furthers
and helps the industry of everybody else. Each country thus gains that double set of producers, that double
production of wealth, that double set of home markets,
which, as we have seen, are everywhere insured by the
reduplicative operation of the home trade.

The framework of industry, compact, self-supporting,
all embracing, knit, morticed, and clamped together,
not only defies, but moderates even the storm of political convulsion. Industry is thus not only developed
everywhere and spread over all lands, but distributed
to all persons and perpetuated to all time. Capital may
be turned over and reproduced, not only every year,
but sometimes every month.

But, besides natural disadvantages, there are temporary and accidental ones, against which it is necessary

that the industry of many countries should be artificially assisted.

What will be in the highest degree advantageous and profitable to the next generation, or even a few years hence, is not so now. Immense future gain may require a present and temporary sacrifice. Individuals will never make that sacrifice; private enterprise looks only to the present, or, at farthest, to the next year or two. It is public wisdom alone which must overrule this blind cupidity, and provide for the future, and for generations yet in the womb of time, by artificially directing industry into those channels which will be ultimately and permanently beneficial. Such was, as we have seen, the public wisdom of ancient Egypt and modern Holland; such was the wisdom of Lord Burleigh, and Cromwell, of Colbert, and Napoleon. Such was the wisdom of Peter the Great; such is still the traditional wisdom and inflexible policy of his successors. Contemplate the grand result. Over the immense extent of Russia, all the industries of all nations are beginning to thrive. Russia is at this day preparing her own cotton-fields in Central Asia and on shores of the Caspian. Silently and deeply are being laid the foundations of an independent and self-sufficing power, before which (when our vain theories are forgotten) the earth will admire and tremble.

One of these temporary and accidental disadvantages against which public wisdom has to guard, is the necessary and invariable inferiority of *infant* manufacturing industry. No matter that the infant is capable of soon becoming not only a man, but a giant, if not protected during infancy, he will languish and die.

Established manufactures enjoy the factitious advantages of great capital, skill, and experience. Production on a large scale, in immense quantities, creates a cheapness which unprotected infant establishments elsewhere

—though their natural advantages may be much greater
—cannot rival. They are smothered as soon as they
are born. Accordingly all manufactures, however
great, have been and ever must be, cradled in protection. Go to the Great Exhibition and find, if you can,
those that were not. So far from protection producing
monopoly, it is protection alone that can prevent the first-
established manufactures from enjoying an unjust and
undeserved monopoly. It is protection alone that can
establish a wholesome rivalry, or even secure the certain
development of manufactures, where there are the greatest
natural advantages.

Nay, this is a case where protection is essential to ultimate CHEAPNESS as well as plenty. Mr. Burke's maxim
is here no paradox,—"Make things dear," says he,
"that they may be cheap."

But it is not only new states or new industries that
require protection for their development—old states, and
old industries sometimes require it, for the preservation
and very existence of their most valuable industry.

In old countries, the land which cannot run away,
ever has been, and ever will be, the obvious and convenient subject of taxation—the sure resource of the
Minister of Finance in the crisis of the State. Accordingly, in England, we see it loaded with tithe, land-tax,
income-tax, hop-tax, malt-tax, poor-rates, church-rates,
highway-rates, county-rates. * So in France, it is
crushed under an immense weight of direct taxation.
If by a compensating duty the price of corn is raised to
a corresponding amount, and no more, then these taxes
fall where they ought to fall on the nation at large.
But if not, and if corn comes in from new or more fertile countries, where it is only necessary to scratch the
soil, and the price consequently falls too low, huge tracts

---

* This passage was written, it may be remembered, in 1849.

of the old country may become unprofitable under till-
age, and be smitten with an artificial barrenness.   The
people then lose a large portion of their natural and
healthy employment; the independence of the State is
compromised; the stamina and physical vigor of the
race itself is touched.   Corn is cheap enough, the loaf is
big enough, but where is the money to buy?

Moreover, the true gain of every country is ample
wages to the laborer.   The laboring classes are THE NA-
TION.   They are the producers, and they are, moreover,
the greatest consumers.   Their expenditure makes the
great home market.

But in the fierce struggle of universal competition, extending over the whole earth, the remuneration of the
laborer must be everywhere beaten down to the level
of the worst-paid laborers in the world, whether free-
men or slaves.   The industrious and virtuous English
workman must starve, unless he will consent to be, with
his wife and children, as badly fed, clothed and lodged
as the most wretched of his competitors.

But it is objected, if free exchanges be good between
two provinces of the same country, why not also between
different countries?   If they are good between the Pas
de Calais and the Department of the North, between
Suffolk and Norfolk, why are they not good also between France and England, or between Germany and
England?

This objection is an example of that reckless and head-
strong generalisation, which, to carry out a theory, will
overlook or overleap broad distinctions.

First, suppose that one province should lose, and
another province of the same country gain, what is that
to the country of which they are both members?   Its
aggregate gain is exactly the same.   But, suppose France
or Germany to lose, and England to gain by unregulated

exchanges, this is all very well for England, but not for France or Germany.

But there are good reasons why, in ordinary cases, two provinces of the same country will both gain by free and unregulated exchanges, though of two countries, politically and geographically distinct, either or both might lose.

An extensive area of mutual exchange is essential to production on a large scale.

The taxation, the climate, the soil, the style of living, the rate of wages, being very much alike in two provinces of the same country, neither province is matched unfairly against its neighbor.

There is still that mutual vicinity of consumers and producers which, as we have seen, is essential to variety of employment, to the utilisation of all products and of all hands.

But there is a distinction between an *extensive* area for unregulated exchanges and an *unlimited* one. An extensive area is essential to the development of production on a large scale, and at a cheap rate; but an unlimited one is not. On the contrary, an unlimited one endangers the security and certainty of the home market, and the wages of the laborer. Various German states have recently greatly augmented their mutual industry by joining the Zolverein. But if they had gone further and thrown their markets open to England, they know very well that at that time they would have impoverished and ruined themselves. Now their protected industry begins to supersede ours.

Nay, that free exchanges even between provinces of the same empire are good, is itself a rule not without exceptions. Before the Union between England and Ireland, there were not only Irish linen manufacturers, but Irish wool-combers, Irish carpet manufacturers, Irish blanket manufacturers, Irish hosiers, Irish broad-silk loom-weavers, Irish calico-printers; for there existed be-

fore the Union, Irish protection against English manufactures. That protection was by the Act of Union
gradually withdrawn. These last industries are now all
extinct. Ireland has certainly lost something by the
change. Has England gained? It may be doubted.
Ireland is now not so much a customer as a pauper dependent on English alms. No one desires to see the
old state of things restored, but it raises some serious
questions, as we shall see by-and-by.

To conclude, then, because an extensive area of mutual exchanges is beneficial, that therefore the larger it
is the better; and that an unlimited area of unregulated
exchanges must necessarily be best of all, is to conclude
without reason and against facts. On the contrary, to
determine the extent, and the component parts of that
area of unregulated exchanges, which will best nourish
production and best distribute its results, is a most difficult problem. In almost every case its true solution
varies. In every case it is the problem for the great
statesman.

Then it is objected, if each country produce what it
is by nature fitted for, industry will everywhere be more
productive, and everbody will have more.

Alas! we have seen that many countries would at
once cease to produce at all. In order to gain in one
or two places one or two per cent. in favor of the consumer, you will sacrifice in scores of places 98 or 99
per cent., which the producers used to have, and used
to spend every year, and often many times a year. The
ultimately cheapest manufactures will be often prevented or destroyed by the mere monopoly of priority.
Instead of multiplying the sum-total of the products of
human industry, you will not only greatly diminish
them, but contract the area over which they extend.
And the most numerous and important class of all, the
laborer, instead of having more, will—by being every-

where driven to compete with the most wretched competitors—necessarily almost everywhere have a great deal less.

Next it is objected that, looking at the different climates and different capabilities of countries, it is manifestly the intention of Providence, that there should be universal free and unregulated exchanges.

It is unfortunate for this assertion that for the thousands of years during which man has existed on this earth, such exchanges should not have existed.

Each nation, by regarding its own interests, has promoted, and will promote them, and so the general interest of the whole human race will be effectually furthered and secured.

Let us, as Englishmen, look to the interests of the United Kingdom. Let us, at any rate, secure British and Irish industry, leaving other countries in the same way to secure theirs. This practical division of solicitude and labor will conduce far more to the general diffusion of industry and wealth, and the solid advancement of mankind, than a Quixotic and presumptuous assumption of the care of Providence over the whole human race. We do not, in ordinary social life, find the doctrines of professed cosmopolites either very exemplary or very useful. It is by the conscientious performance of his own duty on the part of every individual in his own family and humble sphere, that the happiness of the whole mass is best promoted; it is by the undivided attention of every workman to his corner of the building, that the most magnificent edifice rises. So it is by the care of its own industry on the part of every European country, that population, wealth, industry, commerce, science, learning, and the arts have been diffused and will be maintained throughout this glorious Europe.

Lastly, it is said the artificial regulation of the areas within which exchanges take place will destroy international trade.

Experience has already demonstrated the contrary. The places and the subjects mutually beneficial exchange on terms advantageous to both sides. We are still to import our wine, our cotton, our tea, our dyes, our sugar, our spices, our timber; nay, even the corn and provisions, and everything else that we really want. But by proper regulation, we are to take care that these imports shall, as far as practicable, come either from our own Colonies, or at least from countries that will deal with us again. Imports will thus have their corresponding exports. We shall thus double and not diminish the international trade. And it will be everywhere a commerce, not between wealth at one end, and indigence at the other, but between opulent and populous nations, emulating and rivalling each other.

Perhaps the candid reader will not now think it quite so certain, that if all countries practised free-trade, all countries would necessarily be gainers. It is possible he may be disposed to believe that many, perhaps most countries, and the most important classes in them, would be very great losers.

And certainly the great majority of nations and governments are, and seem likely still to remain, of this opinion.

So that if the maxim at the head of this chapter were as demonstrable as it is disputable, it would still be but a metaphysical abstraction, and a very poor foundation for a wise and practical statesman to legislate upon.

CHAPTER VII.

" Protected manufactures are sickly."

A METAPHORICAL expression, constantly repeated, little contradicted, and therefore by the half-informed believed. Whatever a man hears or reads constantly without contradiction he is apt to believe. Sale, the translator of the Koran, by constantly poring over it, is said to have become a Mahometan.

But this proposition is so far from being true, that a slight review of the history of any manufacture disproves it.

All great manufactures had their origin in the protective system. Take our own, the greatest, and, until lately, least sickly of any. All our own manufactures took their rise in a system of protective duties, so high as to amount to prohibitions. In addition to this, owing to the fearful hostilities that raged in Europe for nearly a quarter of a century before 1815, we enjoyed a further accidental monopoly of the manufacturing industry of the world. And this stringent protection has not only created manufactures, but created them where they would not naturally have existed, in spite of great natural disadvantages. Other nations have coal and iron ore as well as we. The United States are even richer in this respect. But other nations have also what we have not—they have native raw materials. It has been justly observed, that Great Britain is singularly poor in the raw materials which constitute the basis of the greater portion of her manufacturing industry. We have no cotton, no silk, no fine wool. Even our best iron for the manufacture of hardware comes from Sweden: our oils, gums, colors, woods, from the ends of the earth.

Next to us in manufacturing industry is France. Her manufacturing industry, though still inferior to ours, has nevertheless, since the peace, augmented in an even greater ratio, but under strict and jealous protection.

No political parties can differ more widely than do the partisans of the exiled Head of the house of Bourbon (really including the larger portion of the upper and educated classes) from the Orleanists and middle classes; or than these again from the republicans, propagandists, socialists, and ultra-reformers.* Yet on the subject of protection (with the exception of some theoretical writers and wine-growers in the south) they are all agreed. Protection to French industry, from the time of Colbert downwards, has been, and will be the policy of whatever party is uppermost in France; and in this policy, and this alone, will the dominant party receive the support of all parties. The few French partisans of free-trade being mostly speculative and literary men, we might have supposed that the French newspaper press, rich as it is in literary talent of the first order, or that at least a considerable portion of it, would be favorable to their views. But it is not so. Nay, the very newspaper which has been for many years the advocate of progress and liberal views, the *Constitutionnel*, is and always has been, the most determined champion of protection. In fact, among all classes, and in all parts of the country, in the metropolis,

---

* This passage was written before the accession of Napoleon II., who, perhaps, will be recorded as having done more for France than any previous monarch.

and in the provinces, the doctrines of protection prevail and flourish. The stupendous natural boundaries of the country, the very Alps and Pyrenees themselves, do not repose on their everlasting foundations more securely than the artificial barriers that protect and foster the native industry of France.*

After France comes Germany. Let any one, before the late struggles, have visited the countries embraced by the Zolverein. To say that protection has there *produced* manufacturing prosperity, would be to beg the question. But one thing is certain, that exactly *coincident in time and place* with the most stringent protective laws, has arisen a manufacturing industry and production of wealth, without an approach to a parallel in all the former history of Germany. On every side are seen rising mills, factories, workshops, and warehouses, teeming with an industrious and busy population; and so far from agriculture being neglected, it never made more rapid progress, to say nothing of the mining and metallurgical industry, which has also received the most astonishing impetus. Yet with us—the richest country in the world—the Zolverein, in proportion to her vast extent, multitudinous population and increasing wealth, has little trade. But as she has protected herself from the influx of our manufactures, she has undoubtedly been growing richer and busier. Nay, hardware, the product of protected German industry, is actually finding its way into Birmingham itself, and articles of German manufacture are superseding articles of Birmingham make. The more protected are beginning to beat the less protected manufactures on their own ground. The Birmingham people have no

---

* Look at the overwhelming majority for protection, including all parties in the recent debate of the National Assembly, 1849.

power to retaliate: German tariffs take care of that. German thinkers, deeper and more independent than the English, have exposed the shallowness of those theories which have turned our heads. Princes, ministers, philosophers, and people are agreed to maintain the protection which has so abundantly justified their sagacity.

Look next at Russia. Examine the protective and jealous tariff of that infant but colossal state; then contemplate its results. Take the testimony of that most unexceptionable witness, Mr. Cobden. He has recently visited the protected textile manufactures of Russia, which, but for protection, would never have had existence. And what does he say? That the Russians are to be our customers for cotton goods, and to take them in exchange for the boundless importations of corn from the Black Sea? Vain delusion! According to him these protected manufactures, which should, in conformity with our received theories, have been sickly and stunted, are now so advanced and flourishing as to threaten a rivalry with Great Britain herself. And every branch of human industry and art is, by the same means, beginning to flourish and expand in an empire which, stretching from west to east, and from east to west again, in almost unbroken continuity around Europe, Asia, and America, extends in latitude from Archangel nearly to Constantinople, embracing, notwithstanding its sterile tracts, some of the finest climates and soils in the world, connected and concentrated as they will soon become by its new iron highways. Within her borders are cherished and naturalised the productions of all lands. We have just seen in England specimens of the finest steel from native Russian iron, fabricated in Russia, not only into the swords, bayonets, and lances of an overwhelming military power, but into table cutlery and tools. that you might suppose to have been turned out at Birmingham and Sheffield; while the gold and silver plate, the diamonds, the jewelry, the exquisite silks, the gold and silver tissues and brocade, dispute the prize with Paris and Lyons. Storch, the political economist, about the year 1815, persuaded the Russian government to give the free-trade system a trial. It was tried. It dismally failed, and was abandoned. All are now agreed that domestic production is the true policy of Russia; and all find, that in Russia, as everywhere else, it is the sure road to prosperity and power.*

Take now a small state, Belgium. In proportion to her area, her manufacturing industry is perhaps greater than that of any other country, not excepting the United Kingdom itself. But in Belgium, not only has the protective system long flourished, but the protecting duties are now higher than ever. Belgium is the very Paradise of protection. Nay, there is even a bounty on exportation. Superficial observers call it an absurd tax on the many for the benefit of a few. But those who know the facts of the case, and will be at the pains to trace its effects, and assert the liberty of independent judgment, find it the cheapest mode in a season of great danger and difficulty, of supporting the apparent surplus of an immense population. Many who censure the king and government of Belgium, for this flagrant breach of dry and barren rules, would have found greater difficulty in preserving that little and defenceless kingdom, not only in peace, but prosperity, amidst the storms of surrounding revolution. Here again, as elsewhere, the advantages of the proximity, or, rather,

---

* Will it be said that the vast extent, the great population, and varied climate of Russia, form an exception to general rules? What then must be said to the almost equal extent, much larger population, more varied climates, and boundless sea-coasts of the British empire?

the contiguity of agriculture and manufactures are apparent. Protected manufacturing industry has overflown on the soil. Land, by nature a mere sand, has actually but artificially become the most fertile in Europe, and supports a larger population than any other.*

Cross the Atlantic, and look at the past and present policy of the United States. For some years after the last war, † low import duties were tried. The effects were ruinous; ‡ they were abandoned for duties avowedly protective. Our economists prognosticated mischief, but the result was prosperity, and a vast extension of the cotton, woollen, and iron manufactures. Branches of industry, which in the presence of free imports from England would never have had even a beginning, now threaten rivalry.

Protection! protection! is now the instinctive cry of the nation, and the settled policy of the government. Enormous duties, though lately somewhat moderated, are at this hour levied on all our manufactures for the avowed purpose of protection. American cotton-mills have risen up, § and are beginning to buy away, on the spot, the cotton from our Manchester manufacturers. A powerful party are actually calling for an increase of protection, although American protected manufactures are beginning to make their appearance in our market.

Who is the man of all the American citizens, ‖ by age, experience, sound practical wisdom, high character, and great natural talent, best qualified to occupy the presidential chair? Impartial judges will say, Henry Clay. It is well known that he, though a Southerner,

---

* See the chapter on the Theory of Rent.
† This passage was written before the late American civil war.
‡ See Mr. Carey's detailed and accurate history of these changes and their effects.
§ And of late in the South as well as in the North. 1850.
‖ This passage was written in 1850.

is a staunch advocate of protection, and declares free-trade to be a flattering illusion, destructive, in his judgment, to the solid interests of America. What, says Daniel Webster? His talent, penetration, experience, and judgment, no man doubts. He once was a free-trader, but he now declares that free-trade is erroneous in theory, and would in practice inflict mortal injury on his country. But the actual President, General Taylor, is an avowed protectionist. *   More enlightened society is not to be found in the world than in the city of Boston ; yet there, as elsewhere, and among the most enlightened and influential classes, the doctrines of protection reign triumphant.

What is the consequence of this policy? Or that we may not be charged with the old sophism, *"Post hoc ergo propter hoc,"* what is coincident with this misdirected industry? No longer (as during the low import duties) general distress, but prodigious prosperity. Notwithstanding a most expensive war, the United States never were so prosperous as at this hour. †

Here are instances of nations adopting the protective system. In every case manufactures have been *created*, not sickly and stunted, but healthy and flourishing ; in almost every case in the face of natural disadvantages ; in all cases industry has been *forced* into an artificial channel, but the result has been solid and prodigious prosperity.

Need we wonder, that in every one of these states, protection continues the universal creed of the people, and the settled, immovable policy of the government?

I mistake. One of these states, and the one that has flourished most under the protective system, has suddenly altered its opinion, and altered its policy. So it

---

* His successor, Mr. Filmore, is yet more decidedly so. These observations were written in 1849.

† This passage was written in 1850.

4

once changed its mixed and free government for a republic. And as it then soon reverted to its ancient
constitution, so will it ere long revert to its ancient
commercial policy. *   That policy will then be trebly
justified, as well by the ruin attending its desertion, as
by the prosperity following its original adoption, and
its final resumption.

But the maxim that protected manufactures are
sickly and stunted, must not escape so easily. There
are other tests of its truth.

Where are the great and flourishing manufactures
that have never enjoyed protection?—that were not
produced and cradled by it?

Let the Great Exhibition of 1851 reply to the inter-
rogatory.

Stand in the centre of the magnificent transept, and
look around. Then go and explore the naves, the
sides, the galleries. The marvels of industry created
and nurtured by protection shine everywhere, above,
below, around, and on all sides. But what has unprotected industry to show? If unregulated exchanges be
(as you say) not only the most congenial and invigorating, but the natural atmosphere of manufacturing
industry, surely you can point out some specimens of
its rise and luxuriant growth, under such obvious and
favorable circumstances. We will be content with a
specimen. *Ex pede Herculem.* You may search and
ransack as long as you please. No trophy of a GREAT
MANUFACTURE, not indebted to protection for its incep-
tion, is to be found there. Not (we may be well assured)
because it is excluded, but because it exists not.

If unprotected manufactures are anywhere to be found,
they are the sickly and stunted ones.

---

* Written in 1850.

Look at the two nations in Europe that most freely admit foreign commodities. They are Ireland and Turkey.

I say Ireland, because she has, and has had for many, many years, perfect free-trade with the richest manufacturing nation on earth, and now has railways to distribute that trade. With the single exception of the linen trade, which, as we shall hereafter see, was actually created and maintained by protection, and assisted by annual government grants for a long series of years, has she any but manufactures of the most sickly complexion? Alas! Ireland is but another name for everything that is capable, but withal wretched and abortive.

Look at Turkey. Her customs duties have been and are low, her commercial system is what is called a liberal one. The ruins of Asia Minor attest that it once did, and still might, maintain a multitudinous population. Now Asia Minor is a desert. No part of the vast dominions of the Sultan exhibit any good effect of his liberal tariff.

One reason why Canada has not advanced so rapidly as the neighboring districts of the United States is, that Canada had no manufactures, but the United States had. Canada had none, because our manufactures smothered all infant ones. The United States have manufactures, because they have protecting duties. Till recently we gave Canada, as an equivalent, protection in our markets, as we were protected in hers. We have taken it away. What is Canada doing now?

The *facts* are, everywhere, that protected manufactures are healthy and robust; unprotected manufactures, sickly, stunted, and precarious.

A nation that manufactures for itself prospers.

Nor are the reasons difficult to discover.

A nation that manufactures for itself, as well as grows

food for itself, produces two values and creates two markets instead of one.

A manufacturing nation grows rich much faster than a mere agricultural one, for an obvious reason.

An agricultural people turn over the greater part of their capital only once a year. The manufacturers sometimes turn it over three, four, or a dozen times a year—that is to say, they may *create* the total amount of their circulating capital many times in the year.

Neither manufacturing nor agricultural industry is any longer limited by the accidental capacity of foreign markets. Manufactures create a market for food; food, for manufactures. Both may increase by each other's help, and manufactures to an unlimited extent.

One great cause of our alternations of manufacturing prosperity and distress, and the absence of steady progress, is the want of a due balance between the production of food and raw produce, and the production of other things—a balance to be restored by encouraging and developing the employment of the people on the land, not only in England, Scotland, and Ireland, but in the Colonies, and by the importation of food from abroad, giving, however, the preference to those who will reciprocate on fair terms. What fields we have! But we are spell-bound.

CHAPTER VIII.

" Pas trop gouverner—Don't over-govern."

"It is," says Mr. Burke, "one of the finest problems in legislation, what the State ought to take upon itself to direct by public wisdom, and what it ought to leave with as little interference as possible to individual exertion."

Such is the modest and diffident tone of wisdom and experience on this thorny subject.

How different from the positive and disdainful language of many modern theorists. Instances of injudicious interference on the part of government are easily pointed out in the ancient legislation of this and other countries. Immediately the people, educated and uneducated, depreciating what they are pleased to call paternal government, rush as usual to the opposite extreme, denounce all interference by public wisdom, and paralyse its most beneficial action.

Twenty years ago it was generally considered as settled, that the business of government was to do as little as possible. Its duty was summed up in a few words, "Keep the peace, coin money, and leave all the rest to the people." *Pas trop gouverner* was to be the pole-star of statesmen. They were to look down on sublunary affairs like the gods of Epicurus, and trust to the natural course of events, as necessarily beneficial. A policy far from distasteful to rulers, whom it saves not merely from the labor of thought, but from the responsibility of action. The fashionable doctrine was that the interests of individuals and the interest of the public (which is but an aggregation of individuals) necessarily and universally coincide. Individuals know their interests better than the government, and may and should be left to take care of themselves. The ignorant and prejudiced vulgar are to receive no impulse, in the shape of direct legislative enactment, from their governing and more enlightened superiors. *

Don't, it is said, treat men as *children;* treat them as being what they are, *grown men.* Let mankind learn by experience.

But who does not see the fallacy that lurks under such advice? It treats the successive generations of mankind and the existing multitudes of men as if they constituted a single individual, living to the age of the patriarchs, and possessing the experience not only of past times, but of other places and hemispheres.

But what is the bulk of any nation really?

Station yourself at the gate of a churchyard or cemetery, and observe who are carried in: the young are carried in, and a proportion of middle-aged persons: very rarely will you see an old man carried in.

---

* In France, even before the late revolution, public opinion as to the true functions of government had undergone a great change. The let alone system had begun among reflecting men to fall into discredit. Let us hear what M. Chevalier, himself a professor of political economy, says on this subject :—" J'ai eu à cœur de combattre des préjugés accrédités en France, et par la France dans le reste du monde, en vertu desquels le gouvernement devrait se réduire à des fonctions de surveillance subalterne, lui qui, comme son nom indique, est appelé à tenir le gouvernail."

" En France, il y a vingt ans encore, les publicistes les plus distingués, les économistes dont la reputation était la mieux assise, et la mieux meritée étaient presque tous de cette opinion négative. Les théories d'économie publique les plus repandues posaient en principe, que le gouvernement ne doit rien faire par lui-même, qu'il est essentiellement mal-adroit . . . *En fait une réaction s'opère dans les meilleurs esprits,* elle renverse des idées éphémères."

The bulk of every nation, therefore, are young and inexperienced, and ever must be so.

As to their knowledge of the experience of past generations, they know of it about as much as they know of transactions, or social experiments, in the planet Jupiter, a hundred years ago.

The state of Ireland, and the state of England too, are, however, rapidly undeceiving those who held these extreme notions. Public opinion is undergoing a change, and it will soon be demonstrated that there reside in every enlightened and wise government powers of active interference for good unknown and unsuspected.

A patient review of existing facts would, indeed, have sufficed to evince the hollowness of the yet fashionable theory, and to show not only that the interference of government in a hundred ways is indispensable to the very existence of civilisation, but that there is no single general rule or theory to determine when it ought or ought not to interpose, that the propriety of interference in each case must be decided on its own circumstances.

Not to amuse ourselves with general terms, let us pass in review some of the cases in which government has interfered, in most cases indispensably, and in all, as is generally thought, beneficially.

It provides defences against external aggression.

It conducts treaties with foreign nations.

It preserves internal peace and order.

It is the corner-stone of family ties, family duties, family affection, family education, by regulating and enforcing the marriage contract.*

It institutes and protects property.

It regulates the transmission of property.

It enforces the repair of highways by the several districts through which they pass, or by those who use them.

---

* Now unhappily relaxed.

It obliges each county to make and repair its bridges.

It maintains ports and harbors.

It surveys and lights the sea-coasts of the realm.

It coins money, and prohibits interference with this monopoly.

It regulates the issue of promissory notes payable to bearer.

It provides a uniform system of weights and measures, and proscribes the use of any other.

It assumes the distribution of intelligence by the post.

By the patent* and copy-right laws it gives bounties on the exertion of the inventive faculties, in the shape of a *monopoly* for a limited period.

By requiring a public specification, explanatory of every patented discovery or invention, it takes care that the secret shall not be hidden from the public, nor die with the inventor.

It imposes a bridle on the acquisition of property by corporate bodies.

It protects the public health by the prohibition of nuisances of a thousand kinds, and by making provision for their removal.

By the quarantine laws, it prevents the importation of contagious diseases.†

It provides for the cleanliness of towns.

It regulates the fares of hackney carriages, and controls the drivers.

It forbids inoculation for the small-pox, and artificially promotes vaccination.

It assumes the distribution of insolvent estates.

---

* The former of these instances of interference may be doubtful in the present state of knowledge.

† Not to be lightly discarded. Medical opinion is veering back to old notions.

It has been found necessary (after signal suffering) to extend quarantine regulations even to animals.

It provides for the maintenance of the poor.

It forbids perpetuities by avoiding all attempts to tie up property beyond a life or lives in being, and twenty-one years after.

It restrains trusts for accumulation of property.

Though it tolerates all religions, it does not leave the virtue and happiness of the multitude without the support and direction of an established faith and worship. *

The government does some little (alas! how little) for the technical and industrial education of the people.

In the above cases government interferes on behalf of *the public.*

But there are many other cases where it interferes to protect the helplessness or inexperience of *individuals.*

It is a sound principle of universal law established by the wisdom of more than two thousand years, that where, in the necessary imperfection of human affairs, the parties to a contract or dealing do not stand on an equal footing, but one has an undue power to oppress or mislead the other, the law should step in to succor the weaker party.

It shields infants by avoiding their contracts and protecting their persons and property;

And married women;

---

* The Church of England would be at this moment more powerful and popular than ever, if she would submit to obvious reforms. Of all modern measures, none have been framed so wisely, or succeeded so well, as the Acts for the commutations of tithes.

Her younger sister, the Established Presbyterian Church of Scotland, has, ever since her final predominance at the Revolution, done more for the virtue, happiness, and general improvement of the community, than any other Church since the first establishment of Christianity. Few things are so much to be regretted as her disruption.

4*

And persons of unsound mind;

And in many ways, the helpless, laboring poor.

It forbids the truck system.

It regulates the employment of women and children in mines and factories.

It controls pawnbrokers—grinding the tooth of usury, and securing facilities for redemption;

It prohibits and punishes, as we have seen, the use of unjust weights and measures;

And the sale of unwholesome provisions;

And the adulteration of coffee, tobacco, snuff, beer, tea, cocoa, chocolate, and pepper.

Nor is it the laboring classes only that the law protects when individuals are liable to be oppressed and over-reached.

Suppose a man gives a money-bond, with a penalty if the money is not repaid at a day prefixed, the law will not allow the penalty to be enforced.

The barbarous old common law exacted the full and literal penalty. Experience showed that the law ought to step in, and shield a man even from the consequences of his own imprudence; otherwise the administration of justice itself would be converted into an engine of oppression, and be regarded not with respect, but with horror and disgust. In the reign of Henry VIII., Sir Thomas More unsuccessfully attempted to persuade the judges to grant relief at law against the penalty of a bond, on payment of principal, interest, and costs; and when they said they could not relieve against a penalty, he swore, "By the Body of God he would grant an injunction!" Equity was compelled to relieve, and at length the common-law judges were by statute enabled to relieve also.

A man binds himself in a large sum, say £1000, to observe the rules of a society. One of these rules, perhaps, is, that he shall contribute a shilling a month for a particular purpose; another that he shall hang his hat on a particular peg. He has inadvertently overlooked or forgotten, but broken, one of these rules. Is he not to be relieved from the penalty, if he pay his shilling a day too late, or if he hang his hat on the wrong peg? The law says he is.

A man in his necessities mortgages his property, and stipulates that if he do not redeem by a certain day, he shall not be at liberty to redeem at all. The law enforces his right to redeem after the stipulated time, in spite of his contract. It disregards an engagement which *may* have been wrung from the necessities, or filched from the inexperience of the mortgagor.

The law formerly interposed between the usurious lender and the necessitous borrower of money. It does so still, it is believed, in every European state, although there are instances of the repeal and subsequent re-enactment of usury laws.

In America, the law, as a general rule, interposes so far as to annul the contract for the excess beyond a fixed rate. Possibly this is a just medium between our former severity and our present laxity.

Mr. Bentham's book overlooks many obvious distinctions between the contract of loan of money* and other contracts.

The law interposes again between the necessitous seller of an expected future interest and the buyer.

The foolish young expectant heir to an estate of £1000 a year sells it for £500. When it was represented to Lord Hardwicke that these acts of folly could not be altogether prevented, the answer of the great magistrate was, "Est aliquid prodire tenus."

In some cases, the law points out to a man the form of his contracts, and the evidence which shall prove them, by insisting that they shall contain certain par-

---

* See *Observations on the Usury Laws.* London: Sweet, 1846.

ticulars, and shall be in writing—a provision, the wisdom of which a single day's experience in a court of justice will abundantly evince.*

To guard against fraud, the law directs the form and manner in which wills shall be executed.

These are rules not laid down before-hand by theory, but pointed out by experience, and not only justified by the practice of ages, but found to be absolutely indispensable.

A man grants an annuity for his life. The law supervises and registers the transaction. Many wholesale schemes of plunder were thus (when the usury existed) nipped in the bud.

The most stringent securities known to the law are warrants of attorney and cognovits. Under them body, land, and goods may be seized. An unlearned person requires these instruments, and the contingencies in which they may be used against him, to be explained to him; otherwise they might as well be written in Arabic. Accordingly the law smites with sentence of nullity all such instruments, unless the unfortunate person executing them has at his elbow, at the time of signature, an attorney of his own choosing, to explain their meaning fully.

A purchaser of gold and silver articles cannot tell whether they are real solid gold and silver or not, or how much of the weight is precious metal and how much alloy : he is constantly liable to be imposed on. The law steps in to his assistance, and provides the assay-mark of a public officer.

A man buys a pocket of hops. It cannot at particular seasons be opened to see if it is of the growth represented, or of uniform quality; a sample can only be taken from the outside. The purchaser is at the mercy

---

* On the Continent, the introduction of notarial contracts saves much litigation.

of the grower. Again the law steps in, and makes it penal to pack falsely.

An attorney sends in his bill to a client; how can the unfortunate client tell whether the charges are usual and fair? The law, having found competition a very inadequate security, provides a public officer, before whom the debtor is entitled to lay the bill for supervision, or taxation as it is called. This officer is endued with a power not only to correct, but to punish overcharges.

A passenger, or emigrant, going on board ship for a long voyage, is ignorant how much room, how much food, how much water, ought to be provided, that the healths and lives of the passengers may not be jeopardised. Experience has long decided that the law must come to his assistance.

The law compels the professional education of medical men and attorneys. Their competition for practice on the one hand, and the ordinary prudence of mankind on the other, are found by experience very ineffectual safeguards against empiricism and dishonesty. The law superadds artificial protection, which, though still inadequate to attain the end proposed, is of great use so far as it goes.

The law discourages gaming contracts, and avoids gaming policies of insurance on ships and lives. Without such provisions the perverseness of mankind would turn, and has turned, insurance offices into gambling houses.

The above are but some instances of the mode in which nearly all governments have found it for the advantage of the community to interpose. An abolition of almost any one of these functions of government would be a step backwards, from civilisation towards barbarism. But, until lately, our modern legislation has been destructive rather than constructive.

What is the interposition of government?

Simply the concentrated action of the wisdom and power of the whole society on a given point. A mutual agreement by all, that certain things shall be done or not done for the general benefit, and an enforcement of that agreement. Why should it ever have been assumed that this latent but most energetic power will be inefficient or necessarily injurious? Because men ought to be taught by experience—that is to say, ruined first and taught afterwards. The interposition of government may sometimes have been mis-directed or abused. But to argue from the abuse against the use is an ancient and transparent sophism. We have already seen that nothing but the force of government holds society together, and prevents the most flagrant and disorganising mischief, springing from a natural state of things. And great as are the benefits we derive from government—from the concentrated action of the whole community—still greater are yet in reserve. What the steam-engine is in practical mechanics, the artificial and concentrated action of the whole community may hereafter be in national economy. *Here*, and not in the *let-alone* system, lies the real hope of the ancient societies, the decrepit monarchies of Europe.

As in individuals, so in communities, we have seen vices and evil tendencies continually springing up, which a wise and vigilant legislation nips as they bud. Are there no rank and monstrous growths of evil that have never even yet been pruned—no wholesome plants that have never yet been set?

The natural, healthy, virtuous occupation of a man is the cultivation of the soil. In every healthy and permanent community it bears its due proportion to other industries. Otherwise you have overgrown towns, now in comparative prosperity, now in unspeakable distress. The moral depravation and physical deterioration of the race soon follow. A good and stable government of a depraved people is impossible: the more popular the government, the worse it is.

Can any reflecting person view, without alarm and wonder on the one hand, the congested and deteriorating population of the cities and towns of the United Kingdom, and on the other the imperfect cultivation even of England and Scotland, to say nothing of the acres of waste but cultivable lands in Ireland, or of the boundless agricultural resources of the Colonies?

Ought not the concentrated action of the whole community to be directed *to the fuller employment of the people on the land?*

The purification of great cities, and the proper use of their refuse, not by diluting and turning it into rivers or estuaries, thus polluting and poisoning the greatest blessings of nature, but by collecting it in other ways and restoring it to the land, may be made to increase our agricultural resources as much as if it enlarged our territory.

Small holdings, with stall-feeding and spade labor, even on lands so barren as to be unprofitable or inaccessible to the plough, together with the unoccupied lands in our own Colonies under our own control, present resources more than sufficient to absorb all the real surplus of our population.

Unhappily our recent policy has been in a direction at variance with the employment of the people on the land.

What stands in the way? Some fancied theories of the political economists about rent,* and the mischief of bringing inferior lands into cultivation. Theories unsound in themselves, and every day practically contradicted by the unexpected fecundity† of untried lands,

---

* See the observations on the modern Theory of Rent—infrà.

† Witness the experiments which have lately been made on Chat-Moss. A few years ago it was deemed an irreclaimable bog. It is now demonstrated, that at small expense it is capable of becoming some of the most valuable land in England. And

and fertilisation by new processes. Theories which
railways, new roads, new manures, the resources of
agricultural chemistry, an improved tenure of large
farms, and the introduction of small ones, will laugh to
scorn as practical guides.

Another opposing theory is, that the interests of the
community and the interest of individuals always coincide.

It is the present interest of many large landowners
in Scotland to dispossess the cultivators and lay down
the land for moors, because the land will then let to
sportsmen for more money. Are these proceedings in
the true interest of the whole community?

We have seen some of the numberless instances in
which when, of two parties, one is weaker or more
incompetent than the other, the law steps in to the aid
of the weaker party, and places both on level ground,
although the public have no direct interest in the transaction. Especially ought the law so to do when the
public have a vital interest in the contract which that
weaker party makes.

A tenant in Ireland takes a farm or bit of land. He
can do nothing but cultivate land. He must take it or
starve. Even if he cultivate at an eventual loss, his
little property could not be better employed. He is
at the mercy of his landlord. He will bid for a farm
at a losing rent, because the quantity of land is limited.
And what is much worse, he has neither the knowledge, nor the *power*, to engraft on the contract stipu-
lations securing to him the benefit of improvements.
If he make improvements, he knows they will belong
to his landlord; and so they do. But, in general,
he *will not* make them. Unless the law interpose,
there exists, therefore, an effectual practical bar to improvement and to the full cultivation of the land.

what is true of Chat-Moss is true of the Irish bogs. See the
observations on the Theory of Rent—infra.

Here the law ought to interfere. It might easily, in all cases, secure to tenants the full benefit of proper improvements. It might thus at once secure the landlord from any danger of being obliged to repay them, and yet improve his estate. It is mere trifling to say the landlord and tenant *can* do this now. The fact is, they *do not*, and the tenant *cannot:* both are sufferers, but the greatest sufferer is the public. *

A vast unperceived change has come over the country within the last two hundred years. The masses—the bulk of the people—now live entirely on wages. On the rate of wages hangs the weal or woe of the United Kingdom. A difference of a shilling or two in the rate of wages may make many millions sterling difference in the aggregate annual income of the laboring classes, and, of course, in their expenditure and consumption—in the market they create. The laboring poor are the great customers.

One great series of measures in a right direction have lately passed—the *Factory Acts.* They have been successful measures. So has every measure in the same sense: witness the laws against the truck system. Humanity is the profoundest policy.

These measures, it must be admitted logically, lead to others. Modern political economy condemns them all; but experience will be found to justify much further progress in the same direction: it is interfernce for the bulk of the people. Such interference is, however, indissolubly united with a protective system. Those who by law are bound to treat men *as men*, must not be exposed to unfair competition with those who are at liberty to treat them as slaves and machines. It would be easy to show that the apprehensions of the political

* These observations were written in 1849. This matter is too serious to be settled on mere commercial principles. Indeed, in the case of land, the quantity of which is limited, mere commercial principles are inapplicable.

economist, that legislation of such a tendency would diminish the fund out of which labor * is paid, and unduly stimulate population, are utterly groundless; nay, that the effect would be the very contrary—to increase markets, increase industry, augment the fund out of which wages are paid, and introduce habits of forethought and caution among the laboring poor.

Minor cases, in which the still further interposition of government is imperatively required, crowd upon us.

Can the people be safely left even to bury their dead as they like? Churchyards and other crowded cemeteries were not shut up till government interposed.

Can they be trusted to remove the refuse even of small towns and villages (to which the earth-closet system may easily be applied), and employ that refuse on the fertilisation of their lands? Do they not convert into poison and death the provision which providence has made for indefinite reproduction? For the earth, our mother, LENDS, but she will not GIVE.

Do not frightful and frequent accidents call for more efficient inspection of mines?

Do not shareholders in railways require the protection of public auditors?

It is now too late to repair the incalculable loss and mischief occasioned by abandoning the setting out of the iron highways of the land to competition and the let-alone system.

But two remediable railway evils cry aloud for the interposition of public wisdom.

What man of business can understand, much less verify, the published accounts of railways?

---

* See the observations on Wages—infrà.

Public, able, trustworthy, and disinterested railway auditors are indispensable. They need cost the public nothing. The railways should bear the expense, which would be inconsiderable. But the auditors must be appointed by government, must give their undivided attention, and be as entirely independent of the railways, as judges are of suitors.

A second evil is the absence of central control over the traffic, and especially the passenger traffic.

Mr. Cardwell's Act, passed several years ago, for the regulation of traffic on railways and canals, was a sound and useful measure; but unfortunately it did not go far enough, and gave the control to an unfit tribunal.

Railway travelling, as now conducted in England, is a serious, unnecessary, and increasing addition to the perils of human life. Competiton between railways forces every railway to run supernumerary trains more than half empty, and at dangerous speed. On the continent the trains are fewer, but full. Yet no railway in England dare reduce the number of its trains, lest some rival line should supersede it, and engross the traffic. The consequence is danger to the public, incessant and unnecessary wear and tear of way and rolling stock, and great increase of wages and all other expenses to each and all the railways.

Some railway tribunal, composed of practical men, should be appointed to guard the true interests no less of the railways than of the public: for in this matter they happen to coincide. Mr. Cardwell's Act gave jurisdiction to the Court of Common Pleas; but that court is a very unfit tribunal in railway matters, however useful it may have been in those branches of specially delegated jurisdiction with which it is familiar, such as interpreting the Reform Acts, carrying into effect the plain intentions of parliament, and finally settling all difficulties by declaring the law.

Ought there not to be cheap, * certain, public communications by steam with the Colonies?—steam vessels, that shall be bridges in peace, and if not, floating castles, yet effective cruisers in war.

The policy of the Romans was as much wiser and grander than ours as their means of locomotion were inferior. Contemplate the ruins of the Appian, Aurelian, Emilian, and Flaminian ways. On four feet of masonry repose huge blocks of basalt, surmounted by slabs of marble a foot thick, and ten feet square, jagged with a chisel to prevent the slipping of the horses. Some of the Roman roads have borne the traffic of two thousand years. Radiating from the Imperial City in right lines, here ascending, there piercing mountains, or spanning morasses, and recommencing beyond the sea, they penetrated and bound together, Italy, Gaul, Spain, Britain, Germany, Greece, Asia Minor, Syria, and Northern Africa. These vast constructions were achieved at the public expense, by a people wise enough to appreciate their utility and magnificence.

Ought there not to be government supervision and government guarantee of the Savings Banks? †

Many such questions may be put.

The true admonition at this day is not, "Do not over-govern." It is, "Do not under-govern." Government has practically abjured half the functions of which the people have a right to expect its discharge. The vessel of the state now never so much as attempts to

---

* Experience both in Europe and America has demonstrated that such communications cannot be achieved by private enterprise alone: hence government aid has been wisely granted to lines of steamers connecting Great Britain with British India, with the Cape of Good Hope, with the British West Indies, and with British North America. But they are not yet the bridges which entice the footsteps of the emigrating multitude to our own colonies.

† This was written in 1850

stem an adverse current, but on principle resigns itself
to the stream. *

Let any individual abandon himself to the natural
course of events, and we know what will soon become
of him. Let a number of individuals, a community,
do the same, and their fate will be the same.

---

* It must be recollected that these observations were penned in
1849. Much has been done since.

CHAPTER IX.

" What is the good of Colonies ? "

So say the ultra-free-traders.

"Give me ships, *colonies*, and commerce," said the greatest administrative genius of modern times.

Well does it behove the rulers of the British Empire to see to it, that they commit no mistake in this matter. A mistake here is irreparable. The world is now occupied. No more colonies are to be had. Repentance and a change of public opinion, however soon it may arrive, may yet come too late.

Almost within living memory, through an indiscretion of our own government, we lost America. A little conciliation, and that vast confederacy might at this moment have been proud to call themselves members and subjects of an empire encircling the globe.

Steam, as an effectual means of communication by land and ocean, has not existed twenty years.* The wonders of the electric telegraph have but just burst on our astonished sight. Our fashionable but ephemeral anti-colonial theories, modern as they are, are nevertheless older than iron highways, Atlantic steamers, and the electric telegraph. They therefore leave entirely out of their calculations the connecting and concentrating efficacy of these momentous modern discoveries.

Steam has transformed the little peddling manufacturing villages of the last century into Manchesters and

---

* This passage was written in 1849.

Birminghams. On towns, and on a small scale, such are its effects; on empires, and on a large scale, its effects will be proportionate. Uniformity in language, manners, opinion, law, government—simultaneous and concerted action over enormous portions of the earth's surface, hitherto impossible—are now suddenly rendered not only possible, but perfectly easy. Time and distance are annihilated. The aggregation of vast masses of mankind under one governing power, will minimise the expenses of government, consolidate its strength, augment its efficacy, and ensure its duration. We already see the approaching shadows of those gigantic confederations which a coming age will witness. The two colossal empires that even now loom in the distance are the United States and Russia. Possibly a third may be descried, and a greater than either of the other two, unless it pleases Providence only to show us the mighty possible future of Great Britain, and then to dash our insipient greatness by allowing us to persevere in a disintegrating policy, in spite of the plainest warnings.

Let us consider for a moment what our colonial empire consists of, and what it can do for us.

Our noblest dependency is the Indian empire. It has been lately increased, and to an enlightened policy rendered more valuable than ever, by the acquisition of the Punjaub. Two of the greatest rivers in Asia are now ours, and may easily be made available, not only for internal communication, but for the fertilisation of vast districts. A new field for British skill and science and in a healthy and temperate climate, has just been opened up. The revenues of the new province are already so large that it need be no expense. Within our own borders, India now presents us with the productions of all lands and all climates—cotton, silk, fine wool, sugar, spices, rice, and every other natural production that can be desired, in inexhaustible profusion.

And these immense natural riches are India's means for the unlimited purchase of Manchester, Birmingham, and Sheffield goods. Her custom-houses are ours. Trade with India alone, under proper regulations, is capable of soon becoming almost as great as the whole present foreign trade of Great Britain.

Turn to the West. We have Upper and Lower Canada, with the magnificent St. Lawrence. Inexhaustible forests, and supplies of wood, on our own soil. Every Canadian already dines off an English table-cloth, with English knives and forks, clears and cultivates with English tools, sets his foot on an English carpet, sleeps on an English bed, is clothed from head to foot in English manufactures; and till lately, he was satisfied and proud to be a British subject.*

We have New Brunswick, with its timber and ship-building capabilities. Nova Scotia, with the most magnificent and commodious harbors in the world. In the harbor of Halifax alone 1000 ships can ride safely, to say nothing of the harbors of Margaret's Bay, St. Mary's Bay, the Basin of Mines, the Annapolis Basin, Picton Harbor, and Cumberland Basin. There is a neighboring power that forms a juster estimate than we do of these means of maritime greatness and imperial wealth.

We have, in the same part of the world, Cape Breton, Prince Edward's Island, and the Hudson Bay territory.

The West India Islands, so cruelly treated,† might,

---

* Written in 1850.

† Slave labor is abolished and prohibited throughout the West Indies. But those Colonies are nevertheless unjustly and cruelly matched against slave labor. The same blow has smitten and destroyed at once and everywhere the whole British West Indian interest. Plantations are abandoned to the jaguars and other wild beasts; mills and machinery silent and decaying; roads obliterated by the rank growth of the jungle; dykes that fenced large and fertile districts against the sea, left to ruin. The white population are everywhere ruined, if not disaffected. The blacks

since the introduction of steam, be just as valuable to us as new counties, with a tropical climate, in the English channel, or as sugar plantations, with a congenial climate, in Suffolk or Yorkshire, were such changes as possible as they are imaginable.

We actually have, within a run of a few days, almost of a few hours, several provinces adapted by nature to supply us with tropical productions.

First, there is the noble island of Jamaica, the aggregate imports and exports of which island alone used to be about five millions sterling a year, and which, if it were treated as it ought to be, like an English county, might be, and soon would be, much more. We have then the long list of Antigua, Barbadoes, Dominica, Grenada, Montserrat, Nevis, St. Christopher, St. Lucia, St. Vincent, Tobago, Tortola, Trinidad, the Bahamas, and the settlements of Demerara and Berbice—all once most flourishing and loyal dependencies, many of them now sinking to decay. Alienated by a policy unexpected, because incredible, but in the near neighborhood of a great and rising state, whose policy is altogether different.

---

forsaking the chapels and schools, shunning the face of the white man, neglecting marriage, and casting off not only Christianity, but the decencies and restraints of civilised life, are fast relapsing into their original barbarism. A tropical climate and teeming soil nourish their indolence, inflame their sensuality, diminish their wants, and easily supply them. High wages cease to be, as in England, a temptation to labor. Upon a strict calculation. even on mere sordid pecuniary and mercantile principles, the gain to the British empire by a little lower price of sugar is a miserable percentage upon the loss of *income* to British subjects, to say nothing of CAPITAL annihilated. Those who may be inclined to think this description of the present wretched state of the West Indies overcharged are implored to peruse "LORD STANLEY'S FURTHER FACTS CONNECTED WITH THE WEST INDIES." A more demonstrative and melancholy exposure of the folly of that system which would always leave capital and labor to themselves, without regard to domestic interests, never was written.

5

Our European dependencies are chiefly valuable as naval and military stations, the outposts and sentinels of what yet is, but possibly for no long time, the greatest naval power that ever existed.

Gibraltar, the key of the Mediterranean, has been ours for nearly 150 years.*

The strong fortress of Malta, taken from the French in 1803, was ceded to us at the peace of 1815.

The Ionian Isles—viz., Corfu, Cephalonia, Zante, Santa Maura, Ithaca, Cerigo, Paxo—passed under the British protection, or, more properly speaking, the British sovereignty, in 1815. These islands supply us with large quantities of currants and olive oil, and take in return cotton and other manufactures, and colonial produce. The revenue of these dependencies about pays the expenses of government, leaving us the trade.†

The small island of Heligoland, in the North Sea, is useful, especially in the time of war, as a dépôt, and as a pilot and packet-station.

Besides the Colonies and dependencies above enumerated, we have also in the Northern Hemisphere, on the western coast of Africa, the settlement of Sierra Leone, the settlement on the Gambia, and the settlements of Cape Coast Castle, Accra, Dix Cove, Annamboe, and Fernando Po.

In the North Atlantic we have the Bermuda Islands.

Such is a mere outline of this colossal empire in the Northern hemisphere.

But we have yet to enumerate our vast possessions under the Southern Cross.

In the South Atlantic Ocean we possess St. Helena and the Ascension Island.

---

* Written in 1850.

† This passage was written before their relinquishment. which may have been a wise measure, though already regretted by them.

We then come to the Cape of Good Hope* and South Africa—the half-way house, as it were, on the road to our possessions in the East and in Australia.

Then we have the Mauritius.

Next comes the great and beautiful island of Ceylon, well fitted for every tropical production, especially for coffee, cinnamon, and the cocoa-nut tree.

The island, or, rather, the continent of New Holland, (the whole of which is a British possession) is twenty-eight times as large as Great Britain and Ireland put together. Although this immense territory has not been ours sixty years, already, on the coast and its neighborhood, are extensive and flourishing settle-

---

* A niggardly policy has endangered this noble and indispensable dependency. Unwise economy has, as usual, necessitated extraordinary expenditure. The English people now grudge the expense of upholding, or, rather, recovering our dominion. Suppose, then, frankly confessing our poverty and the decline of our power, we surrender the Colony of the Cape of Good Hope to its ancient mistress—Holland. Its value in the eyes of the Dutch would at once be apparent. Dutch ships of the line, with ten thousand troops on board, would be descried from Table Bay. The Dutch with their colonial system would be but too welcome. No more disturbances in the interior, or anywhere else. The Dutch and not the British flag would thenceforth wave, not only over the Caffres, but over the Southern Ocean.

No doubt to hold and rule the British Empire, there must be great naval and military strength. But the larger the Empire is, the ampler the imperial means and resources. A narrow shop-keeping policy did not acquire our dominions and cannot keep them. And such a policy is no more the road to imperial wealth, than to imperial power. It is true that our recent anti-colonial system has not only severed the strongest ties that bound the Colonies to the mother country, but weakened the arguments for the integrity of the empire. Why should we be at the exclusive cost of defending Colonies, which for all commercial purposes now belong to others as much as to ourselves? Why should the colonists desire the connection? Why not prefer America, Holland, or France? Why not prefer independence? which last would really be to prefer the strongest or nearest naval power in the next war.

ments. Indeed, all but the first are of only a few years standing.

On the East is Sydney, with an extensive territory.

On the South-east, Port Philip.

On the Southern coast, the settlement of South Australia. *

On the West, Swan River.

These settlements enjoy a dry, temperate, and peculiarly salubrious climate. All the vegetable productions of the South of France and the South of Europe flourish here. So well adapted are they to sheep pasturage, that the fine Australian wool is rapidly superseding foreign wool in the British market. The soil and climate are well fitted for the growth of the vine. Although the manufacture of wine is but in its infancy, yet wine, both red and white, of excellent quality, has already been produced in considerable quantities. There is reason to expect that before long the export of wine will be a flourishing branch of commerce. Although the mineralogical wealth of these vast territories is still unexplored, yet copper is known to exist in abundance, and *even gold has been found.* †

The same general remarks apply to the island of Van Diemen's Land.

Norfolk Island has hitherto only been used as a penal settlement.

The temperate and healthy climate of the three islands of New Zealand renders them peculiarly eligible for emigrants; and though the settlements are in their infancy, they promise, ere long, great prosperity.

Such is an imperfect and bird's-eye view of the vast

---

* Queensland and the settlements on the north-eastern coast did not exist when this passage was penned.

† Written in 1849.

dominions of the British Crown in both hemispheres. If they do not compose a state without a parallel for greatness and universal prosperity, the fault must be in the policy of the imperial government.

It is true the ocean flows between, or, rather, amongst the members of this vast confederation. But that very ocean is at once the cheapest highway, and would be, with a wise policy, the source of maritime strength and greatness equally overwhelming and durable. With such an empire Great Britain is, more than ever, Queen of the seas.

Go to the hall of Greenwich hospital, and see in the pictures that line the walls the more than Roman valor and contempt of life to which Great Britain owes this imperial greatness. But the names of Blake and Shovel, of Elliott, Duncan, Howe, Collingwood, Jervis, and Nelson fall coldly on the ears of an unconscious and ungrateful public. *

Their heroism has won for us means of *unlimited* production, purchase, and trade; with harbors, rivers, ports, and custom-houses † under our own control; advantages of which we seem equally insensible and unworthy. We have incurred the cost of acquisition, but refuse to reap the benefit. We prefer to find,

---

* But the public should not be unjustly censured. Anti-colonial and other cosmopolitan theories were not first introduced by them, but by theorists in high places. The difficulty and anxiety which all the industrious classes in this kingdom experience in getting a living and disposing of their children has depressed their spirits, and nearly extinguished the great sentiment of national pride. Their main object necessarily is to make their limited and precarious income go as far as it can, no matter what the ultimate danger to the country, or to the permanence of that income itself.

† Since this passage was written we have taken away from the Colonies their advantages in our own markets, and, as a consequence, allowed them to fence themselves with protective tariffs against us.

among foreign nations, hostile tariffs, and jealous rivalry.

Is not the closer and closer union of the members of this great family the secret of their true policy? " UNION IS STRENGTH," should be the guiding star of our course.

The ancient colonial system, though not so dangerous as the modern anti-colonial one, is nevertheless not the true and durable one.

The great Lord Chatham was not only a protectionist, but an ultra-protectionist; jealous even of the colonies. "They shall not," said he, "make so much as a nail." The ultra-free-traders, on the other hand, wantonly expose the colonists to every disadvantage, and allow them no protection against those foreigners who enjoy ovewhelming advantages. The colonists are over-weighted, and required to run against those who carry no weight. The true policy would differ from Lord Chatham's, for it would treat the colonists as if they inhabited an English county, giving them full liberty to grow and manufacture what they pleased. It would differ from the system of the free-traders, for in place of disadvantages, it would give them, in common with all their fellow-subjects, an advantage in the imperial markets, and take in return a reciprocal advantage in the colonial markets. British markets, till lately the first markets in the world, instead of being opened as now to all without distinction, would give a preference to British subjects. It requires little foresight to perceive how powerfully self-interest would have bound the Colonies to the mother country, and the mother country to the Colonies. National pride would have joined with national interest to cement the union. England would not be prouder of her vast dominions, than these dominions of the confederation to which they belong, and of the royal and imperial head of which they are the members. Full scope in every quarter of the globe would be given to Anglo-Saxon energy and enterprise. In no long time not only would the colonial trade of the British empire have been more than all the foreign trade is now, but our external trade, instead of leaning on a sandy and precarious foundation, would repose on a solid and enduring one.

But it is said, Nature never intended such vast territories as India, at the other end of the globe, to remain subject to this little island: we must lose our colonies some day or other.

In the first place, it is forgotten what natural physical advantages the inhabitants of a northern and temperate region have over the listless and indolent natives of a tropical climate. The supremacy of the one, and the subjection of the other, is not only in the order of nature—it is for the advantage of both. British India never knew the blessings of peace and regular government, till it passed under British sway.

As to all your Colonies in temperate regions, you have it in your power—at least you *had* it in your power— to make a continued connexion with the mother country their interest and their pride.

But assume that at some future time you are to lose a portion of your dominions. What is this but saying that the British Empire is like all other human things, mortal? Is that any reason for prematurely breaking it up? for sacrificing the ultimate advantages which survive even the severance of a long connexion? Is the present, and the next, and the following generation to count for nothing?

But Colonies are expensive.

Whoever will sit down and count the real pecuniary loss to the mother country, and compare it with the real pecuniary gain, will soon discover that even now the Colonies are a prodigious gain to the mother country.

He will find it, even if he addresses himself to the calculation under the influence of two palpable but almost universal errors: first, that national expenditure is a *pure loss;** and secondly, that all the good derived from trade is the *profit*, in the narrowest sense of the word.

Much more clearly will he see it, if rising above these popular delusions, he remembers that national expenditure is, to a very great extent, but *a transfer of value;* and that everything produced within the limits of the British Empire, is an *addition to its wealth.*

But if the Colonies are a gain *even now*, persecuted and distressed as they are, what will they be under a wise and truly British policy? If they would be of value to almost any state, how much more to a state overflowing with population, and staggering under a load of debt? But what you do, you must do quickly. It is very doubtful whether you have not already really lost some of your greatest Colonies, which might have been among your best customers. When interest and affection have both been loosened, and cease to cement the union, a nominal allegiance only awaits the favorable opportunity.

Indeed the pecuniary burthens of Great Britain are among the strongest reasons for drawing closer the bands of connexion with the Colonies. Without them she will soon sink to the rank of a fourth-rate power. Her obligations, public and private, might then grind her to powder. With her Colonies, and the sure, open, boundless field which they present, her debts and liabilities are dust in the balance.

Men of fortune! if you live to witness the severance of Great Britian from her Colonies, you will find your wealth of every kind vanish like Aladdin's palace: your land may remain, but its principal value will be gone.

---

* This question will be examined hereafter.

Once more. As the Colonies grow, the more they enrich both the mother country and themselves. Both she and they can more and more easily sustain the expense of government and mutual defence. The greater they become, the less they cost.

Lastly: Pursue the disintegrating theory to its logical consequences. Canada is expensive; give it to the United States. The West Indies and the Cape of Good Hope are expensive and discontented; throw them into the lump. The East Indies are expensive; abandon them to the Native Princes or to Russia. Gibraltar and Malta are expensive; the Spaniards, French, or Russians will gladly take them off your hands. Australia is expensive; let them set up for themselves, and shut out your products, as all emancipated Colonies ever have done and ever will do.* Ireland is very expensive; leave her to the Irish. The Islands and some of the Highlands of Scotland are little better than waste land. Some counties are threatening to fall into the same condition. What will be left? A fraction of a bankrupt island in the Northern Sea. Do you get rid of your debt with your dominions?

But if you are to retain your relative rank with Russia and the United States, you must not go backward, but forward. If you even stand still, you are overshadowed. You have only to retain your Colonies, make them an integral part of the mother country, and you will be greater than either.

Bind them up in one Great British Zolverein.

No doubt there are *political* measures that deserve the attention of our rulers.

Before the Reform Act, some at least of the Colonies had a voice in the Legislature, and were, though not nominally, yet really, and very effectually represented. Now no Colony is represented there, directly or indi-

---

* Unfortunately this fear is already partly verified.

5*

rectly. Laws are made, or decisions arrived at, deeply affecting the Colonies, by utter strangers, very imperfectly acquainted with their real interests.

Is Thetford to send two members, and are neither Jamaica nor Canada to be even heard by one? And can the prerogative select no colonial subject whose wealth, influence, or information would be an accession even to the Upper House?

But what is to be said of the *Colonial Office*—of the machinery which directs in England the Imperial government of the Colonies? Can anything be more inadequate? Persons are not to blame, but the system.

It may happen that a minister of eminent talent and conciliatory manners is at once Secretary of State for the Colonies, and leader of one of the Houses of Parliament. It is unreasonable and impossible to expect him to give daily unremitting, undivided, and patient attention not only to the details of colonial affairs, but to the questions pregnant with momentous consequences which are every day arising. The late Mr. Justice Maule used to say that every man in England had more to do than he could do: certainly the Secretary for the Colonies is, without any fault of his own, in that predicament.

Sometimes a minister for the Colonies has had no very profound previous knowledge of the subject.

A story is told of Lord Palmerston, on his accession to the administration of colonial affairs, that, on entering the Colonial Office, he said to one of the subordinates, "Have the kindness to tell me Which are the Colonies, and Where they are?"

No doubt for a few years during nonage, the parent must expect to contribute, and possibly somewhat more than an equal share, to the assistance and defence of the child. But the time in the case of most Colonies has already come, when these proportions are reversed, and in other cases England already is at no expense at all. The time is approaching when the gratitude as well as the true interest of all the children may prompt them, and adult age and strength enable them effectually to succor and defend the venerable parent. and repay superabundantly the debt they owe.

The position of the Colonies when England shall be again at war with a naval power, demands the most anxious study. Without forethought there is no foresight.

Are we to have them as allies, or as enemies. It may not be in their power to remain neutral.

Our great harbors and estuaries on the east coast of North America are now within six days' steam of Ireland. They are already nothing less than the outworks of Ireland. They may become, if turned against us, the most formidable means of offence. Our possessions on the western shores of America overlook our commerce in the Pacific, and as to all our other Colonies (not to say military and naval stations), what are they to be in war, friends or enemies?

Is it not a question worthy also of immediate and anxious study, whether one or more boards or councils, like the East India council, composed in a large proportion of persons intimately acquainted with the Colonies, should not be instituted?

CHAPTER X.

" Protection would destroy external trade."

ONE answer to this assertion is an appeal to facts. No nation has adopted the theory and practice of protection to the same extent as England: no nation has at the same time enjoyed so extensive and lucrative a foreign trade. For centuries the protective policy has been unquestioned and triumphant: for centuries our foreign trade has been steadily augmenting. The strictest protection in the world has coincided with the greatest foreign trade in the world.

In truth, the domestic activity, industry, and prosperity, fostered by the protective system, is the surest basis of a permanent and extensive and mutual foreign trade.

In the first place, with protection and a certain home market have arisen *the means of purchase.* Under a strict and jealous system of protection we have seen the rise of Manchester, Birmingham, Sheffield, Merthyr, Leeds, Glasgow, Huddersfield, Bradford, Nottingham, Coventry, Leicester. We have seen skill and machinery brought to perfection. Protection has not blunted the invention or superseded the ingenuity of our countrymen. On the contrary, our cottons, and woollens, and hardware, *were* the best in the world.* What England would have been *without* protection from foreign manufactures we know not. She might have been

---

* But there is reason now to fear that competition, to lower the price has diminished perfection, and increased adultera'ion.

what Ireland now is without protection from British
manufactures. But it is certain that *with* protection the
means of purchase have been created and multiplied in
a degree marvellous, and transcending all anticipation.
Had the manufacturing prosperity of England been
matter of ancient history, looking at its diminutive size
on the map of the world, it would have been deemed
incredible and fabulous. Our means of purchase are
immense and inexhaustible. All we now want is markets—but markets for the support and existence of these
means of purchase, as well as for their increase. A
sure market created them; insecure and precarious
markets will destroy them, and leave in their place a
wretched and discontented population. Thus with
protection has arisen the first indispensable pre-requisite
for foreign trade—things to give in exchange for foreign commodities; in other words, the means of purchase—exports.

Next, a judicious system of protection would neither
indiscriminately prohibit, nor indiscriminately admit,
foreign articles. It would subject the claim of every
foreign commodity to be admitted into the first market
in the world (and as well the *places* from which, as the
terms on which, it should be admitted) to a separate and
rigorous inquiry.

The following commodities would, it is conceived,
make good their claim.

First: Articles which our soil and climate cannot
produce, such as tea, coffee, sugar, cocoa, indigo,
cochineal, spices, gums, oils, and many others.

Secondly: Articles which we could produce at home,
but of inferior quality and at a disproportionate cost.
Wine, for example, could be manufactured in England;
but the cost would be many times the cost of Spanish,
Portuguese, or French wine, to say nothing of its infer-

ior quality. It may, as we have seen, be perfectly true, that by buying foreign articles instead of home-made articles, the nation, under ordinary circumstances, loses the entire value on one side of the exchange; and yet, on the other hand, true that to manufacture wine instead of buying it from abroad, would be a losing process to the nation at large.

Thirdly: The raw material of manufactures, such as cotton, silk, wool, timber, hides, and many others. Some of them cannot be had at all, except from abroad, and others not in sufficient abundance to supply the industry of our artisans. The old rule was to admit them, but in a state as little manufactured as possible.

Fourthly and chiefly: The produce of our own Colonies and dependencies.

We now* import annually from the United States of America raw cotton to the value of more than ten millions sterling. But this supply is precarious, depending on political and other causes, to say nothing of what is alleged, that the fertility of the best cotton-producing lands in America is being exhausted, or at least is impaired and declining. The whole of this amount of cotton, and as much more if it were wanted, might, under a proper colonial system, be supplied by our own East Indian dependencies.

This sum of ten millions sterling is now entirely American income. It, and much more, might have been entirely income of British subjects.†

This sum of ten millions now constitutes a market for American produce, and at present (though it is to be feared, but for a short and precarious season) for some British produce. It, and much more, might have con-

---

* 1849.

† These observations would apply with still greater force to the substitution of home-grown flax for cotton, if that were possible.

stituted a permanent, certain, and increasing market for British produce.

No one under present circumstances advocates a duty on raw cotton. But suppose British East India to be attainable in a sufficient abundance, cotton to be but one per cent. dearer than American cotton, the popular political economy would still say, "Buy American." See the consequence. The British empire loses ten millions and gains a hundred thousand pounds: that is to say, it loses nine millions nine hundred thousand pounds sterling per annum; and moreover loses a market of that annual amount.

Nor is this all. When American cotton is brought over in American ships, the freight constitutes income of American ship-owners, a market to American industry, a nursery for American seamen. If it came from British India it might have constituted income of British ship-owners, a market to British industry, a nursery for British seamen.

We say nothing of the uncertainty of the American supply,* a falling-off in which precipitates at once populous English cities, whole English counties, into ruin; nothing of the rapidly-increasing cotton manufactures of the United States, buying away from us the cotton in their own markets, and by our policy enabled to do so; nothing of French or other competitors for American cotton.

We say nothing of the obvious, and truly English and imperial policy, which counsels an intimate connexion with our dominion in the East, greater than Alexander's, and capable of multiplying ten-fold the prosperity and greatness of the British Empire. A dominion which, as long as it remains ours, prevents us from being overshadowed by those enormous states

---

* This passage was written many years before the cotton famine.

and confederations of mankind, which the improved modes of communication will assuredly produce—by the vast extent either of the American Republic, or of the Russian Empire.

We say nothing of the prosperity of a hundred millions of Indian subjects, who never knew the blessings of peace and order till they were submitted to the British sway; whose well-being and ultimate civilisation is bound up in their connexion with Great Britain.

If it be objected that an increase in the price of the raw material will injure the export of the manufactured article, the answers are manifold :—

First : There will in the long run be no increase at all in the price of the raw material. It is even probable that by the introduction of railways, and improved means of cleaning the cotton, our own Indian cotton might become both cheaper and better than ever American cotton has been.

Next : Even if there were for a short time a small increase in the price of the raw material, that would hardly be appreciable in the price of the manufactured article ; for that price is compounded, not only of the value of the raw material, but of many times its value in labor, machinery, rent, profit, and freight.

Again : Supposing even some small temporary decrease in the foreign sale, an entirely new market to the extent of ten millions per annum is opened up in India. That market is not a precarious one, depending on the caprice and fluctuating policy of other states, but a certain and permanent one, under our own control.

What we ought to have done, and might have done, with cotton, we used to do with sugar. We had tropical provinces in the West Indies almost as valuable and prosperous as English counties; supplying us from our own soil with sugar, and taking payment entirely in British articles. We could add to them, if need were, the East Indies and the Mauritius. There is no limit to the possible production of British sugar; there is no limit to the production of the articles which would pay for it.

Alas! a very different policy has prevailed. We see only a part of the sad consequences in the ruin and disaffection of our noble West India possessions, and the gradual but certain decline of the great West Indian trade.

As with cotton and sugar, so almost with every tropical or natural product that can be named, our Colonies would supply us, furnishing certain and increasing markets in return.

Our foreign trade may have already reached, or even passed, its culminating point: our colonial trade is but just rising.

By giving the Colonies a preference, the protective system, so far from diminishing, would ultimately securely and infinitely increase the external trade.

Fifthly: The protective system would not exclude, or even tax, except in a slight degree, the importation of the food of the people.

The advantages of a low exchangeable value of food cannot be over-rated. But there is one thing of much greater importance than even its cheapness, and that is its *accessibility*. Food should not only cost as little labor as possible, but be (as under proper regulations it would be) attainable by him who has labor to offer.

With a view as well to the steady low value as to the *accessibility* of food by the people at large,—with a view to the full and various employment of the people in its production,—with a view to the improved and complete cultivation of the soil,—a judicious financial system of protection would give certain advantages to its production at home and in the Colonies.

A protection to this extent—a protection not overlooking the contingency of war, and countervailing national burthens on the land, is just and politic.

A protection extending further, for the mere purpose of keeping up rents, is utterly indefensible.

Whether the duty should be a fixed or a graduated one may be very doubtful; but there can be little doubt that it should be a *discriminating* one. The neighboring ports, that take nothing from us, might otherwise (as they are already doing) shut out our better but more distant customers.

And what encouragement is there to deal with us, when we treat those who do, and those who do not, exactly alike, except that we take care to secure to those who do *not* deal with us the full advantage of proximity?

The absence of any duty whatever on either the import or export of corn under any circumstances is, in a limited and populous territory, a perilous experiment. There can be no greater mistake than to conclude that the price will on that account always be low and equable.

It is believed that the late Lord Lauderdale, in his book on political economy, was the first to explain and fully illustrate a well-established principle which may be shortly stated thus:—When a commodity of first necessity, but of limited supply, runs short, the price rises not in the arithmetical ratio of the deficiency, but in a ratio so much greater that it may almost be called a geometrical ratio.

Take a besieged city short of bread. The real deficiency may be but 10 per cent.; but bread must be had, cost what it will. The price might rise 100 or 500 per cent. and much more.

In the last war we ourselves actually contended that provisions imported into France were contraband of war.* But, although that be not so under ordinary circumstances, suppose England at war with a great maritime power to be, as she now is, dependent on foreign supplies for bread to eat, and to lose command of the seas, to what might not the price of bread rise, even supposing the deficiency to be accurately known? But there are no means of knowing the deficiency, and it would assuredly be exaggerated by the panic fears of the public.

We will not dilate on the horrors of famine, or of the pestilence that follows it.

In one of these islands we have already witnessed a sudden famine in our own time, although from an unforeseen and different cause.

It is not to be expected that such warnings will have any effect, for it has been often and truly observed, and very lately by Lord Palmerston, that nations have no prevision.

Again, the Irish millers justly complain that their trade is stopped by the importation of fine flour instead of corn. The rearers of stock also reiterate the complaint in another shape, and say that their industry is deprived of the benefit of the bran and coarse meal.

Lastly : To deal with those who deal with you again, DOUBLES instead of diminishing external trade.

---

* See our minister's representations to Mr. Jefferson in 1793, and to Mr. Randolph in 1797.

CHAPTER XI.

" The distress of the country is owing to taxes, and the expenditure of government."

THE multitude are sure to say this, when mistaken legislation has impoverished them. But it is a fallacy.

We have but to look back on modern European history, or even to open our eyes on what is now before us, and we shall see nations highly taxed, prospering as much, and a great deal more, than many others taxed very little, or scarcely at all. Take Holland as an example—always a very highly-taxed nation, yet always very prosperous. Take Great Britain herself from the revolution of 1688 till a very recent period.

Nay, we have seen an increase of taxation followed by no diminution of prosperity, and a diminution of taxation attended with no increase of prosperity.

Nor do the reasons of those phenomena lie far beneath the surface.

It is comparatively easy to discover who ultimately pay the *direct* taxes, such as the income-tax, and the assessed taxes. These taxes are a mere transfer of value from the hand that pays, to the exchequer that receives and distributes again. The NATION AT LARGE is neither poorer nor richer for the tax or the transfer.

The incidence of *indirect* taxation is a question of great difficulty. The learned in such matters have not settled, and probably never will settle, on whom the indirect taxes fall. Very different opinions are entertained. Some think they fall always on the onsumer; others that they are not paid by the laboring classes, whose wages, we are told, rise to what is necessary to keep up the supply of labor. It is clear, however, that in some proportions or other they are paid by the people at large.

It may be said of both direct and indirect taxation in the aggregate, that the people at large, in some unknown proportions, *pay* the taxes. *

And it may also be said with truth, that, in time of peace and domestic expenditure, the people ultimately *receive* the taxes again. When they suffer from taxation, it must be either because foreigners receive the taxes, which in that case amount to a tribute, or else because taxation causes a vicious distribution of property, or lastly, because it subtracts from the employment of productive labor.

Let us examine a little more closely how the taxes are spent.

Take the larger half. In round numbers nearly thirty millions are paid every year to discharge the interest on the national debt, funded and unfunded.

No doubt, wherever the stock is held by foreigners,

---

* Yet there is an exception. It may sound paradoxical, but it is true, that there is a species of taxation by which the people may sometimes be even gainers.

Customs duties on imports are not always paid by the consumer. They are often paid in whole, or in part, by the foreign importer. It often happens that the foreigner makes in the British market a great deal more than is sufficient to remunerate him. He can often afford to pay a duty, and yet sell at the same price. In this case the whole duty is so much gained; or, more frequently, he can afford to pay the duty and raise the price of his commodity to a less extent than the duty. Here the difference between the duty and the rise in price is gained. Lord Stanley (in a speech deserving for other reasons the perusal of every man in England) lately called the attention of the House of Lords to these considerations, and their bearing on an import duty on provisions.

the dividends received by the foreigner are in the nature of tribute, and impoverish the country, just as the payment of tribute would do.

It is to be feared that during the late troubles in Europe* (coinciding, as they have done, with a great excess of our imports over our exports) the portion of the debt due to foreigners has been very much augmented. The purchase of stock by foreigners, distrusting the investments of their own country, tends to redress an adverse balance of trade, but leaves us in debt to them, with interest to pay till the debt is discharged. When it is discharged, it will be by selling the stock, and taking the produce out of the country without any return.

Nevertheless, much the larger portion of the debt is still due to British subjects resident in the United Kingdom. The contribution of the dividends by the nation on the one hand, and the receipt of the dividends by a portion of the nation on the other, can be no direct loss to the whole nation. A, B, and C pay to A, one of the three; A, B, and C together are as rich as they were before.

Nor is it clear that the artificial distribution thus introduced is very disadvantageous.

It is proved by actual returns that the number of large fund-holders is inconsiderable in comparison with the number of small ones; and even of that number of large fund-holders many are trustees, many more are public companies, such as insurance companies, who represent a plurality of persons in moderate circumstances.

It is probable that the bulk of the dividends are ultimately received by a multitude of persons, not much above the poorer classes. So that as far as the bulk of the public debt is concerned, the taxes are received

---

* This passage was written in 1849.

again by a numerous class of the nation, and those not in affluent circumstances. What the awful effects of a suspension of public credit would in this country be, it is fearful to contemplate; but as a set-off to those calamities, the suspension of the payment of dividends would afford no relief. By as much as one portion of the nation would, by the suspension, be richer; by so much, another portion of the nation would, by the same suspension, be poorer.

It is said that the dividends are subtracted from productive expenditure, and added to unproductive expenditure.

This is assertion only. It is doubtful whether either proposition be true. It is probable that the greater part of what is handed over to the tax-gatherer, would be spent by the tax-payer much in the same way as by the receiver of the dividend. And if there be cases in which the tax-payer would employ his contribution more for the advantage of the nation, than the receiver of the dividend, there are, on the other side, cases where the receiver of the dividend employs it better for the nation than the tax-payer. In how many cases are dividends received by trustees for infants, who afterwards employ their property in trade—by bankers for their customers— by public companies of acknowledged utility for their members, or their customers?

It seems, therefore, to be true that the interest of the debt does not, so far as it is paid to British subjects, impoverish the nation: it is a mere transfer of value.

Then it will be objected, "According to you, the national debt is no evil." By no means. We do not assert that no mischief was done by the *creation* of the debt—we only say that none is done by the honorable *payment of the interest.* The value that evaporated in gunpowder can never be recovered back. The evil lay in contracting the debt. If it had never been contracted, the public creditor might perhaps have had what he now has, and yet the nation has been obliged to pay him no dividend.   In fact, as long as the punctual payment of interest is continued, so long is the full mischief of the past wasteful expenditure of the public resources postponed.

When the day arrives that a half-year's interest cannot be paid, then at length will yawn that awful chasm in which the national wealth has been swallowed up. On that fatal morning, no matter how rich you are, your banker must dishonor your check. The comfortable balance due to you has vanished with the banker's balance due to him from the government. You can have no credit with your tradesman. Your humble neighbor is no better off. There are no funds to pay wages, and none even for public charity.

There remain to be considered the civil and military expenditure.

This also, so far as it goes to British subjects, is but a transfer of value.   Yet it is clear, that large bodies of men on land or sea, kept in unproductive employment, are a loss so far as *industry, otherwise productive*, is thus diverted to unproductive purposes.   It is hard to see that it is loss to a greater extent, but that extent probably falls very far indeed short of the whole amount.

Still, as a general rule, taxes paid to British subjects are but a transfer of value, though they may, and no doubt do, in many cases produce injurious effects.

But to regard the public revenue of the nation as so much value destroyed, or, in popular language, so much money thrown into the sea, is a very gross delusion.

Another consideration will fortify this view.

The annual public revenue of the United Kingdom has been since the peace, in round numbers, fifty millions a year.*   Fifty millions for thirty-four years amount to seventeen hundred millions sterling, without

---

* This passage was written in the year 1849.

the interest.   Can any man believe that we are in the same condition as if this sum of near two thousand millions sterling had been paid in tribute to a foreign country ?

But we have seen above, that to import from abroad commodities that we might have produced nearly as cheap at home, unless we secure the employment of the displaced labor in some other way,* is really a *dead loss* to the nation—is really a *tribute* paid to a foreign country.   That tribute is now paid, and paid unnecessarily, to the extent of millions, and tens of millions.

What, then, are we to think of the wisdom of financial reformers, who, disregarding a fatal drain of life-blood like this, begrudge a few millions, distributed within our borders, for the defence and security of the empire ?

How is it that we have borne the burthen of our public expenditure so long, and have been, nearly all the while, richer and more prosperous than all other nations ?

None will attribute the distress we now experience to taxes and government expenditure, who are not resolved to shut their eyes to the true causes.

In truth, under a wise but very different policy, the public burthens of the United Kingdom would not be felt.   Out of evil good might be made to come.   The very taxes themselves, if directed to that end, might be made the means of developing the producing forces of the country.   The resources of the British Empire are far more than adequate to much heavier ones.   This is not conjecture or assertion merely ; we know that they have actually been found so.

---

* See ante, Chapters IV. and V.

6

CHAPTER XII.

" Increase of exports and imports is the index of national prosperity."

QUIETLY assumed.   But is it consistent either with reason or with facts?

We have seen how much more important home production is than foreign production.*   Yet the superseding of home production by foreign production, is a process which necessarily increases imports, and will generally be followed by an increase (though it may not be a proportionate one) of exports also.   When you buy from abroad, to the value of a million sterling a year, shoes, which you used to make at home, and annually export to pay for them a million worth of cotton manufactures, which your own shoemakers used to consume at home, you increase the annual imports a million sterling, and you increase the annual exports a million sterling also.   But your manufacturers of cotton goods get no more than they had before.

Now look at your shoemakers.   They have lost an income of a million sterling a year.   Their expenditure to that extent is gone.   The home market to that extent is gone.   The annual product of the labor of the country is diminished by a million sterling a year.   And there is no compensation for all this.   Thus a real blight on industry, a real loss to the nation, *may* show itself, not only in increased imports, but in increased exports.

So, on the other hand, suppose Ireland, assuming but

---

* Chapters IV. and V.

not affirming it to be possible, instead of importing flax from abroad, should henceforth grow an adequate supply of flax at home. That would wonderfully relieve her distress. But flax would no longer figure in her imports, nor the articles that pay for it, in her exports; for they, or their equivalent, would be used by her own people, now idle and starving; and the flax manufacturers would be supplied to the same extent as before. Here would be an example of improvement, indicated by a decrease both of exports and imports.

Superficial observers point to your exports and imports, and say, distress must be imaginary, because these have both increased. If there are customs duties, then they further point to the customs, and say, truly, your revenue has increased.

But patient and unprejudiced enquirers, who, distrusting alike great names and popular notions, will sift the matter to the bottom, find out the true state of things to be this: domestic exchanges are unregistered and do not figure in any returns. Supersede them by foreign ones, and these foreign ones are immediately doubly registered, published, and paraded both as exports and imports. When domestic production and mutual domestic exchange flourished, there was no register of their existence. When half the benefit leaves the Englishman, and passes over to the foreigner, there is no register of the illness or death of the dying or deceased domestic industry. But the entry of the superseding foreign industry into the home market is registered, and the departure of the products of home industry, to be enjoyed and spent by a foreigner, instead of being enjoyed and spent by an Englishman, is registered also. And the new direction which the exchanges have taken, being no longer latent but public, government could, if they thought fit, lay hold of both exports and imports in their transit, tax them, and then point to an increase of revenue.

So far, therefore, from an increase of exports and imports, necessarily betokening an increase of the annual products of the land and labor of a country, or the improved condition of the people, reason shews us that they *may be* symptomatic of the very reverse. They certainly, therefore, are no criterion or index of national prosperity.

Now let us see whether FACTS shew them to be such a criterion.

The most prosperous of all nations, for the last fifty years, has been the United States. Yet the exports and imports of the American Union, notwithstanding its vast augmentation in population,* are not very much greater than they were in forty years ago. It is the unregistered home production, and home trade, doubling and quadrupling over and over again, that has created this unexampled prosperity.

Next to the United States comes the United Kingdom. The increase of exports and imports with us, though great, has not until recently been at all proportionate to the increase of wealth.

Now, indeed, for the reasons just given, the increase of exports and imports may indicate a decay of domestic production.

It cannot be repeated too often that a nation, whether she buy from abroad or produce at home, can have no more than she produces. The development of her domestic producing forces is therefore the true and only sound test of her prosperity.

---

* This passage was written in 1849.

CHAPTER XIII.

" All commodities should be rendered as cheap as possible."

No word is so seductive as the word *cheap*, yet no word has more meanings. " The world," says Horne Tooke, " is governed by words." A word so alluring and yet so ambiguous, is, of all other words, surest of conquest and dominion. Accordingly it has subjugated the popular opinion of England.

First, cheapness, in its strict and proper sense, means cheapness in money. A thing is in this sense cheap when it fetches but little money—but little of the precious metals; when a little money will purchase it. This is the first sense of cheapness.

But, secondly, cheapness may also be taken, and by political economists is often taken, to mean a low exchangeable value, that is, a low value, estimating that value in other commodities. In this sense a ton of iron is cheap if it can be purchased with but little corn, but little cloth or silk, but few hats or shoes. This is the second sense of the word cheapness.

A third sort of cheapness is a cheapness produced by low wages of labor: the cheapness of shirts made by poor needle-women at fourpence a dozen.

Cheapness, fourthly, is taken to mean a low value as estimated in the labor bestowed on an article. When little labor has been employed, and little is necessary to produce an article, then it is said to be cheap.

Let us now briefly examine how far these several sorts of cheapness are beneficial, and to whom they are beneficial.

Take the first sort of cheapness—cheapness measured merely by money.

It is an observation lying on the surface, that this sort of cheapness may be brought about, not only by the abundance and accessibility of other commodities when compared with the precious metals, but by the scarcity and inaccessibility of the precious metals when compared with other commodities. So when Dr. Johnson was told that eggs were so cheap in the Hebrides, that several might be bought for a penny, "It is not," says he, "that eggs are in plenty, but pennies are scarce."

It is further evident, that if society were starting afresh, if there were no existing debts or obligations, then this sort of cheapness would be a matter of perfect indifference. The dearness or cheapness of things would depend on the aggregate amount of the precious metals, compared with the aggregate mass of all other commodities. If there were much gold and silver things would be dear: if there were little gold and silver things would be cheap. But the little gold and silver in the one case, would be worth as much as the larger quantity of gold and silver in the other case, and would effect the necessary changes equally well.

In itself, therefore, this first sort of cheapness is a matter of perfect indifference.

But suppose an old society, in which the industrious classes are oppressed with very large engagements, public and private; suppose a public debt of 800 millions sterling, and an amount of private debts and mortgages far exceeding even that immense sum; then this first sort of cheapness is no longer a matter of indifference, it is a matter of supreme importance.

If it were brought about by lessening the labor necessary to produce other commodities, then it might be a blessing to all parties. But that would be cheapness of the fourth description.

If, on the other hand, cheapness in money value were brought about by diminishing the quantity or augmenting the value of the precious metals, say, for the sake of illustration, by one half, would that be a national benefit or a national evil?

It is manifest, that it would at once double the national debt, that it would at once double every mortgage, that it would at once double every debt and pecuniary liability.

It would, on the other hand, double the real income of all tax-eaters, mortgagees, and creditors. Every fund-holder, for example, would receive two bushels of corn instead of one, two yards of cloth instead of one; in other words, two bushels of corn and two yards of cloth, instead of one, must be sold to pay him.

It would be, in great measure, a transfer from the industrious to the idle classes. Every man in trade would find his stock-in-trade decline in price, and the proportionate amount of his debts and incumbrances augment.

While the *appreciation* of the precious metals, or of the currency, is going on, there will be universal distress and paralysis of industry. On the other hand, it has been truly observed by David Hume, that a progressive *depreciation* of the precious metals is always accompanied with an expansion of industry.

It is said in answer to this, that the poor suffer in their wages by a diminution in the value of money. The answer is, that they gain much more than they lose by the additional demand for labor; and that their wages, as a general rule, will accommodate themselves to the difference.

It seems therefore clear that a mere cheapness of the first sort, a mere *cheapness in money*, though in itself a matter of indifference, is, to a country overburthened and bound down like England, with pecuniary obligations of all sorts, so far from being a *benefit*, that it is the greatest possible *curse and calamity*.

One-sided free-trade, without reciprocation, causes the first description of cheapness by augmenting the value of money. *

We now come to examine the second sort of cheapness—that is, cheapness in the sense of a low value measured in other commodities.

One, or *some* commodities may, it is true, be cheap in this sense; but *all* commodities, or even *the bulk* of commodities, cannot. The cheaper you make some, the dearer you make others by that very process. If the cheapness of commodities is measured merely by the quantity of other commodities for which they will exchange, the dearness of some is what makes the cheapness of others, and the cheapness of these is what makes the dearness of the first.

This second sort of cheapness of *all* commodities is therefore impossible—it is a contradiction in terms.

The third sort of cheapness—a cheapness attained by low and inadequate wages of labor—is a murderous and suicidal cheapness.

The cheaper things are with this cheapness, the dearer they are to the laborer. The less of them the laborer can get, the less he has to spend. The cheaper things

---

* To what extent would not recent measures have augmented it, but for California and Australia? The *value of money*, and the *rate of interest*, are two very different things, as we shall see more fully hereafter, though often carelessly confounded together when the newspapers speak of *dear* and *cheap* money.

are with this cheapness, the more the incomes of the working classes fall off. The more surely you ruin the largest and best of all markets, which is the expenditure of the laboring classes. *

Where foreign goods made by laborers, worse fed, worse lodged, worse clothed, than the Englishman, are introduced into the English market, they bring with them this cheapness. It is contagious. Those foreign goods, if no other employment can be found for the Englishman, might as well, so far as he is concerned, be infected with the cholera or the plague.

Now for the fourth sort of cheapness, viz., a low value measured by the labor necessary to produce a thing.

This fourth sort of cheapness may be, and ought to be, a gain to all classes of society. This is the cheapness created by more fertile soils, improved methods of cultivation, more powerful manures, improved machinery, the subjugation to human uses of the great powers of nature, such as steam, electricity, and mechanical and chemical agencies. This cheapness results from a more complete and extended dominion of man over nature. It is the gift of a beneficent Providence, to be wisely improved, and directed to the benefit of the masses.

I say, to be wisely improved and used; for even this cheapness is of itself but the raw material of national wealth and happiness. Alone, it will leave the masses of the people as miserable as it finds them. We know this by sad experience.

Very few things are of more importance than cheap food. That a low price of corn brings down *rents* is no objection at all. If that were all, it is a mere transfer

---

* Every Chancellor of the Exchequer in England, every collector of the Octroi in France, knows by experience, that the greatest expenditure is by the laboring classes, because they are the most numerous.

6*

of wealth from the rich to the poor, tending to redress
that fearful inequality of condition between the very
rich and the very poor, which is one of our greatest
miseries and dangers. You could, if you chose, bring
about this cheapness by the better cultivation and increased fertility of your own dominions; and it would
then be a great and unmixed national blessing. But
if you attempt it by discouraging domestic or colonial
production of food, and introducing food grown by
worse-paid laborers, the poor will be greater losers by
such a cheapness than even the rich themselves. They
will have far less cheap bread than they had dear bread
before. Kilrush market is now abundantly supplied
with the cheapest Indian corn and the cheapest Russian
wheat. Look at the laborer.*

Nothing can be more ungrateful and short-sighted
than the complaints of machinery superseding human
labor. Where it does so it is a mitigation of the prime-
val curse. The hand might as well complain of the
spade or the plough. Regulations of trade-unions pro-
scribing the use of machinery are utterly indefensible,
and if not now indictable misdemeanors, ought to be at
once made so. But then, on the other side, improved
modern machinery is a new and highly artificial thing.
It will disturb the old and simple relations between
the workman and his employer—and sometimes, perhaps,
to the injury of the workman. Mr. Mill complains
that improved machinery has not yet lightened the toil
of a single human being. At all events, nohow and
nowhere does the workman (and he is THE NATION) get
his full share of the benefit. Why? Because men are
slow to perceive that the introduction of so artificial an
element will necessitate other artificial arrangements.
The Factory Act is a right beginning—but only a beginning.

---

* This passage was written in 1849.

Of the four sorts of cheapness, therefore, the first, though in itself a thing indifferent, is injurious *to us*— the second, impossible—the third, destructive—the fourth, but a means to an end.

For the benefit of the masses, it is not enough to make things cheap, even in the best sense of the word. What is wanted is, to make them *accessible, attainable,* by the multitude. By making things cheap, you do not necessarily make them accessible. Nay, there are some modes of making things cheap, which as we have seen will make them less accessible to the multitude than they were before.

What the masses want is the *means of purchase.* If the means of purchase be wholly absent, it is a matter of supreme indifference to them, whether things be dear or cheap. The only means of purchase which they possess are the wages of their labor. In a word, *employment* is their *means of purchase.*

You may have cheapness without full and various employment for the masses; that is *cheapness,* but without *plenty.* You may have full employment for the masses at good wages without cheapness, that may be competency, or even plenty, without cheapness. The aim of all good legislation should be to unite the two blessings—cheapness and plenty. But if, as often happens, in the imperfection of human affairs, you have to choose not only between two evils, but sometimes also between two good things, inconsistent with each other, which of the two is to be chosen—*cheapness* for the benefit of a few, or *plenty* for the benefit of ALL?

Undoubtedly, plenty. Then the study of every government, in order to produce plenty, permanent plenty, plenty widely diffused and extending to the masses, should be the *full and various productive employment of the people.* The test of every measure ought to be, and used to be this—Will it promote the productive employment of the people?

It has been already shown, and on the authority of Adam Smith himself, that the production of articles at home which can be made or grown somewhat cheaper abroad, though it should not produce cheapness, does promote the productive employment of the people—does give them the means of purchase—does produce plenty, permanent plenty, plenty widely diffused, plenty extending everywhere to the masses of the population; and that the opposite policy, even under the most favorable circumstances, though it should and will create cheapness, will destroy the means of purchase, and introduce a real and spreading want.

We have already seen * that Adam Smith himself declares and proves that foreign production, compared with domestic production, gives BUT ONE HALF THE ENCOURAGEMENT TO THE NATIVE INDUSTRY OF THE COUNTRY.†

And this under favorable circumstances, and with reciprocity.

---

* Chapter IV.

† It is not pretended that Adam Smith is everywhere consistent with himself on this subject: he certainly is not, for this admission alone destroys the theory of free-trade. Mr. Horner himself, speaking of Adam Smith, calls him a loose writer.

CHAPTER XIV.

" Free importation is the source of plenty ; protection, of scarcity."

THERE are two sorts of plenty. One sort of plenty is a mere relative plenty, where there is more than individual consumers can buy *and pay for.* Such plenty as now exists in an Irish market, where the starving poor eye wistfully, but in vain, English hats, clothes, shirts, shoes, American flour, and Indian meal. This mere relative and spurious sort of plenty free importations and one-sided free-trade may tend to create ; and doubly, for they at the same time tend to diminish and destroy the means of purchase.

But another, and a much better sort of plenty is an abundance, at once absolute and *accessible ;* when there is as much as the masses want, combined with *accessibility ;* when there is enough for the multitude, and the multitude can *get at it* and enjoy it.

This is the sort of plenty at which governments should aim : this is the only plenty by which the masses profit. But this plenty depends on the *means of purchase* enjoyed by the multitude ; their means of purchase depend on their full and various productive employment—on their producing as much as possible *at both ends of the exchange.*

Production at both ends of the exchange creates at once not mere *relative* plenty, but *absolute* abundance on both sides, and the means of purchase on both sides. It you produce on one side only, you sacrifice half your abundance ; you are dependent on the capricious and variable extent of a foreign market not under your own control; and you are subject to a periodical check and glut. Produce at both ends, and *in due proportion*, and what would otherwise cause a check and a glut, will but augment the means of purchase, as well as the overflowing and superabounding plenty. You have at once abundance combined with accessibility. A universal glut is, as M. Say has well demonstrated, an impossibility. Suppose that in this country wheat, raw cotton, wool, and timber could be produced in abundance as unlimited as knives and pocket-handkerchiefs, who does not see that the consequence is, not a glut, but an enormous consumption, an immediate plenty and ease of circumstances, for the whole population all round?

Nay, suppose we had on the other side of us, no further distant than Ireland, another country as large as Ireland, unoccupied, able to grow not only wheat, wool, and timber enough, but cotton enough, and sugar enough, and all other tropical productions enough, to supply all our deficiencies. Again, there is at once the same immediate abundance, and ease of circumstances.

But we actually already *have* this imaginary Ireland. Steam has brought our Colonies, and therein timber and wool, our sugar and cotton, and corn-growing provinces, almost as near to us as Ireland once was.

Moreover, the real Ireland is *half waste*, England but imperfectly and partially cultivated, some of Scotland actually laid down to waste every year. The resources of the East and West Indies and Canada are not only not developed, but some of them positively discouraged.

The means of producing on both sides of the exchange—the means of producing all things, and in all climates—the means of producing plenty in the best, fullest, richest sense of the word—we already have; plenty not only to satisfy the wants of all, but plenty to confer on all the means of purchase; plenty unlimited, universal, permanent.

But we are "*magnas inter opes inopes.*" Our theories blind, paralyse, and starve us.

CHAPTER XV.

" England has a greater capital than any other country."

IN one sense this position is true; in another sense,
it is at least doubtful, perhaps false.

What is CAPITAL? A question that has engendered
endless strife among political enconomists. But these
disputes are mere logomachies. Every man has a right
to employ the word *capital,* or any other word, in any
sense he pleases. If he will but tell us exactly what
he means, then, whether he employ the word in the
right sense or not, is a mere question of propriety of
language. It comes to this—Is the word when used
in this man's sense, good and usual English or not?
A trivial question of no scientific importance at all. *
"I will never quarrel about words," says Mr. Locke,
"with him who grants my meaning."

But though it be a matter of no importance in what
sense you choose to use a word, it is of the last
importance, first, to let us clearly understand in what
sense you do mean to use it, and next to keep strictly
to that sense without changing it.

This, however, is no easy task. There are many
words that continually change their sense with the

---

* Not that purity of style is to be undervalued. It consists in
never unnecessarily employing any word, or a word in any sense,
not justified by the usage of the best authors. Purity of style is
not only a great and rare literary merit, but is essential to the permanence of every living language and every literary reputation.
Without it the writers of one age are barbarous, if not unintelligible to the next.

subject and context. Capital is one of these words. The controversies about capital are therefore like the disputes about the color of the chameleon.

If by capital you mean the aggregate of mere visible and tangible things, possessing exchangeable value—such as cultivable land, or the improvements of land, buildings, railways, ships, stocks of food, clothing, or specie—then, in this sense of the word, it is by no means clear that England has the greatest capital of any nation in the world. It is doubtful whether in this sense, France, the United States, or even Russia, do not surpass her.

It is at least evident, that when we say England has the largest capital in the world, we include something else in the word *capital*. What is it?

We include the power of raising money, or means for enterprises, great and small of all sorts, public and private. In other words, CREDIT.

What is CREDIT? Faith in the solvency and punctuality of the paymaster.

This is the saving faith of commerce. This is the faith that can perform miracles and remove mountains.

An intending producer is about to create wealth by producing, but, alas! he has no money. There is an impassable gulf between him and his creation of national wealth. Let him but satisfy the capitalist that he can find a *market* for his commodity, and that so he can and certainly will repay advances, and straightway his acceptances are discounted, he is put in funds, and the gulf is bridged over that lay between him and the production of wealth.

This is the prospective miracle of credit.

Now see its retrospective miracle.

A nation has contracted a debt of many hundred

millions. While the interest is punctually paid, the
debt is by credit transformed into the most valuable of
property. Cease to pay the interest and many hundred millions of property disappear as one. There
is universal bankruptcy. This is the great gulf that
yawns behind a national debt. But resolve to pay
the interest to the fraction of a grain of gold, and let
the capitalists understand that. Credit again comes to
the rescue, and bridges over this other chasm, more
dismal and unfathomable still.

Touch a country with the talisman of credit, and
capital, even in the other and material sense, springs
up instantly. It does not accrue from savings merely,
as modern political economy poorly and inadequately
teaches, but starts up in huge masses. Instantaneously
are created the very incomes themselves from which
savings are made.* You now produce first and pay
afterwards.

The hindrance and stumbling-block to production,

---

* Take for example the Liverpool and Manchester Railway
Company, or the New River Company. For every hundred
pounds expended, there are two hundred pounds, or possibly a
thousand pounds of value created. Nay, if it is believed before-
hand, and rightly believed, that the enterprise will be profitable,
the projectors and original proprietors may not only have their
capital permanently doubled, but all the money offered on loan
and prepaid by strangers before they turn a spadeful of earth.
This multiplication of capital does not come from savings.

Such joint-stock undertakings are but samples of thousands
of private enterprises.

We hear of capital *sunk* in railways. Suppose a railway to
have cost five millions, and to yield but a moderate return, say
4 or 5 per cent., and its shares to be at par. Every shareholder who has contributed his hundred pounds still has it.
A value equivalent to the whole amount spent still exists in
the aggregate value of the shares of the Railway. But, in the
mean time, that railway has conferred on the country the benefit
of spending its value. It has created a net spendable gain of
five millions sterling. (See Chapters IV. and V.) If no part of
this five millions would otherwise have been productively employed, then the whole of this five millions is not only net gain,
but additional or surplus net gain owing to the making of the

want of money (as it is called in popular and inaccurate language) is taken out of the way. The greater, the more various the production on all hands, the more the means of payment abound and overflow, the ampler and the more insatiable the markets. The vast increase of wealth, material, visible, and tangible, in its turn augments and justifies credit; and credit again multiplies material and solid wealth. National burthens themselves are, as by the wand of the magician, transmuted into national wealth.

Nor is there any reason why this general confidence and affluence should necessarily end (as it has too often done) in a glut or a check.

We have already called attention, more than once, to the admirable remarks of M. Say, who proves that a general glut of all commodities is impossible. Industry once aptly organised—the more you produce all round, the more you may. We have already seen that every interchange of two domestic productions opens no less than four home markets. It is these sure markets that sustain production, and make it certainly and

---

Railway. And so of every part of it, which but for the making of the Railway would not have been productively expended. That proportion is perhaps in every case very large. So that wherever we see a moderately successful railway we behold a monument of capital *created*, not of capital *sunk*. In the end it may perhaps be found that capital created by some railways is a compensation for the destroyed capital represented by the national debt. For only a part of that debt has been really spent. Where a railway does not answer, there it does indeed represent capital sunk. Had the making of railways been decided by public wisdom, instead of being left to the cupidity and jobbing of individuals, this set-off to the gain of railways would not have existed.

You thus augment capital, not merely by savings, but by creating at once the very gain or income out of which savings are made.

What has been the amount of capital in the British West Indies, *suddenly* annihilated by the opposite policy?

What an immense amount of capital are we now *suddenly* creating in *foreign countries*, by our new commercial policy?

permanently profitable. It is this certain and durable profit that begets trust in the solvency of the paymaster, that creates, diffuses, and maintains credit.

While this organisation of industry lasts, CREDIT and CAPITAL in their material sense last and grow too. Indeed, much that is called CAPITAL is at bottom but an apt organisation of industry, which can scarcely ever be except under one fiscal administration.

Now put forth your hand and touch the ark of public or private credit.

Touch first private credit only.

You have but to disarrange the mutual and profitable interchange of British productions, each affording the other not only a full but secure market. Let but one great branch of industry lose its market. Three more markets are (as we have seen) at once closed. A series of markets is ruined. A check, a glut comes.

English industry becomes unprofitable. The English producer is the ultimate paymaster. The means of the paymaster disappear. Trust in his solvency and punctuality vanishes. Credit no longer sustains industry. Capital, in the larger sense, disappears by millions at once. Boundless wealth, material plenty, and industrious energy, give place to universal distrust, idleness, and poverty.

At this hour Irish property, West India property, Manchester property, illustrate the partial collapse of private credit.

Private credit once seriously and generally impaired, public credit can no longer be preserved. Property is gone. Universal ruin and public confusion follow. Where now is England's capital?

Already it is the United States, and not England, that are finding the capital to obliterate the Isthmus of Panama, and pour the commerce of the world over the vast and populous shores of the Pacific.

CHAPTER XVI.

" Free-trade for Ireland, and the evils of Ireland will work their own cure."

Never!

> Rusticus expectat dum defluat amnis ; at ille
> Labitur et labetur in omne volubilis ævum.

A better state of things in Ireland will never *grow,* will never come of itself. A better state of things may be *made,* may be *created* there ; *might* be created immediately and permanently ; *will* be created when the *let-alone* policy is finally abandoned in despair, and the hollowness of existing notions of political economy is demonstrated by experience, and generally recognized.

According to received theories Ireland ought to be very prosperous. She is a very large and an eminently fertile island, in a temperate latitude. She has safe and capacious harbors, noble rivers, immense water-power. In spite of calumnious assertions to the contrary, her poor, *when employed and fed,* are the most able-bodied and laborious of mankind, doing a large proportion of the hardest work both of England and America. Our wise men assure us that it is a vulgar error to suppose that absenteeism has been injurious.* Above all, *Ireland has had perfect free-trade for many, many years, with the richest nation on earth ; and the let-alone system has had free course.*

---

* See the Chapter on Absenteeism.

But in Ireland, as everywhere else, do not facts rebuke those received theories?

What is Ireland's condition? We do not venture to describe it.

Who is responsible? Common sense says, and all Europe and America repeat it—"Those who have governed Ireland are responsible."

But who are they? Not the English members alone, but the Irish members of the imperial parliament. Indeed, it may be truly said that it was the Irish members themselves—Mr. O'Connell and his followers— who enabled the ministry of the day to carry the principal measures of one-sided free-trade.

But it is unjust to charge Great Britain with the want either of a kindly feeling or of generosity to Ireland. There is now, and has long been, an earnest desire to serve her. The truth is, that partly from the pressure of other business, but partly and chiefly from the influence of empty and pernicious theories, Ireland (except in the imperfect way in which the peace has been kept) has not been governed at all. On sound principle, as has been thought, every social and economical abuse has been allowed to run riot.

Proprietors have, on principle, been allowed to lock up their lands with charges constituting a *mortmain*, worse than the mortmain of the middle ages—preventing not only alienation, but cultivation.*

To interfere with contracts between landlord and tenant, so as to give the tenant (what the public welfare requires he should have) an interest in the improvement of the land, has been denounced as contrary to principle! †

---

* Since these observations were written, the Incumbered Estates Court has addressed itself to this evil.

† Written in 1850.

To interfere with the mode of cultivation, shocked the political economists.

To distribute artificially not an excessive, but a congested population, and so to put a stop to those clearances which inflict the misery of an invasion, was to interfere with the rights of property. To encourage artificially any Irish industry, and so to compensate in some degree for the artificial and direct discouragements to which it had been subject for so many years, till it was effectually over-laid and finally smothered by the manufacturing industry of England, would still be deemed monstrously absurd.

But it is said, the population of Ireland, even if properly distributed, would yet be too large to be provided for.

But on this subject many who have studied the agricultural resources of Ireland, and compared them with the existing population, think otherwise. Sir Robert Kane tells us, not only that there is no redundancy of population, but that Ireland might with ease maintain *two and a half times* its present numbers; that all fears of a surplus population (especially with the drain of people now going on) are preposterous; that it is the unequal distribution of the population, and not its aggregate amount, that is to be deplored and corrected. It is not denied that there are districts where the population is congested; but then it is proved that there are others infinitely more extensive, where there is not a fourth part of the population necessary to do work which would be most profitable work, and work which might be done almost without any capital at all. What is wanted is to *get the people at work on the land;* which, if it do not come about naturally, must be done artificially.

Besides the land already tolerably cultivated, there are, we are told, in Ireland no less than SIX MILLIONS OF ACRES of waste land, of which THREE MILLIONS OF

ACRES are peat bog. Successful experiments, both in England and Ireland, have recently demonstrated, that this last sort of waste may at small expense be converted into the most fruitful soils.*

Next it is said that capital is wanting to employ the poor.

We have already seen how the ambiguity of the word CAPITAL deludes us.

But we are further deluded by our English notions. We assume that Ireland is necessarily to be everywhere parcelled out in large farms, and cultivated by day-laborers, in receipt of wages, after the English system. But it is still a matter of controversy, not only in England and Ireland, but on the Continent, and particularly in France, which, on the whole, is after all the best—large farms or small farms—*la grande, ou la petite culture.* It is certain that in Belgium mere occupation of the most arid and sandy deserts in Europe by peasant-squatters without capital, has gradually transformed those deserts into the most fertile land. It is the opinion of many practical persons, well qualified to decide, that small pieces of land occupied by the laborer and his family, not as heretofore, at a high rent with an uncertain tenure, with licence of indefinite subdivision, but if not in fee, at least for a term, with security for the reimbursement of improvements, and prohibition of subdivision, is the sort of cultivation which is best for a large part of Ireland.

But the practicability of schemes which should properly distribute the destitute poor over Ireland lies in this: that no exclusive theoretical and premature choice

---

* There are two pamphlets which ought to be read by all who have no leisure to peruse the larger works on Ireland. "A plea for the rights of industry in Ireland;" and "The Irish difficulty, and how it must be met;" both by Mr. POULETT SCROPE. Before long, justice will be done to the sound views of this gentleman, and his energy in disseminating them. (1850.)

of any one of these modes of cultivation need be made.
The one which circumstances should render necessary
or preferable in every district would be adopted.   The
option would be with the owners or occupiers there.
Many experiments at once in progress under different
circumstances—many districts with their several ener-
gies no longer dissipated over the area of Ireland at
large, but concentrated within their own limits—the
efforts of every locality converging to one point, and
their lights collected into one focus, might soon fuse
and evaporate every difficulty throughout the land.

An expense for arterial drainage would no doubt be
in many districts necessary.   But this is an improvement in which several districts might join, which would
materially assist in the employment of the poor; for
which government aid may or might be had; and
which is absolutely certain to repay the advances many
times over.

The land of Ireland, when but moderately cultivated,
will produce an enormous superfluity.

Whence is Ireland's salvation to come?

From a parliament? From a popular assembly,
English or Irish?

Alas! "perorating" members, "wind-bags of parliamentary eloquence," as Mr. Carlyle calls them, are
poor saviours. A popular assembly is a legislative
make-shift for ordinary occasions; and long debates are
good for this reason—that the more the members talk,
the less they do. But history shews that the just and
clear views, the unfettered and decisive action of a single mind, must make or save a nation.

Thus, Peter the Great laid the deep and strong foundations of modern Russia. So Napoleon brought the
new order and enlightened legislation of modern France
out of the chaos of the Revolution.

Who laid the foundation of Anglo-Saxon greatness?
Not a popular assembly, but Royal Alfred; not the

7

less royal that his incessant and self-sacrificing labors
were prosecuted in a palace that we should call a hovel.
We are told that the wind and drafts that whistled
through, made his candles gutter ; so that he was obliged
to read and write by a horn lantern.   There in gloom,
and pain, and sickness, sat the Lycurgus of the great
Anglo-Saxon race.   The legislator of a thousand years.
Illustrious man ! before whom the pageantry of all the
potentates, and the eloquence of all the parliaments of
Europe shrink into insignificance.

What would an Alfred now say to poor and disor-
ganized Ireland ; to its millions of acres of waste but
cultivable land ; to its ruined commerce and manufactures ; to its people crying for work and wages, but
idle and starving—some flying for their lives from
their native country—others shut up in workhouses ;
to its aristocracy and gentry absent and overwhelmed
with debt? What would he say to counsellors who
should try and persuade him that active and instant
measures would infringe some *let-alone* or *free-trade*
theory ; that this frightful condition of the most fertile
of all lands was inevitable and incurable?

We know not what he would say.   Peradventure he
might think there was no time for *saying*.   But we
know that he would ACT—act instantly, act in spite of
all obstacles, and act effectually.

Is our hope in free-trade ?

Let us see what free-trade has done for Ireland's
manufactures.

For near half a century, Ireland has had perfect
free-trade with the richest country in the world, with
which steamboats and railways have now connected her
more closely than ever.   What has that free-trade done
for her ?

She has now little employment for her teeming population, except upon the land.   She ought to have had,

and might easily have had, other and various employ-ment, and plenty of it. Are we to believe the calumny that the Irish are lazy and won't work? Is Irish human nature different from other human nature? Are not the most laborious of all laborers in London and New York, Irishmen? Are Irishmen inferior in understanding? We Englishmen, who have personally known Irishmen in the army, at the bar, in the church, know that there is no better head than a disciplined Irish one.* But in all these cases, that master of industry, the stomach, has been well satisfied.

No! the truth is, the misery of Ireland is not from the human nature that grows there—it is from mis-taken legislation, past and present.

As to England's past legislation, for a long course of years, Ireland's manufactures were systematically discouraged and stifled, while England's were, at the same time, protected and cherished. The Colonies, and even England and Scotland, were protected against Irish manufactures.

"Ireland," says Dean Swift, writing in 1727—"Ire-land is the only kingdom I ever heard or read of, either in ancient or modern story, which was denied the liberty of exporting their native commodities and manufactures wherever they pleased, except to coun-tries at war with their own prince or state; yet this privilege, by the superiority of mere power, is refused to us in the most momentous parts of commerce."

The masculine common sense of this great writer bewails in a hundred places the importation of English manufactures, and the consequent absence of Irish ones, as the plague and curse of Ireland.

---

* "The minds and bodies of the Irish people," says Sir John Davies, Attorney-General to King James the First, "are endued with extraordinary abilities of Nature."

"One cause of a country's thriving," he says, "is the industry of the people in working up all their native commodities to the last." Another: "The conveniency of safe ports and havens to carry out their own goods as *much manufactured*, and bring in those of others as *little manufactured*,* as the nature of mutual commerce will allow." Another: "The disposition of the people of the country to *wear their own manufactures, and import as few clothes, furniture, food, or drink as they possibly can live conveniently without.*"

But he adds: "Both sexes in Ireland, especially the women, despise and abhor to wear any of their own manufactures, even those which are better made than in other countries. . . . I would be glad," says he, "to know by what secret method it is that we are to grow a rich and flourishing people. The only trade worth mentioning is the linen of the north, and some butter from Cork. . . If," says he, "*we do flourish, it must be against every law of nature and reason, like the thorn at Glastonbury, which blossoms in the midst of winter.*"

All will now at length allow, that the *old* English policy of preventing or destroying Irish manufacturing industry was not only unjust, but highly disadvantageous to England as well as Ireland, inflicting as it did on Ireland the curse of inveterate pauperism and mendicancy. But the mischief has been done. It cannot be undone, by merely removing restrictions on Irish industry. This will only perpetuate the evil. Trade has always a tendency to run in the same channel. English manufactures, originally created by a jealous system of protection, and therefore, at least, until lately, the first in the world, permeating every Irish village where there is a penny to spend, effectually choke and smother infant Irish manufactures.

---

* Dean Swift's notions were like those expounded in Chapters IV. and V.

Misery has produced discontent, insubordination, insecurity. Now, neither Irish nor English manufacturing industry will flourish on Irish ground without some temporary but extraordinary inducement,* as a compensation for the extraordinary and accidental disadvantages to which it would be subjected. The destruction of Irish industry by the ancient English policy is not only a case for repentance, but for *restitution*, or at least compensation. Like other sinners, we are very willing to confess that we have done wrong; ready even to promise that we will do so no more. But a proposal for compensation—a proposal that we should give any Irish industry, or even any English industry on Irish ground, a partial and temporary advantage, so as to place Ireland, as nearly as we can, in the same state as if she had always been fairly treated, as an integral part of the empire—a proposal to make up for past delinquencies, and really restore industry to its *natural* channels—I say such a proposal, just and natural as it is, would at present be received in England with derision.

But at length it will be seen that by merely leaving things alone, although you make Ireland an integral portion of the British territory, you are but perpetuating the old injustice. She will certainly not *make* her cloths, her silk and cotton goods, her hats, her leather, her shoes, her ploughs, her spades, her knives, her steam-engines; for it is cheaper to buy every one of them from England ready made. But she has·not the means to buy to any great extent. She will continue to do as she always has done. She will *do without*. She will be ragged and wretched as ever.

BUT INVERT YOUR ANCIENT POLICY. Give the artificial but *temporary* stimulus of some direct encouragement to a few branches of *Irish* industry. Consider

---

* Written in 1850.

how you created your own manufacturing industry.
See how every European kingdom has done the same.
Reflect for a moment that you are but doing what a
native and independent Irish parliament would be sure
to do. Native industry, native manufactures will, in
Ireland, as elsewhere, be the necessary and certain
result.

Such measures need be but partial and temporary.
We have seen that it is a mistake in political economists when they assert that capital comes from saving
only. A new field once opened to profitable Irish enterprise, Irish wealth will start up in masses. Moreover, English capital and credit, on Irish ground, employing cheap Irish labor, tempted and stimulated by
some temporary advantage for a few years, will soon
be able to compete in Ireland with English manufactures. Native Irish industry will strike deep root,
and extend widely. Security of life and property will
follow, or rather, accompany industry. Noble rivers,
unequalled ports and harbors, large cities, and now
even railways, and until lately political tranquillity invite to this great act of justice and sound policy.

Such manufactures might be selected, as Ireland
shall, in the judgment of well-informed men, be deemed
suited for.

The amount and species of encouragement to be accorded need only be such as will countervail the
temptation to employ industry in England, *rather* than
in Ireland; as will compensate any risk, real or imaginary; as will amount to a temporary premium of
insurance. In short, it should be as much as would
place Ireland, not on a seeming and pretended level,
as now, but on a *true and actual level with England*.
It should be no more than is absolutely necessary for
this just purpose, and last no longer than the necessity
continues, which time would be very short.

Then, and not till then, will the union be as intimate and inviolable as between England and Scotland.

England's gain in the result cannot be calculated. But she will be no loser even in the process. The wealth that native manufactures will at once pour into Ireland's lap will not be *abstracted* from the United Kingdom, but *created* in Ireland. So far from being a worse customer to England, Ireland will be a better. Now she cannot buy—then she will be able. Now she is in the receipt of alms, then she will have the means of earning her bread. I speak of the commercial policy, the mere sordid and immediate pecuniary advantage of such a course. But there are nobler and more generous motives which will actuate Englishmen, if they can be disenchanted of their theories, and brought to see that such a policy would be really beneficial to Ireland.

There is no novelty or strangeness in this suggestion of partial and temporary encouragement of infant Irish manufactures. Enlightened and impartial foreigners have made it before. For example, the Baron Dupin, in France, and Mr. Webster, in the United States of America, have given it as their opinion, that little good is to be expected without it, from any course of British legislation for Ireland.

Nay, we have more than theory or authority to guide us. We have in the past history of Ireland herself, actual experience both of the advantage of artificially developing Irish manufactures, and of the ruin attending the withdrawal of encouragement.

There is one, and but one great industry in Ireland still eminently prosperous, and rivalling Manchester itself. I mean, of course, the linen manufactory of Belfast.

Did that great industry come of itself? Far from it.

A French Protestant, a refugee from the persecutions of Louis the Fourteenth, settled in Belfast and introduced the trade. King William the Third encouraged it with a large annual grant. This grant was continued by succeeding sovereigns. A linen board sitting in Dublin under the sanction of government regulated the trade. It was afterwards encouraged by a parliamentary grant, continued to 1826.

At length, when the industry had grown robust enough to stand of itself, artificial supports were withdrawn, and now it is one of the first industries in Europe. Where would that industry have been if the "let-lone system" had been followed?

The Scotch fisheries were at first created by actual bounties.

The Irish fisheries have, if not for bounties, at least for direct encouragement, a much more urgent claim. The poor fishermen were obliged, in the stress of the Irish famine, to part with their boats and tackle, and have never been able to replace them. They are idle. The western and southern coasts of Ireland swarm with fish. The population are ready enough to consume, and ready enough to produce in return.

Surely this is a strong case, at least for a loan on the security of the boats and tackle, though its repayment were much more precarious than it really would be.

Before the Union Irish protecting duties existed on many English manufactures. Among others there was a duty on English woollens; a duty on English calicoes and muslins so high as to be nearly prohibitory; a duty on English silk. There were duties on English cotton yarn, cotton twist, and cotton manufactured goods.

The Act of Union continued the duties on woollens and several other articles for twenty years. It continued the high duties on calicoes and muslins till 1808. They were then to be gradually reduced till they should fall to ten per cent. in 1816, and to nothing in 1821. The duties on cotton yarn and cotton twist were continued till 1808, and were then to be gradually reduced to nothing in 1816. The linen trade was encouraged by a parliamentary grant withdrawn in 1826.

Now see the effects, first, of protection, and, next, of its withdrawal, or, rather, a specimen of the effects.* -

Before the Union there were under protection, Irish woollen manufactures, Irish carpet manufactures, Irish blanket manufactures, Irish silk manufactures, Irish calico manufactures, Irish flannel manufactures, and Irish stocking manufactures. These manufactures are now smothered and extinct.

---

* It has been stated by Dublin tradesmen acquainted with the facts, that in 1800, they had 91 master woollen manufacturers, employing 4918 hands. In 1840, the master manufacturers were 12, the hands 602.

Master wool-combers, in 1800, were 30—the hands 230. In 1834, masters 5—hands 66.

Carpet manufacturers—In 1800, masters 13—hands 720. In 1841, masters 1—hands 10.

Blanket manufacturers in Kilkenny.—In 1800, masters 56—hands 3000. In 1822, masters 42—hands 925.

Broad silk loom weavers in Dublin, in 1800.—At work 2500. In 1840, 250.

Calico looms in Balbriggan, in 1799, in full work, 2000. In 1841, 226.

Flannel looms in the County of Wicklow, in 1800, 1000. In 1841, not one.

In the City of Cork.

	1800	1834
Braid weavers	1000	40
Worsted weavers	2000	90
Hosiers	300	28
Wool combers	700	110
Cotton weavers	2000	210
Linen check weavers	600	none.

7*

But what ought they to have been, with increased population and power of consumption, with the application of steam, with improved mechanical and chemical agencies? What would, and must they have been, but for the blight of English competition, withering at once the power of producing, and the means of purchasing? What might they be made EVEN NOW, should England, instead of blindly chasing the phantom of cheapness, no matter of what sort, at once and seriously address herself to developing the unexplored but prodigious productive power of Ireland?

But England is at present spell-bound and paralysed by her epidemic yet ephemeral theories. Unless it be in comformity with her new doctrines, she will not listen to the most obvious measure of true policy for Ireland. She will support an artificial system to maintain myriads of Irish poor in idleness, but will not hear of an artificial system to marry them to industry. "Buy," says she, with bitter irony, to the penniless Irish—"*buy* in the cheapest market. Don't make for yourselves, when you can buy of me cheaper than you can make." Accordingly, the Irish do as all nations so situated needs must do—they *go without*. Innumerable Irish hands, ready to labor—immeasurable quantities of Irish materials ready to be wrought

---

Cotton spinners, bleachers, calico printers—thousands employed utterly extinct.

The linen trade protected and fostered till 1826, was not in those days confined to the North of Ireland. In Clonakitty, in the county of Cork, £1200 a week was expended on the purchase of coarse linen webs, so late as 1825. In Mayo, £111,000 was expended in purchasing the same species of web. In 1825, the sum of two millions and a half sterling was expended in Ireland in the purchase of coarse unbleached home-made webs.

I am obliged for these specimens of the ruin of Irish industry to Mr. Butt, Q. C. at the Irish Bar, who informs me that they could be very much extended.

up—innumerable consumers, too anxious to consume, and to produce in return—are, as if by enchantment, kept asunder. Without temporary encouragement, Irish industry is undersold, smothered, rendered impossible. Universal, hereditary, and national idleness, poverty, and discontent are the necessary consequences.

What sort and what degree of encouragement should be accorded to Irish industry without detriment to England, is a problem for a great statesman to solve.

CHAPTER XVII.

*" The currency should vary, as it would vary, if it were
entirely metallic."*

HERE we have the principle of the Act of 1844.

Here, also, we have the old fallacy, that a natural
state of things is necessarily good; that it is to be imi-
tated, not to be corrected and improved.

Men talk glibly of variations in the currency. Few
reflect on the awful extent to which such changes
affect the prosperity of all ranks. The laborer, the
pauper, and the beggar are as much interested in the
currency question as the manufacturer, the shopkeeper,
or the great proprietor of land or funds, and even
more.

Sudden and great alterations in the amount of value
of the circulating medium are at best transfers of property—gigantic robberies; they are often much worse;
they involve wanton *destruction* of immense property,
and *stoppage* of industry. The standard of value
should be as fixed and immutable as human art can
make it—and human art can make it much more invariable than if it were entirely metallic. The Act of
1844 makes it not only variable as the wind, but as
subject to tempests and hurricanes.

The cure provided by the Act of 1844, for an adverse
balance of trade, and for every export, or tendency to an
export of the precious metals, is a sudden and great
diminution in the quantity of the currency—a rise in
its value—next, a great and sudden rise in the rate of

interest—a fall in the price of all things—a fearful injury to all the industrious classes. "I will," says the law-giver, first "take no precaution whatever against an adverse balance of trade. Such precautions I consider puerile. Next, when the adverse balance comes to be felt, I will take no measures to mitigate its pressure, but you shall feel all its consequences just as if the currency were entirely metallic. That is the natural state of things, and therefore must be a good one."

Let us see what the old system was, and how it acted; and next how the new system has acted, and will act.

There is an intimate connection between a currency at once safe and invariable, and a moderate, judicious, and discriminating protective system. Under the old system of protection, imports were systematically controlled by import duties, exports were for the most part free. There was therefore a constant tendency in exports to exceed imports—a constant tendency in the balance of trade to be in favor of this country. You might consequently, on extraordinary occasions (as in the event of a bad harvest necessitating an extraordinary import of grain and export of bullion), safely allow the money market to be relieved by an extraordinary issue of notes, securely depending on the ultimate balance of trade, which, in the long run must, in consequence of your artificial tariff, be in favor of this country. What you expected always eventually happened: the balance of trade brought the bullion back. The issue of notes was then, in easier times, contracted to its safe and ordinary amount. You passed through the crisis with little or no alteration in the value of money, or rate of interest. When the bullion went away, notes, by supplying its place, broke the shock to credit; when bullion returned, the withdrawal of those notes still preserved the equilibrium. The paper portion of the currency, over and above its other advantages, was then an ingenious contrivance in the nature of a spring or elastic band, which, enabling you safely to expand the currency in times of distress, and to contract it again in times of prosperity thus equalised and averaged the tension. Lord Ashburton has shewn how the currency often was relaxed in periods of severe pressure with perfect safety. And this occasional relaxation in times of difficulty was the ordinary course of proceeding long before the Bank Restriction Act. Its advantage was well understood even as early as the beginning of the last century. Addison, writing in the time of Queen Anne, says, "When the bullion leaves us, we make credit supply its place." There was in the paper currency a union of convertibility with elasticity. There was a compensatory and self-adjusting action which artificially secured uniformity of value, and made a mixed currency, partly metallic, partly paper, a much better and more invariable standard of value than a mere metallic currency could possibly have been.

Now let us see what the new system is.

In the first place, the balance of trade is on principle ignored and neglected. Yet it is clear that variations in the rate of exchange can never do more than correct slight differences. That if a large and unfavorable balance arise from a permanent cause, it must be, and always is, corrected by payments in bullion.* If there is a balance to pay, it must be paid either in the precious metals, or by a sale to foreigners of English securities, which in the long run is still a payment, though a postponed payment, in the precious metals. It must, as it always has been, and will be, paid at last in the precious metals.

You can now no longer rely on an average favorable balance of trade: there may not only be (as there will certainly be) periodical drains of the precious

---

* Mr. Mill admits this, Vol. i. p. 164.

metals, but there may be a perennial stream running out, not as formerly less than the perennial stream running in, but much larger.

How is it now proposed to meet the drain when the misery begins to be felt?

Not as before, by supplying the void with notes. That is no longer consistent with the preservation of a metallic basis to the currency; for we are told, and truly told, that if new notes were issued as fast as gold went out, the drain of gold would be continually going on, till all the gold had left the kingdom, the Banknote would be inconvertible, and another Bank Restriction Act would be inevitable.

No, it is to be stopped violently by a diminution in the quantity, and consequent rise in the value, of the whole currency, just as if it were entirely metallic. No notes are to be issued in place of the gold that goes out. Nay, the law may even contract the notes as the gold goes out. Prices of everything are to fall. The industrious classes are to see their property thus taken from them, and their debts and incumbrances thus really augmented. Industry is to be paralysed, trade stopped, and the pressure of the public burthens indefinitely aggravated; while the transactions of the empire are being dwarfed and stunted to fit a short allowance of the circulating medium of the civilized world.

Then it is said prices will be effectually beaten down, and so at length imports will be checked, exports promoted, and an adverse balance of trade *naturally* redressed. Never mind, though this desirable and necessary result should be produced by the diminution or cessation of the ordinary operations of industry and commerce, and the bankruptcy of otherwise solvent houses.

But has it been duly considered what the *currency*, the *medium of payment*, the real *money* of the United Kingdom really is?

How are payments in fact made?

First, in *coin*—in gold, silver, and copper.

Secondly, in *Bank-notes* payable to bearer on demand.

But these first two species of money only carry on the retail or small dealings of the kingdom.

Thirdly, in *bankers' checks*, also payable to bearer on demand. Bankers' checks are transferable by mere delivery. They possess the qualities of money. As in the case of money and bank-notes, honest acquisition confers title. The payment not only of large but of small amounts in bankers' checks, is enormous and incalculable. Checks not being subject to stamps,* no means exist of ascertaining their amount.

Fourthly, in *bills of exchange*. The returns from the Stamp Office of money received for bill-stamps, will not show the exact aggregate value. But it is quite clear from the amount of stamps issued, that the mere inland bills of exchange issued and circulated in the United Kingdom, in a year of ordinary prosperity, amount to *many hundred millions sterling.*†

Lastly, payments are made in *money of account*. By money of account is meant transfers in traders' and bankers' books. Formerly, in some trading cities, as in Amsterdam, Genoa, Venice, and Hamburg, this money of account being payable in imaginary new and perfect coin of the state, and not in the mixed, worn, or clipped coin of the actual circulation, bore an *agio*, or premium, and was called, as it really was, *bank money*. If such money as this existed here in bankers' books only, it would still, though of no more value than so much *coin*, be not improperly termed *bank money*. But money of this description exists, not only in bankers'

---

* Imposed since these observations were written.

† Foreign bills drawn abroad, but circulating here, are not included in this estimate ; for they are not subject to stamps. Their aggregate value must be very great.

books, but in the books of merchants and others. It has therefore been called, and not inaptly, *money of account*.

This is the money in which the *largest* of all payments are made, and in which great payments are most *frequently* made. The spread of banks over the kingdom, their multiplication in the Metropolis, and the improved modes of communication, especially by railway, give every day an increased circulation to this *money of account*, and economise and supersede the use of coin and bank-notes in payments of any considerable amount.

And even in the smaller transactions where gold is used, the same sovereign now circulates in London in the morning, in New York in the afternoon, and does as much work as four or five sovereigns would have done twenty years ago.

These are the various sorts of money in modern use in Great Britain and Ireland.

It will be seen at a glance how insignificant the aggregate amount of coin and notes is, compared with the aggregate amount of bankers' checks, bills of exchange, and money of account.

But then the quantity and value of these checks, bills, and money of account, depend entirely on the quantity and value of the coin and notes. Diminish the quantity of coin and notes by five per cent, and you may augment the exchangeable value of the residue, even of the coin and notes, by twenty or fifty per cent; for when the quantity of money or of any other article of first necessity, but of limited supply, is diminished, its exchangeable value rises in a much higher degree than the degree of diminution. Added to all which there is the effect of uncertainty and panic. That, however, is the least part of the mischief. Touch the coin and notes, the other and greater currency shrinks at once, like the sensitive plant.

And no one can tell the proportion in which, when you curtail the lesser currency, the greater is actually curtailed; in some instances it may be in a less proportion, but in many instances a far greater proportion. The enhancement in *value* of the greater currency is the same, but who can tell or conjecture what the diminution in *quantity* is?

The whole currency of all sorts may not inaptly be compared to radii diverging from the centre of a circle to a portion of its circumference. Contract or draw closer together these radii never so little; and though near the point of convergence, you lessen but insensibly the space they occupy, yet, at the circumference, that space is marvellously diminished. Or if the reader will pardon a more popular illustration—The currency is like an expanded fan. Contract the bones of the handle near the joint but a little, and the large expanse of gauze, silk, or feathers, is doubled up and vanishes. Contract the coin and notes by five millions, and you may be contracting the greater currency, the sustenance of trade and labor, by fifty millions, or more. It is mere matter of conjecture. Apprehension or panic, which your measures are sure to create, may derange all calculations.

In the Autumn of 1847, a diminution in the quantity of the lesser currency actually diminished the quantity of the greater by *much more* than a proportionate amount. As in other commodities, so in money, *actual* exchangeable value depends not only on the *true*, but on the *erroneous* judgments, or even feelings, of the public. The predictions of philosophers, who teach from their closets that these things always depend on certain general laws, will, in actual experience, be found strangely wide of the mark.

We see, therefore, how cruel and barbarous must be

the operation of the Act of 1844, on a country with debts and engagements such as ours.

This is now, unfortunately, no longer matter of prophecy, but of actual experience.

The Act operated for the first time in the autumn of 1847. And it is not too much to say that such commercial distress and ruin was never seen in England before. How far further it might have proceeded, if government had not been compelled to announce their interference, no man can predict.

Nor let it be pretended that the mischief was in the crisis itself, and not in the law. The first answer is, That as soon as it was *announced* that the Act would be suspended, the mischief abated; though the Act never was really suspended at all. If government had adopted that course earlier, many a merchant-prince now ruined, would have been saved. Next, the most opposite authorities agree in attributing the mischief to the Act of Parliament, and to that alone. Lord Ashburton declared that the importations, large as they necessarily were, were not more than, under a wiser management of the currency, the country could have easily borne. Mr. Mill says, " the crisis of 1847 was of that sort which the provisions of the Act had not the smallest tendency to avert, and when the crisis came, the mercantile difficulties were probably *doubled* by its existence."*

And why was the industry of the country subjected to this horrible torture? That an adverse balance of trade might be corrected by what is called the natural flow of the precious metals. That a theory might be carried out. In vain did men, grown grey in business, remonstrate against the measure three years before. It was carried in contemptuous defiance of their warnings.†

---

* *Principles of Political Economy*, vol. ii. p. 21.
† Since these observations were written twice again have the government been compelled to interpose.

Which is best, the old method of *prevention, or miti-gation,* of an adverse balance, or the new measure of *cure?*

We shall see what other measure of *cure* will be tried next.

In the meantime we are preparing for a renewal of the crisis. The imports now greatly and permanently exceed the exports. A nation that intends to *secure* an adverse balance, to be paid at some time or other, ought to tax its exports, and let its imports come in free. This is exactly what we now do by our one-sided free-trade, with this disadvantage: It is not we but the foreigner who taxes our exports when they come as imports into his country: instead of taking the tax on our exports ourselves, we give it to the foreigner. We take the disadvantage of the adverse balance: he takes the revenue.

In 1848 and following years, owing to the political troubles that afflicted Europe, an enormous influx of movable capital from all parts of the Continent, seeking a secure but temporary investment in this country, postponed the day of reckoning and accumulated the arrears. At this day the enormous credit established by England abroad, and her annual revenue from foreign bonds, stocks, and securities, appear to postpone the day of reckoning. As before, men of experience warn, but the warning is not only unheeded, but ridiculed. "If you will not hear reason," says Dr. Franklin, "she will surely rap your knuckles."

Few subjects are so intricate as the distribution of the precious metals among the countries of the world. Many considerations are overlooked by those who prophesy that the evil will work its own cure. David Hume says that a progressive increase in the quantity of the precious metals, and their declining value in any country, is favourable to a progressive increase of industry. And no doubt that is so. A stream, therefore, of the precious metals poured into a country, produces effects exactly the converse of the effects which its dereliction produces in the country which it is leaving. This fertilising stream, in the country to which it goes, stimulates industry, multiplies transactions, creates its own demand, and counteracts its tendency to return. Our industry is crippled—our neighbor's is augmented. We permanently need the bullion less—he permanently needs it more.

To confound a low rate of interest with a low value of money is a very common mistake. The *rate of interest* might remain as low as it is now, if twice the quantity of gold were put into the sovereign, and the value of money thereby doubled; for the interest would in that case be as much augmented in value as the principal.

A low rate of interest is consistent, and often coincident, with a high exchangeable value of money, and a high rate of interest with a low exchangeable value of money.

Thus of late value of money, measured in other commodities, has been high. Its purchasing power has been and is very great. But the rate of interest has nevertheless at the same time been very low. Good bills are discounted at 2 per cent. per annum. On the other hand, during the war, when the currency was notoriously depreciated, the value of money measured in other commodities was very low. Its purchasing power was then very small. But the rate of interest was then very high. The discount of the best bills was 5 per cent., and would have been more had the law allowed it.

When, therefore, in the inaccurate language of city articles in newspapers, we read of the *plenty* of money or the *low value* of money, or that money is *cheap*, that is ambiguous and inaccurate language.

It is quite consistent with this intelliegnce, that by a high exchangeable value of money, the price of commodities is injuriously depressed, that the profits of trade are low, and the pressure of the taxes unfairly augmented. The announcement may betoken or promise anything but prosperity.*

What are the circumstances on which the rate of interest depends is a point on which political economists are not entirely agreed. Most of them, however, coincide with Adam Smith, that it is regulated by the current rate of profit—that most will be given for money where most can be made of it. Hence, though the value of gold in London and its value in New York, or Sidney, are at this moment nearly alike, the rate of interest is higher in New York, and higher still in Sidney, because the profits of trade are greater in America than in England, and greater still in Australia.

---

* Yet it may well be, that a sudden *increase* of the relative quantity of money *beats down* for a time the rate of interest; and that a sudden *decrease* of its relative quantity, *raises* for a time the rate of interest. But these effects will be transient. Eventually the larger relative quantity of money in the first case, will in the aggregate be worth no more : and the smaller relative quantity in the second case, will in the aggregate be worth no less, than the original aggregate quantity of money was before either alteration. The ultimate and permanent effect will be felt in *prices*, not in the *rate of interest.*

All this assumes that the goodness of credit, public and private, remains the same. Of course where from any cause credit is affected, another element enters into the calculation of interest, viz., the degree of risk. And not only the *real* risk, but the *apprehended* risk. Where the fears of the public exaggerate the apprehended risk, we say there is a *panic*. A panic may temporarily raise the rate of interest to any conceivable amount. A rise in the value of money often increases real risk. A trader's means of payment may be, and often are, destroyed by unexpected low prices.

CHAPTER XVIII.

" Higher wages will but increase population."

THE fashionable political economy has many pleasing theories: it is distressing to see them fall either before a rigorous analysis, or before the yet more convincing logic of experiment.

But then, by way of set-off, political economy has one theory very dark and gloomy* indeed. We are told that to augment the comfortable subsistence of mankind, is but to increase their numbers—to create ultimately only a larger collection of wretched families, who are to succumb at length to vice and misery, the appointed checks of population.

Twenty years ago, the doctrine of the anti-populationists reigned supreme. A great law of nature had been discovered. Rich unbelievers in Malthus were assailed with ridicule and contemptuous pity :† persecution, it is true, was reserved for poor and practical unbelievers only.

But of late, this specious but disheartening theory has been much more closely examined. Old facts have been more carefully sifted, and new facts have afforded a wide field for induction.

The opinion of sceptics in political economy will of course weigh little. Let us therefore see what orthodox believers in political economy, and eminent professors of the science now say.

---

* Mr. Carlyle calls it " THE DISMAL SCIENCE."

† Obvious mistakes had been discovered—the world had not been made big enough. There was danger of want of standing room.

And Mr. M'Culloch shall speak.

"The principle of increase," says he, "as explained by Mr. Malthus, and more recently by Dr. Chalmers, appeared to form an insuperable obstacle to all permanent improvement in the condition of society, and to condemn the great majority of the human race to a state approaching to destitution.

"But further inquiries have shewn that the inferences drawn by the authorities now referred to, *are contradicted by the widest experience.*

"*That the too rapid increase of population is almost always prevented by the influence of principles which its increase brings into activity.*

"That a vast improvement has taken place in the condition of the people of every country, *particularly of those in which population has increased with the greatest rapidity.*

"And that so far from being inimical to improvement, we are really indebted to the principle of increase, for most part of our comforts and enjoyments, and for the continued progress of arts and industry."*

So that according to this great authority, Mr. Malthus's inferences are now contradicted by the widest experience.

Good men *felt* all along, that there must be something unsound in a theory which would extinguish benevolent and philanthropic exertion. It now appears they were right.

"The heart is wiser than the schools."

When, therefore, we are distressed to see the pleasant theories of political economy gradually dissolve, and new views take their place, it is a consolation that the gloomiest picture is as evanescent as the sunniest.

The two following propositions constitute the theory

---

* *Principles of Political Economy*, preface, p. 14.

of the anti-populationists, not long ago triumphant, but lately fallen into distrust and discredit.

First, that the increase of mankind proceeding in a geometrical progression, while the increase of the means of subsistence advances only in an arithmetical progression, population increases faster than subsistence.

Secondly, that the price of labor, when left to find its natural level, is, to use the words of Mr. Malthus, "a most important political barometer, expressing clearly the wants of the society respecting population." In other words, that the increase of a population will be in proportion to its comfortable circumstances.

But it is now difficult to reconcile the first position with well-known facts.

Mr. Malthus published the first edition of his book in 1798. Since that period (or, if you please, since the conquest), which has augmented most—population or the means of subsistence? Which have done most—the mouths that have come into the world, in diminishing food, or the hands that have come with them, in augmenting the means of producing it?

Protectionists tell us, that in the article of food alone, our means of producing, even within the narrow boundary of the British islands, are yet unlimited. There are many millions of uncultivated acres, of fertility till lately unsuspected. The resources of drainage and improved cultivation are but beginning to be opened up. Agricultural chemistry is in its infancy. The elements of fertility have but just begun to be scientifically understood. You have yet to spread the manure and sewerage of your cities on the soil. You have yet to witness the boundless gratitude of your mother earth, when you plant her now starving and naked children on the waste. They point to your Colonies in both hemispheres, where the precious grain of the Anglo-Saxon race is sown and germinating. There you have, not petty territories, like France or Spain, but vast

8

continents preparing to receive your productions, to pour back in return their food and other natural riches, and, if need be, to receive more people than you can send. They add that steam has, since the days of Malthus, laid these Colonies of yours, with their boundless fields, alongside your coasts.

The free-traders on their part bid you look to the valley of the Mississippi, able to supply all Europe with food. They tell you that you could, and ought, to draw your supplies from that and many other inexhaustible foreign sources.

We have not in the present chapters of this little book now to discuss which of these two counsel the true policy. But both protectionists and free-traders agree in this, that since the days of Malthus, however the population may have augmented, the means of producing and acquiring food have been augmented not only in an equal, but in an infinitely greater degree.

Now look at all other material things besides food. The difficulty is not to produce, but the difficulty seems now to be, not to *over-produce*. Steam, and mechanical powers, with chemical agencies, have laid the riches of all nature at our feet in inexhaustible profusion.

The means of subsistence, therefore, have not been wanting to population. There was in 1798, no real danger of too great an increase of men and women. Providence had gifts in store, not suspected by those who distrusted His prescience and His bounty.

Indeed, it has been truly observed by Paley and by M. Thiers, that there never yet has been a nation which even fully cultivated *its own soil;* and if we are to judge of the future by the past, there never will be.

But how often has population been wanting to the means of subsistence! Where are the dense populations that anciently lined the banks of the Nile, the Indus, the Tigris, and the Euphrates? The fertile land remains in Asia Minor, Arabia, Syria, Persia, and

Northern India; but in many parts of these countries huge cities and the myriads of human creatures with which, under their ancient monarchies, they once swarmed, are gone!

But the second position, that the rate of wages governs the rate of increase, and that the increase of a population is therefore always in proportion to its comfortable circumstances, is quite as irreconcilable with established facts.

Comfort, and a station in life, we find beget prudence. Poverty produces recklessness. The middle and upper classes do not breed like the lowest. Few populations have ever multiplied like the most wretched Irish.

There is nothing, therefore, in a true theory of population to scare either governments or benevolent individuals from persevering endeavors to better the condition, *and raise the remuneration,* of the lowest class. On the contrary, there is everything to encourage such philanthropical endeavors. It is the truest, soundest policy.

In the wynds of Glasgow, and cellars of Liverpool, population multiplies as fast as anywhere else. And what a population! The moral degradation deep as it is, is not deeper than the physical deterioration of the fathers and mothers of the coming race.

.　.　.　. nequiores mox daturos
Progeniem vitiosiorem.

We have thought it worth while to improve the breed of oxen, sheep and pigs. Our sleek and comely animals seem another race from the lean and long-legged creatures of France. But there is reason to fear that the reverse operation as to human creatures, is proceeding in the great cities of both countries.

Compare the swarms of fragile women, of slight, deli-cate, and half-begotten men in London, Paris, Lyons, and Manchester, with the men and women, represent-ing a by-gone race, but now living in the country dis-tricts of Normandy, and frequenting the markets of Dieppe or Caen, and you will see what is going on. *

There is no reason to fear an increase of population.

But there is great reason to fear the increase of a population morally depraved, and physically deterio-rated.

---

* Written in 1849.

CHAPTER XIX.

*"It is preposterous to interfere with a man's management
of his own property."*

LAND, as has been well observed by Mr. Mill, is a
commodity distinguishable from all other commodities
by two peculiarities. First, land was not made by anybody. Secondly, land exists in limited quantity.

Land is not, therefore, to be dealt with on mere
commercial principles.

On the one hand private property in land, and the
stability of that property, is the first essential to its
due cultivation. On the other hand proprietors should
not be at liberty to prevent or even impede its due
cultivation.

We constantly hear complaints, that land is encumbered and tied up with settlements, estates for life,
charges, terms for years, and encumbrances of every
sort; and that the relations between landlord and tenant, at least in Ireland, are such that the land cannot
be properly cultivated.

But this evil exists, not because the law has interfered so much, but because it has interfered too little.

That land may be freely bought and sold, the legislature has from time to time passed many statutes of
mortmain. With the same view, the Courts of Law
have abolished all indestructible entails, and have destroyed perpetuities, by prohibiting settlements of pro-

perty which would endure beyond a life or lives in being, and twenty-one years afterwards.

But such is the imperfection of human affairs, and the necessity for constant legislative superintendence, that one mischief is scarcely eradicated when another springs up. A new sort of *mortmain* has now presented itself, in the shape of settled and encumbered estates : an evil of portentous magnitude, not only impeding the sale of land, but preventing its cultivation ; making the most important and productive of all labor impossible, even in the midst of a superfluity of unemployed laborers ; and smiting large portions of England, and one-half of Ireland, with an artificial but invincible barrenness.

Owners of land have from generation to generation been left at liberty to manage, charge, and settle their lands as they thought fit. The law has interfered no further than to prevent indestructible entails, perpetuities, alienation in mortmain, and trusts for accumulation extending beyond a certain period. The *laissez-faire* system has had full swing.* Proprietors have done as they would with their own. No enlightened and provident legislation has looked forward to the interest of the public. Nay, there is at this moment nothing to prevent the proprietor of half a county from indulging his caprice by ejecting the occupiers, dismissing the inhabitants, and laying it down as a forest or deer-walk. No chimerical apprehension : the thing has been done in Scotland over and over again, and, recently, to a very great and most pernicious extent. This is only a direct mode of doing that which is accomplished indirectly and circuitously by allowing a title to become such an entangled and trackless wilderness of charges, judgments, life estates, terms for years,

---

* Since these observations were written, the Incumbered Estates Act has operated in some degree in Ireland.

and mortgages, that a sale of any portion of the land, and the proper cultivation of all of it, becomes impossible.

The evil is gigantic, and the remedy proportionably difficult. *

Among others, these suggestions appear to deserve consideration.

No judgment should hereafter bind the land except from the time of actual seizure by the sheriff. †

Mortgages and charges of every kind should be made apportionable without the consent of the incumbrancer.

At present, if an estate is charged or mortgaged, the whole settlement or incumbrance weighs on every acre. No portion can be sold by paying, or securing its fair proportion of the incumbrance. Cases often happen, in which an owner of incumbered land desires to sell a portion of his land. It is his interest to sell. It is the interest of an anxious purchaser to buy. It is, above all, the interest of the public that the sale should take place. But the sale cannot now be effected without the consent of the mortgagee or incumbrancer, and very often he cannot legally consent. An owner with the approbation of a protector of the settlement should be invested with the power of selling any portion of his estate, notwithstanding incumbrances. The *fair proportion* of incumbrance chargeable on the part proposed to be sold, should be subject to a calculation. The amount of purchase money for which no valid discharge can be given, should be paid into the Bank of England, or invested in the funds. A public officer,

---

* Since these observations were written, a mode has been devised of giving a clear parliamentary title to persons who desire it. But its operation has been very limited.

† These observations were written in 1850.

practically conversant with titles and legal business, should supervise and approve the transaction. If litigation be necessary, it may take place; but the purchase-money lying at interest, and not the land, will be the subject of it. The purchaser should then have by Act of Parliament, a new, clear, indefeasible fee-simple, unassailable by any objection, except that of fraud. *

Mortgagees and other incumbrancers should always have a power of sale, and a power to sell portions of an estate.

Mortgages with powers of sale are of comparatively recent introduction. And one reason why Irish real property is more encumbered than English is, that mortgages with powers of sale have been more uncommon in Ireland.

The time of limitation might, with great advantage, be shortened.

A man who is *sui juris*, has been resident in the country all the time, and has slept on his claim for ten years, might safely be barred.

It is a common opinion that there should be a general register of titles, shewing at a glance every incumbrance on every estate. England, it is said, is almost the only civilised country where such a register does not exist. It is alleged that this would shorten and simplify searches, abstracts, and conveyances. This is not the place to discuss the arguments for and against it. Suffice it to say, that the many eminent real-property lawyers approve it. But on the other hand, there are many very serious practical difficulties, and the great authority of Lord St. Leonards is against it.

---

* Written in 1850.

There are other far more important interpositions in the *management* of real property, which experience has shewn to be necessary.

The law ought to interpose in contracts between landlord and tenant, at all events in Ireland. At present the contract usually made is for the advantage of neither. But the public is the greatest sufferer. Much of the imperfect cultivation of the land is due to this neglect of public interest.

Non-cultivation, or even improper or imperfect cultivation, should, with proper guards and regulations, be a ground of compulsory sale to the public on fair terms. And a scheme will be suggested presently by which no party interested in the land would be a loser, although the public would be great gainers.

Ought a millionaire to be at liberty to abolish the ploughed fields, and pull down the homesteads in half a county, and convert them into a waste, for his pleasure or caprice?

Are all the proceedings in the north of Scotland consistent with sound national policy?

Ought an Irish landlord, like the dog in the manger, to own reclaimable land of which he can make, or does make, no use at all, but on which, or at which, thousands of his fellow-countrymen might live, be happy, and conduce to the wealth of the country? At present this is not always his own fault. But a state of things might be introduced in Ireland which would either correct it, or make its continuance really his own fault. And then its continuance would be a ground, not of forfeiture, but of compulsory sale.

Owners of real estate are for many reasons unwilling to sell and invest in personal property on government credit, but principally for these two reasons: the funds may fall, and so the capital may be diminished, or the

8*

value of money decline, either by a diminution of the value of gold, or by an over issue of paper currency in times of difficulty, and so both principal and interest may be endangered.

But it is in the power of the public to remove both these objections.

Government bonds renewable from time to time, payable (principal and interest) in money, calculated on the price of corn according to the tithe rent charge tables, would be at once a security against diminution of capital and depreciation of money.*

On such bonds as these all the coil of settlements and encumbrances might be shuffled off without any injury to owners or incumbrancers, and to the immense gain of the public.

The government would have the best security for lending their credit—the land itself—which land, however, they need not keep, but could themselves sell, accepting, if they thought fit, such bonds in payment, and so sell as to ensure the true interest of the public, and the due cultivation of the soil.

And it may be observed in passing that this scheme, so far from diminishing, would augment the stability and security of property in land; for it would greatly increase the number of those who are interested in that stability, and would remove the temptation to plunder.

It is respectfully suggested that in the case of voluntary vendors, the scheme is easy, profitable to all parties, free from difficulty, and so important that attention will be called to it again hereafter.

---

* This scheme was suggested in the 8th edition of this book (1850).

CHAPTER XX.

" Beware of having recourse to inferior soils."

IF the domestic production of *food* could but be made to keep pace with other industry, why should any increase of population be excessive?

A parish, we will suppose, contains one farmer, one miller, one baker, one butcher, one carpenter, one blacksmith, one doctor, one lawyer, one draper and grocer, and so on of other trades, and a certain number of laborers in each occupation.

Now, if the population be doubled, and there be two of a trade all round, and two laborers where there was formerly but one, the *proportion* being undisturbed, there is no more excess of population than there was before. Each new comer adds, it is true, a new pair of hands to do the work, but then he also brings with him a new proportionate demand for the work of everybody else. Everybody is as busy as before.

But here comes the difficulty: you can easily have two millers, and two bakers, and two of every trade and occupation except one. But how can you get two farmers? Where are the *new farms* to be had?

Here we see at once the difficulty in which old and advanced communities are apt to find themselves. We see one reason, among many more, why it has been so often said and repeated, that agriculture is the first of arts; one reason why agriculture merits the chief attention of every wise and foreseeing government.

Four expedients present themselves.

(1.) Taking more land into cultivation.

(2.) Improving the cultivation of that which is already cultivated.

(3.) Importing food from abroad.

(4.) Diminishing the demand for food by exporting the population.

If land were as inexhaustible as air, or water, or light, or steam, or mechanical or chemical agencies, the difficulty would always be at once solved by adopting the first and most obvious expedient. "But land," says Professor Tucker, of Virginia, "is a *machine* which but a few possess, but whose produce none can dispense with."

And so it may with truth be said, that improved cultivation of land already cultivated, is an augmented efficiency of the old *machines*.

But in our altogether uncultivated land in Great Britain and Ireland, we yet have new machines in great abundance and potential efficiency. In our Colonies these new machines are innumerable and almost unused. In improved methods of cultivation, and improved and more plentiful manures, we have the means of indefinitely increasing the efficiency of the machines already in use at home.

Our most obvious resource, therefore, should still seem to be the two first expedients: cultivating more land at home and in the Colonies, and cultivating it better. According to the principles already explained, it is to the British Empire *twice as advantageous* to grow in the British Empire as to import from abroad, and creates twice as great a market* for all other British industry, even where there is a reciprocity in our deal-

---

* See Chapters IV. and V.

ings with foreign nations. In the one case, you keep your farmers and their industry at home; in the other, you send them and their industry abroad, and make them parcel of a foreign nation.

But then, it is said by political economists, that in the case of *food*, another element enters into the calculation—RENT. It is asserted that the lands first cultivated are always the best lands. It is added that by having recourse for further supplies to other soils, which must be inferior, or to better cultivation of old soils, you always in both cases cultivate at much greater expense, in proportion to the produce, and necessarily raise the price of the last quantity you require. The price of that last quantity, however small, governs the price of all the rest, and so the price of food is raised throughout the country, and rents are thereby everywhere created and augmented, the best land paying the highest rent.

This is Mr. Ricardo's theory of rent* briefly stated, which theory opposes a bar to solid improvement, by suggesting theoretical objections to the extended and improved cultivation of our own soil. Its paradoxical caution is, Do not cultivate your own soil too completely or too well, for fear of making food dear and unattainable by the bulk of the people.† But, like Mr.

---

* It is believed this theory of rent was first suggested by Dr. James Anderson, in 1801. It was afterwards more fully developed in an essay by Mr. West, a gentleman at the bar, afterwards Sir Edward West, Chief Justice of Bombay, and about the same time by Mr. Malthus. But the clearest and simplest expositions of it are to be found in the works of Mr. Ricardo, and of the elder Mr. Mill. Those who desire to see it satisfactorily disposed, are referred to *An Essay on the Distribution of Wealth*, by the Rev. R. Jones, A. M. It is much to be regretted that this most able writer has not yet communicated to the public his views on the theory of wages and profits.

† And it is intimately connected with his theory of profit. But Mr. Ricardo's theory of profit, though very subtle and ingenious,

Malthus's theory of population, the theory of rent has
of late been much more carefully examined. It turns
out to be built on some untenable hypotheses. It is
accordingly by some political economists much modified,
and by others regarded as more specious than true, and
rejected altogether.*

The hypotheses on which this theory is built, are
probably untenable in any country; they are certainly
so when applied to the British empire.

The very first proposition is not true—viz., that the
lands first cultivated are always the best lands.

It would be singular if it were true. The first settlers
of any country have little topographical knowledge, poor
means of locomotion (even if roads existed), and very
limited power of draining or clearing the really fat and
ultimately most productive lands.

In Great Britain, the soils first cultivated were not
those that are now the most fertile. In England, for
example, the most fertile of all lands are perhaps at this
moment some of the fens. They have only begun to
produce wheat extensively within living memory. There
is every reason to believe that there are still bogs and
morasses in Ireland, that will be yet more fertile than
even the fattest English fens. These Irish lands are
now undrained, and utterly unproductive; though rail-

---

never enjoyed much currency, and therefore we need not waste
time in examining it. It is a singular example of the force of
theory, compelling one of the acutest of men to ignore the best
established facts. Well did Lord Brougham say of Mr. Ricardo,
that "he seems as if he had dropped from another planet."

* See *Laws of Wages, Profits, and Rent investigated,* by Professor Tucker, Philadelphia, 1837; and *An Essay on the Distribution of Wealth,* by the Rev. Richard Jones, A. M.; *Harmonies
Économiques,* Bastia; *The Past, Present, and Future,* by Mr.
Carey, of Philadelphia; and the last edition of Mr. Carey's
Principles of Social Science. Those who do not also agree with
the conclusions of that gentleman must admit the extensive
practical information on which he has based his conclusions.

ways are near, and an able-bodied, active, and hungry population all around.

Take North America. The pilgrim fathers first cultivated what first presented itself—the barren soil of Massachusetts. Their Colonies at Plymouth, Newport, and New Haven, were on high but comparatively sterile land. So in the vicinity of New York, the island of New York, the shore of New Jersey, and the higher part of Long Island, were first tilled. In all these cases, the lower and infinitely better soils were neglected.

France, Holland, Flanders, Italy, Egypt, and many other countries also present phenomena at irreconcilable variance with the very first hypothesis on which the theory of rent reposes. So much so that some political economists have lately maintained that if you will condescend to be instructed by facts, inferior soils are *always* brought into cultivation before the best.*

Take the next position—viz., that by having recourse for further supplies to other soils which must be inferior, or to better cultivation of old soils, you must cultivate at greater expense in proportion to the produce, and so necessarily raise the price of food.

Take first the recourse to other soils. We have seen that in many countries, at least, there are other soils, which so far from being necessarily inferior, are often very superior to the soils first cultivated.

It is not even true, in the British empire, that increasing the quantity of food, by resorting to other British soils yet uncultivated, will necessarily make food dearer.

In the first place, it is not true that all the soils yet remaining uncultivated at home will necessarily be inferior to many that are cultivated already. Many

---

* See *The Past, the Present, and the Future,* by Mr. Carey.

soils which experienced agriculturists declare will ultimately and certainly turn out very good and productive
soils, have not yet been brought into cultivation at all,
even in Great Britain and Ireland.

Many others that had till very lately been deemed
unproductive soils, have in fact turned out most productive.   Witness the experiments on Chat-moss.

Taking experience and analogy for our guide, this
will probably be the case with many more.

Railways, by increasing the proximity of lands to
markets, and of labor and manure to lands, have
changed and augmented the real value of millions of
acres yet uncultivated, or nearly so.

British soils of inexhaustible fertility in the Colonies
and dependencies are yet virgin soils.

So much for the first branch of the second hypothesis, that soils not yet cultivated must be inferior
soils.

Nor is it in practice true, that increased capital and
labor laid out on old soils always yield progressively
diminished returns.   So far is it from being the truth
(as had been hastily assumed), that, on the contrary,
many of the last *doses* of capital (to use the elder Mr.
Mill's expression) applied to land have yielded more
ample returns than any previous doses.   What wonderful increase of fertility has been produced by drainage
alone!   What unexpected and prodigious results have
followed the spreading of the sub-soil on our fen lands!
A day's labor on what were the sandy wastes of Flanders produces five times what a day's labor would have
done centuries ago.

What are we to expect when an enlightened policy
shall have spread the sewerage of our cities on our
soils? *   I say the sewerage, not the mere diluted and

------

* And since Mr. Ricardo's time, that great bar to improvement, *tithes*, which enabled the tithe-owner to take a tenth of the

comparatively worthless sewage-water. Our mother the earth requires what has been taken from her to be returned to her: she LENDS, but she will not GIVE.

Or when, what is infinitely better, we have planted on the soils the poor themselves; for the human animal is a fertilizing, as well as a consuming creature. The highest and best of all farming is maintained by many to be the cultivation of his own small property by the hands of the peasant and his family. The quantity of all kinds of produce is certainly prodigious. But this sort of high-farming is cheap as well as productive. In the British islands alone, you might thus raise an immense additional quantity of food, and at a very cheap rate. There are no wages to pay and no rent.

It is not therefore true that by expending more labor or capital on old soils you will necessarily cultivate at a greater expense, or raise the price of food.

Mr. Ricardo's theory of rent, therefore, is built on some untenable hypotheses. Without fatiguing the patience of the reader by a further examination of a very difficult question, it may be truly said of the theory of rent, that it is at least no *practical guide* for the legislation of this great country.

There seems, therefore, to be no more reason why you should not use your British soils for producing food in, than why you should not use your British machines at home for producing manufactures.

But the consequences deduced from the theory are as fallacious as the theory itself.

---

gross produce of improvements, have been commuted and abolished. The Church has made a great sacrifice. Her wealth is no longer to advance with advancing agriculture. She is stereotyped. But then, in return, she has a permanent, certain, and much less invidious income, with the best security in the world. This note was written in 1850.

Suppose the theory, instead of being practically false, were practically true, it would still not follow that even in a mere *pecuniary* point of view it would not be more profitable to cultivate English soil of inferior fertility, than to depend on a foreign soil of superior fertility.

On the one hand, by supplying a deficiency from abroad, the British Empire loses the entire value of what you import from abroad, and might have grown either at home, or in the Colonies, and you moreover lose markets to that extent.*

On the other hand, by growing at home, and so supplying the deficiency at a somewhat dearer rate, you augment to some extent (if Mr. Ricardo's theory of rent were true) all rent—and cause, to that extent, a vicious distribution of wealth.

According, then, even to this theory, if it were true, you would gain in value, by growing at home, but you would cause some improper distribution of it.

But the theory is not true.

You will not only gain enormously in value in producing, as much as possible, at home and in the Colonies; but instead of a worse distribution, you will ensure a much better distribution.

You will have, *as means for supporting your own poor*, an additional annual fund equivalent to the whole gross value of what you produce in the empire, instead of producing it in foreign lands.

· You will always have more real plenty, and accessibility of food, and perhaps in the long run, a degree even of cheapness, as great, or greater. You will have developed the best producing forces of the country.

These two questions—first, whether it be true that to produce at home, rather than abroad, is more pro-

* See Chapters IV. and V.

fitable by the whole gross value of the product *—and, secondly, whether Mr. Ricardo's theory of rent be practically true or false—are questions not merely theoretical and metaphysical: they are questions of *stupendous practical moment*. Applied to the food of the people, they involve gains or losses to the nation, not of millions, but of tens and scores of millions annually. Applied to the fund for employing the population by paying *wages*, they involve, wages or no wages, industry or idleness, to the same amount.

We who have lately heard the discussions on the corn laws *usque ad nauseam*, need not be reminded of the many other arguments besides mere *pecuniary* ones, urging us to cultivate *as much as possible* our own English, Irish, and Colonial soils, both in the temperate and tropical regions. The healthful industry, the virtue and contentment of the people, the stability of government, the independence and lasting security of the empire, and a supply, permanent, cheap and inexhaustible, not only of food, but of *cotton* and *sugar*, are deeply involved in the question.

We say, *as much as possible*, but supplying any real deficiency from foreign countries.

There yet remains to be considered the fourth expedient by which old societies may escape from the want of food—and that is, by exporting the population, as we have lately exported our English and Irish bone and muscle, not to our own Colonies, but to the United States—a first rate, and possibly, hereafter, a hostile r.

To cure the want of food by exporting skilled artisans and able-bodied husbandmen to foreign lands, is

---

* See Chapters IV. and V.

(to use Dean Swift's simile) like lopping off your feet when you want shoes.

The notion, therefore, that extended and improved cultivation of our own soil will unduly augment rents and make food inaccessible to the multitude, is as false as it is paradoxical—a mere bugbear, scaring our statesmen from the most obvious policy.

On the contrary, the true political economy will spread and plant the population, not only on the dry and level soil, but all over mountains and morasses. True public wisdom will recognise, venerate, and cherish the natural and indissoluble relationship between man and his mother earth. This filial piety is here also the first commandment with promise; for the days of the empire that violates it are numbered.

The caution not to cultivate our soil too extensively and too well, and the fear least there should be too many people in the British empire, are therefore, as we have seen, of all cautions and all fears the most preposterous.

CHAPTER XXI.

*" Don't undertake to employ the able-bodied pauper
productively."*

So say the strictest sect—the Pharisees of political
economy.

"Set the poor to work," says the statute of Elizabeth.

But the political economists have been some time
in power—and what have we seen in England and
Ireland?

The work of the poor taken from them and given to
foreign laborers and foreign artisans.

The market which their expenditure would create,
no longer an English market, but a foreign one, from
which we are shut out.

In both England and Ireland have been erected
buildings called *workhouses*, because no work is to be
done there, but which have been more properly called
coops, in which the able-bodied and necessitous poor are,
on principle, *imprisoned and kept idle*.

The public must, and do maintain the able-bodied
pauper, but refuse to employ him actively and productively. The public is in the situation of a man who
should be bound to pay wages to 1000 laborers, whether
they work or not. Everything which these laborers
could produce would, under the circumstances, be a
saving of loss—that is, a *pure gain* to him.

In the meantime, the numbers of unemployed poor,
and the annual value they unproductively consume,
fearfully augment. The humble tradesman is ruined

by poor-rates. There stand the idle, starving, uneducated paupers, amidst wealth more than fabulous, "an exceeding great army."

A depression of manufacturing or agricultural industry fills their ranks, and exasperates their discontent. The unemployed poor have already pulled down government and threatened to *destroy property* in France, *—and the danger is not less real here, nor possibly so remote as we may flatter ourselves. Modern civilisation is not, like ancient civilisation, in peril from Northern Barbarians, but from Barbarians already swarming within its borders scarcely as yet conscious of their physical power.

"A persuasion," says Mr. Carlyle, "is rapidly spreading, that pauperism absolutely must be dealt with in some more conclusive way. . . . *It must be done,* whether *before* we have 'RED REPUBLIC,' and universal social dissolution, or *after* it. That is now the practical question, and one of the most important the English nation ever had before it. To see such a problem fairly in any form *begun,* would be an unspeakable relief; like the first emergence of solid land again, amid these universal deluges of revolution and delirium." †

---

* This was written in 1850.
† We are tempted to extract the whole passage:
"A persuasion is rapidly spreading, that pauperism absolutely must be dealt with in some more conclusive way, before long; and the general out-look is towards waste lands and colonies for that object.
"Concurring heartily in these two propositions, both the general and the particular, my own sad conviction is, that before either paupers can be 'dealt with,' or waste lands and colonies got to turn out other than infatuations and futilities for them, government must do the most original thing proposed to it in these times—admit that paupers are really *slaves,* men fallen into *dis*franchisement, who cannot keep themselves 'free,' and whom it is bitter mockery, and miserable folly and cruelty, to treat as what they are *not,* and accordingly must take the *command* of said paupers applying for the means of existence: and enlist them, and have *industrial* 'colonels' and 'regiments,' first one,

Yet what this great writer proposes, is, after all, in substance, nothing more than the remedy already proposed by the statute of Elizabeth. That the power which *relieves* should *employ*—should give relief in exchange for systematic *hard work*, for *really useful and disciplined labor.*

This scheme, though it has been abandoned in deference to theorists, must be resumed.* It has been justified by experience. It is now more than ever needed. It is practicable, profitable, and unobjectionable.

It is practicable and profitable.

There are, for example, immense enterprises, highly and undoubtedly beneficial to *the public*, which it would be *most lucrative* for the public to undertake, with laborers whom it must pay, and *does pay, whether it employs them or not.* These enterprises, left to individuals or companies, may never be undertaken, because some of them would not be profitable, unless he that undertakes them, like the public, already have the labor for nothing, or, which is the same thing, be

---

and then ever more: and lead, and order, and compel them, under law as just as Rhadamanthus, and as stern too ; and on the whole must prosecute this business as the vitalest of all, and develop it ever more, year after year, and age after age ; and understand anywhere, that its *industrial* horseguards, and not its red-coated fighting one, is to be the grand institution of institutions for the time coming! What mountains of impediment - what blank, weltering, abominable oceans of unveracity of every kind, the complete achievement of this problem (in the gradual course of centuries) now supposes the annihilation of : all this, alas! is too clear to me. But all this, as I compute, must actually be *done :* whether *before* we have 'red republic,' and universal social dissolution, or after it: that is now the practical question, and one of the most important the English nation ever had before it. To see such a problem fairly in any form *begun*, would be an unspeakable relief ; like the first emergence of solid land again, amid these universal deluges of revolution and delirium."

* "The further," says Blackstone—"the further any subsequent plans for maintaining the poor have departed from it, the more impracticable and pernicious these attempts have proved."

bound to pay for it whether employed or not; or
because the ultimate profit of others, though possible
even to individuals, who must purchase labor, is yet
distant or doubtful.

Not to deal in general observations, but to come to
particular instances, look at the DRAINAGE OF LARGE
TOWNS. The accumulated filth now corrupts the air,
weakens the constitution, deteriorates the race of human
creatures, poisons any neighboring river, and so cuts
off the natural, best, and most abundant supply of pure
water.

To carry off the poison permanently and effectually,
to restore the supply of pure water, to convert the
refuse, not only liquid but solid, into the most valuable and efficacious of manures, fertilising not only surrounding districts, but capable of being made fit to be
carried by railways to the ends of the kingdom, and
so indefinitely increasing the supply of home-grown
food—to do all this, requires nothing more than the
labor of those who now sit in the neighboring workhouses looking at their feet. Such gigantic enterprises
may or may not answer to individuals. They are
certain to answer to the public. The public have the
labor for nothing, or next to nothing—that is to say,
it costs them no more, or little more, than if they did
not *employ* it.

The gigantic scheme for the drainage of the metropolis was not sufficiently studied before it was carried
out. The utilisation of the refuse was not made a
main object. The invaluable product (the surface-
water being mixed with the sewage-water) is not only
diluted and wasted, but washed up again towards London. Every street has been turned into a long bridge,
which will continually need repair, and will ere long
be full of danger.

The difficulty which opposed a better scheme, was

to find a sufficient fall without using the surface-water.

But a plan had been proposed of sumps or reservoirs in several parts of the metropolis, to which the sewage would descend by a heavier fall. In these receptacles, properly sunk, and bricked round with high walls, it might have been without danger deodorised and prepared for use, properly packed, and distributed, by railways or canals, throughout the kingdom.

The earth-closet system also is a great invention, but, among other difficulties, requires the interposition of perpetual manual labor. No objection in the view with which we are now regarding the subject.

Means like these are essential to keep up the productive powers of the land. The earth expects her products to be returned to her again. Our mother the earth LENDS, but will not GIVE. We are squandering the repayments that are due to her.

But suppose such undertakings to be but experiments—they are for the benefit of the public, and the public by the supposition does work which would not otherwise be done by laborers whom it must pay whether they work or not.

It is not in the metropolis only, but in Edinburgh, Glasgow, Dublin, Manchester, Liverpool, Norwich, Bristol, Birmingham, Sheffield, Plymouth, that these fields of employment are now open.* Not only in the great towns, but in almost every country-town and market-town in the kingdom. Railways have at once made the supply of this gratuitous and most beneficial labor, and the diffusion and sale of its valuable produce, perfectly easy and certain everywhere.†

And this labor, amongst many other recommenda-

---

* Written in 1850.

† This passage was written in 1850.

9

tions, is most beneficial, for this reason, that it tends to redress the most dangerous mischiefs, the most fatal of wants, a deficiency of home-grown food. So far from creating pauperism, it tends to destroy it. Such labor is as beneficial, *as if it augmented the surface of the kingdom.*

Arterial drainage, reclamation of arable lands in the three kingdoms on a large scale, ports, harbors of refuge, and a thousand other useful public works of various sorts, afford a further boundless field for employment.

All this is yet more practical and profitable than ever, for railways have mobilised our poor.

Now what are the objections? That these schemes are but palliative. True. But they diminish instead of increasing the evil.

That such schemes might stimulate population, and multiply unduly the competitors for employment. Those who are tormented with fears on this head, are referred to the remarks on that subject already made.*

It cannot be objected that there are no funds. The funds already exist. All that is proposed is to substitute the industry for the idleness of the recipients. Less money, not more, will be thrown away.

Perhaps it will be said that labor naturally employed will be injured or displaced. Not in the least. No product of pauper-labor need ever make its appearance in the market. All the work which will be thus done, may be work *which otherwise would not be done at all.* So far from displacing labor, a great demand for other labor will in many ways be necessarily created. It is not at all improbable that such beneficial works might

---

* See Chapter on Population.

often stop for want of laborers, through the demand for labor which they will have caused to spring up.

Suppose it should in some instances turn out (as perhaps it would) that the enterprise is so successful that it would even have been profitable to individuals —that would, after all, be a mistake not of the most calamitous kind.

The systematic and productive employment of paupers, is one of the means which will hereafter be used to raise the wages and sustain the position of the independent laborer, while it will at the same time augment the funds out of which all industry is supported.*

Then it may be urged: The poor may prefer being employed by the public. Not if the wages are less, or the work heavier, or more ineligible than in private employment—which it may always be made.

Lastly it will be said: The public are undertaking the maintenance of the people. These are the French national workshops over again.

But the English public would then undertake the maintenance of not one individual more than at present. By law the public is accordingly bound to feed them all. The public will only insist on hard and really useful, and in most cases, out-door work, instead of imprisonment, as the condition of relief. The idleness and sham-work of the present workhouses is much more like the French national workshops, than the disciplined and real industry which might be brought to bear on many crying social evils.

What remains to prevent? The old sophism: All this is artificial. It is not the natural state of things. That must be best.† Is it best? Look around you.

---

* See Chapter on Wages.
† See Chapter III.

CHAPTER XXII.

*" Don't attempt to reduce the capital of the national debt.
Let the taxes rather fructify in the pockets of the people."*

THIS has been the practical maxim of every ministry
since the peace.

As long as we can contrive to pay the interest of the
debt, we postpone the fatal consequences of our past
extravagance.

But who can contemplate, without a shudder, the
dawn of that morning when it shall be announced that
the dividends can no longer be paid ?

Every banker, every merchant, every insurance company, is at once insolvent. No checks, no bank-notes,
are of any value. Even specie disappears. Every
man hides or clutches with a death-gripe his sovereign
or shilling. There are no funds to pay wages. None
to support the poor. None to carry on the government,
or preserve the peace. Eight hundred millions of what
was yesterday the most valuable property, to-day exists
not. The just title to all other property is gone too.
All men, with the government and the public, are
absolved from their engagements. The miles of streets,
and the superb squares of the metropolis, are on a sudden tenanted by bankrupts. The French revolutions
of 1789 and 1848, or the present disorganised state of
the South and West of Ireland, are faint shadows of
the misery of that fatal day. But they do yet obscurely
hint into what profound and bottomless depths of ruin
society may fall.

Political economists are in the habit of using the word *capital* in a very loose sense. Take away English *credit*, and so far from having a larger, England has, as we have seen, a smaller capital than many other nations. Where will English *capital* be when the dividends cease to be paid?

Yet the reckless mode in which the larger portion of the debt was contracted has been recently, and within a few months, repeated, and no provision made for the support of public credit.*

It may safely be said that more awfully improvident bargains than most of the 3 per cent. loans never were made by any government. The enormous burthen of the national debt at this day is mainly owing to the practice of borrowing in a 3 per cent. stock, when the rate of interest really paid was much more.

Suppose a hundred millions borrowed in a 3 per cent. stock, taken at 60. Peace comes. The 3 per cents. gradually rise to 100. Not till this price is reached and passed, not till government really owes and must pay £100 for every £60 lent, has it even the power of reducing the interest, and then but very little. If we calculate what has been lost in principal and simple interest on this sum of one hundred millions only, during the last thirty-five years—*i. e.* since the conclusion of the war—by having borrowed it in a 3 per cent. stock; if we then add what will be lost during the next thirty-five years on eight hundred millions of debt—we shall find the result almost incredible. And to the result, large as it is, must be added half-yearly compound interest. The burthens of the country have, by this absurd practice, been much more than doubled.

---

* Written in 1850.

But one cannot help remarking, that as this operation has so dreadfully augmented the debt, so the converse operation, in a high condition of public credit, would in no very long time, and with very little sacrifice, certainly and materially diminish it.

"Death and the sun," La Bruyère somewhere says, "are two things which men cannot look at." It seems that the capital of the national debt is a thing which governments cannot look at.

Thirty-five years of peace have elapsed, and *nothing done to attack the principal of the debt*—or so little as to be substantially nothing. A generation has passed away, but the debt still frowns on us, as it did at the termination of the war. Four things, however, experience and observation have taught us. First, that a sinking fund, unless by that term is meant an excess of income over expenditure, is of no use, and will always be laid hold of on the first real or fancied emergency. Secondly, that no such excess of income over expenditure will ever be borne, as shall effectually reduce the capital of the debt. Thirdly, that even in peace, occasions may and will arise for adding to the principal of the debt. Lastly, that dilapidated public finances are the proximate and certain cause of the dissolution of society, and the signal not only of the downfall of time-honored institutions, but of the misery and ruin of a generation. Indeed, the calamities which other countries have suffered by the collapse of public credit afford but a very inadequate sketch of the ruin of that colossal edifice here.

When, therefore, public men like the late Lord Ashburton (to whose wisdom and prudence the nation is under great obligations) call attention to the state of the debt, and attempt to rouse the public and the government to a serious consideration of this moment-ous evil, they deserve more attention than they receive. It is, however, no wonder that such warnings are disregarded. Debts are the most disagreeable subject to which the attention of debtors can be solicited. The public, deluded by fallacious hopes of benefit, sometimes from political, sometimes from commercial changes, pursues its favorite theory, till the pursuit is given up as hopeless, or experience undeceives it. It then chases some fresh phantom. Persons of more reflection are apt to silence apprehension by the selfish hope that things will last their time. Governments all the while are too happy if, by temporary expedients, they can make ends meet, or, at the very best, secure a small margin of receipt above expenditure; and have no notion of such a degree of political virtue as would lead them to make any sacrifice to ensure the financial prosperity of their successors.

And yet a certain means of reducing the principal of the debt in a few years, at a little sacrifice, seems suggested by the very operation which has made its amount more than double what it need have been.

Consols are now high, and were recently at par and above.* Suppose, when that next happens, that to the holders of a certain amount of consols the option were presented of being paid off at par, or taking *at the market price* a 5 per cent. stock, irredeemable for a certain number of years. The smallest fractional advantage would make the acceptance of the new stock a certainty; power being given to trustees (who are now in general bound by law to invest in the 3 per cents.), to accept the heavier stock, with proper precautions that tenants for life, and owners of other limited interests, are not unfairly benefited at the expense of reversioners. When consols are at par, the value of a 5 per cent. stock, perpetually irredeemable, would be 166 and more. Suppose such a period to be fixed, during which

---

*So they were a hundred years ago, and will doubtless be aga n.

it should be irredeemable, as should reduce its market
value to 125. The stock being taken at that price, the
capital of the debt so dealt with is not only reduced at
once by 20 per cent., but put into a condition for future
effectual reduction of *interest*. The additional charge
would be less in time and amount than that of termi-
nable annuities. At the expiration of the prefixed
period, if the finances permitted it, the holders might
again be offered, instead of a reduced interest, a heavy
stock at a premium, irredeemable again for a certain
number of years, by which a further amount of principal would be again struck off. The experiment might
be tried (if found to answer) on other portions of the
debt, perhaps eventually on the whole debt. Instead
of a 5 per cent. stock, 6 or 7 per cent. stocks might be
created, which would be still more powerful engines of
reduction. It is impossible to predict the result of such
an experiment, but it is not improbable that the effect
on public credit of an engine so certainly at once *and
beforehand*, extinguishing large portions of the capital
of the debt, might be to raise still higher the value of
government annuities. It is obvious that the higher
the credit of government, the easier the operation.
Supposing that the value of government annuities
remained exactly the same, and that no pecuniary gain
to the nation attended the expedient, still the effect
would be to compel the payment of a large portion of
principal every few years in the shape of som additi-
tional interest; the advantage being, that the capital of
the debt is not only reduced at once and *beforehand*,
but the interest is made easily and effectually reducible
in future. There can, however, be little doubt that the
credit of government would rise with the success of the
operation, so as to make the gain great and the loss
little. Had such a mode of dealing with the debt been
adopted,* at the conclusion of the war, the debt, not-

---

* It is not essential that consols should be at par.

withstanding its immense amount, would by this time with very little sacrifice have been brought within a manageable compass. The temporary addition to the interest would be perhaps satisfied out of the ordinary revenue; but if not, the certainty of effectually reducing the principal of the debt, by doing it beforehand, would be a powerful reason for continuing, or even augmenting extraordinary resources.*

The punctuality with which every public engagement, from the revolution to this hour, has been redeemed, and more than redeemed, by the bright and spotless honor of the nation, will not be without its reward. The consequent marvellous strength and elasticity of our most valuable possession, *public credit*, may yet enable some honest and energetic minister to lighten the burthens of the country effectually.

Moreover, the contract with the national creditor is a metallic contract. Many recent discoveries, not only in California, but elsewhere, seem to portend another fall in the precious metals, like that which happened three hundred years ago. Such a fall would diminish the national burthens not only to a proportionate, but to a much greater extent.

The national debtor, or, in other words, the nation, is, in justice as well as law, entitled to the full benefit of the depreciation.†

---

* Like the income or property tax.

† This Chapter, it must be remembered, was written twenty years ago.

9*

CHAPTER XXIII.

"Absenteeism is no evil."

THIS is gravely maintained by Mr. M'Culloch,* and many other political economists.

Mr. M'Culloch lays it down distinctly, that if an Englishman of fortune, drawing his income from England, instead of spending it on English commodities at home, spends it on French commodities in France, England loses nothing, and France gains nothing by his so doing.

Of course it follows, that if all the nobility and gentry of England, all the landlords, fund-holders, mortgagees, all the proprietors of railway, canal, and mining shares were to do the same—that is to say, were to emigrate and spend all their English income in France, on French productions only—France would be no richer for it, and England no poorer.†

Now, this is so manifestly untrue, so contrary to the experience of every French and English shop-keeper and artisan, that one is curious to see by what process of reasoning it is, that so eminent a political economist has drawn so startling a conclusion.

---

* *Principles of Political Economy*, p. 152. We must do Mr. M'Culloch the justice to add that he admits the *indirect* evil effects of absenteeism ; but in a *pecuniary* view he insists that it is in no degree injurious. Yet Mr. M'Culloch is a very acute and sensible writer, and in many parts of his book shows an independence of thought very uncommon among political economists.

† Indeed, this *argumentum ad absurdum* is capable of being pressed still further.

His premises are these : He says, were the Englishman to live at home and use none but foreign articles in his establishment, he would give the same encouragement to British industry that he would do if he were to use none but British articles. *Therefore,* he must, it is obvious, do the same, should he go abroad.

Now if the conclusion be (as it certainly is) untrue, and yet if this conclusion certainly follow from the premises (as he says it obviously does), then the fault must be in the premises. It cannot then be true that the use of foreign articles at home gives the same encouragement to British industry as the use of British articles. And that it is not true, we have already seen evinced by other considerations.* But we are indebted to Mr. M'Culloch for pointing out the logical consequence, if it were true.

No! absenteeism is a great pecuniary evil and loss, both to England and to Ireland.

The number of English who lived abroad, and the English revenue they spent abroad, two years ago, was immense. The French revolution of 1848, and the troubles in Italy and Germany, drove many of the English absentees back to England, and restored to us for a time the benefit of the expenditure.

This is one reason among others why we have not yet felt all the disastrous effects of recent measures.

---

* Suppose not only the landlord, the fund-holder, the mortgagee, and the shareholder, to spend the whole of their incomes on foreign commodities abroad ; but suppose it were physically possible for the farmer, the manufacturer, the merchant, the shopkeeper, the banker, and the laborer, to do the same. See Chapters IV. and V.

CHAPTER XXIV.

" Other nations will follow our example of free-trade."

OUR recent experiments in commercial legislation
have no parallel in the history of mankind. No one
ever set us the example, and no one has since followed
ours.

Before 1846, all great nations and great statesmen
had acted on opposite principles, and always with
eminent success: Cromwell, Walpole, and Lord Chatham
in England ; Colbert and Napoleon in France. Since
1846, no disposition to imitate our policy has been
manifested by any foreign nations. Whatever changes
have occurred, or seem likely to occur, are changes the
other way.*   Hamburgh, the last fortress of free-trade
on the Continent, has determined to join the German
Protectionist League.   Hanover has just done the same.
Switzerland has augmented her import duties.   France
has recently inaugurated the statue of Colbert at Rheims,
his native city.   Belgium and France, not content with
import duties, have resorted even to bounties on exportation. The more popular the governments, the
more protectionist they become. The United States
have elected a protectionist president, recalled their
free-trade ambassador, and sent a protectionist representative to this country. The Southern States have
now joined the Northern in the demand for protection,

---

* The French Treaty had not been made when these observations were penned.

and little doubt exists that the impending change in the American tariff will reimpose duties for the avowed purpose of protection.* Russia maintains the protective policy to which she has returned.

And why should reciprocity be expected when the first markets in the world are already opened for nothing?

So much for voluntary imitation.

On our own Colonies we have *forced* our new policy, and deprived them of many of the advantages belonging to us.

The present disposition of Australia and Canada are the first results.

Dr. Franklin, in his "RULES FOR REDUCING A GREAT EMPIRE TO A SMALL ONE," has these observations:

"I address myself," says he, "to all ministers who have the management of extensive dominions, which from their very greatness have become troublesome to govern.

"In the first place, gentlemen, you are to remember that a great empire, like a great cake, is most easily diminished at the edges. Turn your attention, therefore, first to your remotest provinces, that as you get rid of them, the next may follow in order."

As we get rid of our Colonies, we shall successively close the colonial markets. All emancipated Colonies will do as the United States have done: they will protect and develop their own producing power.†

---

* Since these observations were published in the first edition, the President's Message, and Mr. Meredith's Report have appeared; since the seventh edition, the Message of Mr. Filmore, and the Report of Mr. Corwin. All protectionist alike, but the last.yet more decidedly than the first.

† This Chapter was published twenty years ago: what was apprehended has already in some instances been done.

CHAPTER XXV.

" A return to the protective policy will never be."

A BOLD prophecy; for a return to a more protective policy has happened in America, in Russia, in Holland, in Germany.

Men hastily conclude, that because such great political measures as Catholic emancipation, or parliamentary reform are plainly irrevocable, therefore, a great commercial measure must necessarily be irrevocable too.

But important differences are overlooked. In the first of those great changes we did but follow all mankind—nearly all governments, popular or despotic, in a great act of public justice—the establishment of equal religious liberty. In the second we did but bring back the constitution to its original theory. Whether in so doing we did practically secure better government— whether as an instrument of *good* and economical *government* the old House of Commons was not better than the new—may be matter of controversy. To popularise the legislature may not necessarily be to improve it —to make it either more honest or more efficient. But that the rotten boroughs would have withstood the shock of 1848, may well be doubted. The change, whether for better or for worse, had become inevitable, and the notion of retrogradation is ridiculous.

Moreover, both Catholic emancipation and parliamentary reform differ from a change of commercial policy in another respect. The real effects of the two first measures will only become apparent after the lapse of long tracts of time, perhaps of generations. The real effects of a change in commercial policy are much sooner apparent. They may be plainly visible in a few years.

Much is already *known*, which was mere *conjecture* in 1846. A comparatively uninformed man is really in some respects wiser now, than the wisest of the debaters in 1846.

Much more will be withdrawn from the domain of *conjecture*, and have become matter of certain *knowledge* hereafter.

And why are we to suppose that commercial legislation, which from the commencement of our history has been variable and fluctuating, will all at once become fixed and stereotyped?

No! As it has always changed in time past, so it surely will change again in time to come, perhaps after bitter disappointment.

It would be wrong to say, that a return to protection is PROBABLE, because it is CERTAIN.*

As to the period, it is a question of time and mischief —how much time must elapse, and how much more mischief be perpetrated before the nation not only feels, as it has already felt, but understands and sees that it has been deluded. Probably the period is not distant.

It is not a class, but THE NATION that will insist on the change. When it comes, it will come naturally, irresistibly, and without danger. What dangers may be incurred in the meantime is another thing.

---

* This passage was written in 1849 or 1850.

CHAPTER XXVI.

" To raise the wages of labor is to impair the fund out of which wages are paid."

THIS is so far from being true, that, under a proper system, the converse is true.

In England, under the old system, the wages of laborers, artisans, and sailors have long been much higher than the wages of other European laborers, artisans, or sailors.

These high wages have introduced a high standard of living—that is to say, high in comparison with other European countries. The English laboring poor have hitherto, on the whole, been better lodged, better clothed, and better fed than the French, the Germans, the Russians, or the Italians.* The effect has been visible in the physical and mental qualities of *the race* on land and sea. Mr. Mill admits the enormous effect of *custom* in determining the actual rate of wages. Before him its potent and extensive operation had been overlooked. A zeal for generalisation had referred the rate of wages entirely to supposed general laws. But custom, bodily constitution, climate, artificial regulations, and many other peculiar or accidental circumstances have much to do in fixing the *actual rate* of wages.

Yet these causes, however efficient, are powerless

---

* It must be remembered that this Chapter was written in 1849 or 1850.

in the presence of unlimited competition by foreigners, worse lodged, worse clothed, worse fed than the English. In order to compete successfully with them, the Englishman, too, must be worse lodged, worse clothed, and worse fed. The foreign workmen will inevitably usurp the Englishman's market unless he can meet them on equal terms. Water does not more naturally and irresistibly find its level.

The first step, therefore, towards an amelioration in the condition of the working classes, is security against the competition of those among whom a lower style of living, inferior diet, dress, and houses are habitual. This is the only true and solid foundation for measures tending still further to better the condition of the working classes—THE BULK OF THE NATION.

Without this foundation you are building on a shifting sand.

But this foundation, once securely and irrevocably laid, other measures, tending still further to better the condition, not only of the working classes, but of their employers, and withal to augment industry and increase national wealth faster than ever, become possible and easy.

In the early history of a flourishing country Nature herself protects, and more than protects, the rate of wages. Hired labor is often actually unattainable. Wages are then an ingredient in the cost of production, incapable of compression. But as population increases, and competition between laborers begins, then, of all the ingredients in the cost of production, the item of wages becomes the most easily compressible. An excess of but 5 per cent. in the supply of labor may diminish wages by one half. The surplus laborers, on pain of death, underbid all the rest. Competition between employers compels them all to emulate each other in bearing hard on the necessities and helplessness of the laborer. Under this double competition wages are ground down by worse than hydrostatic pressure.* Articles are cheap, but they are made of human flesh.

The evil (whether artificially remediable or not) is so far from having any *natural* tendency to cure itself, that it perpetuates and aggravates itself, and eats like a gangrene. Each reduction of wages is a reduction of the market for commodities. Each reduction of the market tends to a decrease of production, and a further decrease in the demand for labor. The cheaper things are, the more inaccessible to the poor they become. The vicious circle swells into a vortex, threatening to engulf all solid national prosperity.

In vain we glorify ourselves on our steam, our machinery, our luxury, our science. The poor may sink deeper and deeper. "It is questionable," says Mr. Mill, "if all the mechanical inventions yet made have lightened the day's toil of any human being.

But why should we either marvel or despair?

This is but one of a thousand instances in which the natural state of things comes to be vicious. Modern political economy, indeed sits down in despair, and has no better remedy to suggest than the destruction or exportation of the people. But why is it to be assumed that human art and wisdom are more powerless here than elsewhere? Remedial measures will be demanded by the masses at the hands of every statesman of old Europe.

The subject is, no doubt, one of awful moment. Not only action, but even speech, is perilous; yet silence and inaction present dangers as great, or greater, and daily and everywhere threatening and blackening.

---

* This consequence has been prevented or mitigated by trades unions.

King! minister! whosoever you are! you will soon find you must act, although,

> . . . . Incedis per ignes
> Suppositos cineri doloso.

Is there really a natural and legitimate STANDARD of wages to be religiously worshipped, or is this pretended standard a fiction and false god, before whom we are expected to bow down?

We know of no *natural* standard of wages except the result of competition just described. What is that result? what is that standard? It is this, THE WAGES OF THE WORST-PAID LABORERS THAT EXIST ON THE FACE OF THE GLOBE. In the fierce struggle of universal competition, those whom the climate enables, or misery forces, or slavery compels to live worst, and produce cheapest, will necessarily beat out of the market and starve those whose wages are better. It is a struggle between the working classes of all nations which shall descend first and nearest to the condition of the brutes.

Mr. Malthus, indeed, says that this natural standard of remuneration for labor "is a most important political barometer, expressing clearly the wants of society respecting population." We have seen above that it is no such thing. We have seen that Mr. Malthus' views on this subject are not only at variance with facts, but repudiated by some eminent political economists themselves. Indeed, this natural standard obviously throws away the chief benefits of production itself, and conducts not only to barbarism, but ultimately to poverty and depopulation.

The *natural* standard of wages, therefore, is not the legitimate and true standard.

What, then, is the TRUE STANDARD? What is the standard that will effectually develop and maintain the producing power of a nation?

The TRUE STANDARD, the standard of wages that
will really at once increase and rightly distribute national wealth, and perpetuate it to generations yet to
come, is, WHAT WILL OBLIGE AND ENABLE A MAN TO
WORK HARD AND WORK CONSTANTLY. * Does the
let-alone system tend to this standard? Does the let-
alone system tend to it, either when population is
scanty, or when population is dense?

In the ancient world the lower orders were slaves.
The paterfamilias, on the one hand, compelled his
work-people to labor, and on the other found them in
food, clothing, and lodging. Neither the employment
nor the remuneration of the laboring poor was dependent on competition. Ancient civilisation rested

---

* It ought to be sufficient to allege that this is the just standard : for here political economy touches the kindred but distinct
science of ethics. The rules of morality are in one respect
totally different from those of political economy. Economical
rules are subject to innumerable exceptions : the rules of moral
conduct admit of no exception.

Carry out to its logical consequences the doctrine that the
price of the human organisation, like the price of any other
machine, is to be governed immediately by supply and demand,
and ultimately by the cost of production in the cheapest and
most economical mode that can possibly be devised. Then you
ought, like the ancient Lacedemonians, or the modern Chinese,
to kill off deformed or superfluous children : and when the
parents are so old that they consume more than they produce,
they should also be removed.

The moral sense of mankind revolts at the very mention of
such atrocities. But so it does, at the mere commercial treatment of the poor, which may be also murder on a still larger
scale. That mere commercial treatment is inconsistent, not
only with the first principles of Christian civilisation, but with
the moral instincts of universal human nature. These are a far
safer guide than economical theories. Yet an accurate examination will evince, that the liberal and Christian treatment of the
lower classes, is the treatment that leads directly to national
wealth. That here, as elsewhere, what is morally wrong, is not
even commercially right.

for thousands of years on the slavery of the working classes. Christianity and modern civilisation have indeed raised the poor from slavery. But much more remains to be done. If you stop here, you will but have emancipated them from masters, who at least had human sympathies, and will have delivered them over to those grim and capricious tyrants and giants—SUP-PLY and DEMAND.

Slavery was found to need legal interference—so will free labor.

The true modes of dealing with the free laboring poor have yet to be learnt. They differ in new and old countries.

When population is scanty, and land abundant, the free laborer is idle and saucy. Artificial regulation has often been found not only useful, but absolutely necessary to compel him to work. At this day, the emancipated negroes in our West India Islands, having hot sun for nothing, and, as Mr. Carlyle says, plenty of pumpkin for next to nothing, will not work. The best of land is valueless for want of labor. Legal regulations in that island, compelling the laborers to work, are by many deemed absolutely necessary, even for the sake of the laborers themselves; for they are rapidly relapsing into their original barbarism. So when you export your free laborers to Canada or Australia, they soon cease to work for wages, run away, and become proprietors. So even in England 500 years ago, it was found, by experience, that the poor need not and would not work. A great plague in the fourteenth century having thinned the population, the difficulty of getting men to work on reasonable terms grew to such a height as to be quite intolerable, and to threaten the industry of the kingdom. Accordingly, in the year 1349, the statute 23d Edward III. was passed, compelling the poor to work, and interfering with the wages of labor. It was followed with

the same view, through several centuries, by a long succession of statutable enactments. The wages of artisans, as well as of agricultural laborers; the prices
of piece-work, as well as of day work; the periods
during which the poor were obliged to work; nay, the
very intervals for meals (as in the Factory Acts of the
present day) were defined by law. Acts of Parliament,
regulating wages, but against the laborer and in favor
of the master, lasted for the long period of 464 years.
Population grew. These laws were then found, and
really became unnecessary and burdensome. In the
year 1813, they were all repealed.

At length the opposite evil makes its appearance.
Formerly, the poor demanded such *high* wages, as to
threaten industry and wealth. Next, their wages are
so *low* as to threaten industry and wealth equally, and
perhaps more, but in another way. Then again, they
are raised by trades unions so as to threaten industry
again.

Does not experience show that the let-alone system is
equally at fault, whether population be scanty or dense?
Weighed in either scale of the balance, it is found
wanting.

We were ready enough to interfere for the employer:
can nothing now be done for the employed?

Leaving the theoretical question and doubtful and
dangerous remedies to those who are far better qualified
to discuss them, are there not THREE safe practical
measures which, in our own old country, would have a
direct and effectual influence in favor of all the working
classes ? *

Never, however, losing sight of the fundamental position, that a population whose wages are high, whether

* We do not venture to discuss the thorny question of Trades
Unions.

naturally or artificially, must not be exposed to competition, with a population whose wages are low.

These measures are FIRST, a system of arbitration for the settlement of wages.*

Until recently, masters could combine to sink wages, but the workmen were not allowed to combine to prevent it, or to raise wages.

This prohibition was no part of the old common law, but a relic of the artificial regulations which formerly existed in favor of the masters, and against the workpeople. Traces of its existence, and perhaps of its necessity, are to be found as early as the reign of Edward the First.

The natural power and right of combination is now by law restored to the workman; but the only weapon which he can wield is intimidation. Intimidation of the master by strikes, intimidation of his fellow-workmen by secret and illegal menace. In this barbarous state of things, frequent strikes not only starve the workmen with their innocent wives and children, and injure the masters, but damage and stop the industry of the country. These strikes generally, however, end by a representative of the workmen in the particular trade agreeing with the representative of the masters on a scale of wages.

What is done at last, after incalculable mischief, in an imperfect and bungling manner, might be done at first in a proper and enlightened manner. All trades are now allowed by law to combine. Trades unions are perfectly legal.† They might, in every trade and occupation, be empowered to name arbitrators to meet arbi-

---

* Written in 1850.

† But where they interfere with the use of machinery or the employment of apprentices, they ought to be, if they are not now, indictable misdemeanors.

trators whom the master should be bound to appoint.
If as would often happen, these arbitrators could not
agree, an umpire previously appointed by enlightened
public authority, taking into consideration all the circumstances, should settle the difference. The award, or
umpirage, would at least produce a scale, the joint
result of practical knowledge and enlarged views.
Without at present going further, all private bargains
would have a reference to that scale.*

Such arbitrations are a great want of the country.
Once properly introduced by public authority, they
would spread everywhere and into every department of
labor. Their utility and general applicability has been
placed beyond doubt by the experience of our neighbors the French.

The " *Conseil des Prud'hommes* " in France exercises
functions of this nature. In the departments these
councils have long existed. Into Paris they were introduced in the year 1844, and they are now established
by law.

In many trades representatives of the workmen are
to meet delegated representatives of the masters. Among
other things this council settles the hours of labor, the
rate of wages, and the conditions on which children
shall be employed. An appeal lies to the " *Tribunal de
Commerce.*"

The deliberations and decisions of these councils
(where they have been acted on) have been found by
experience long, extensive and various, to be eminently
useful in preventing strikes, and yet establishing a fair
rate of wages. The regulations as to the hours and
rates of wages in different trades fill a thick volume.
But this complexity is more apparent than real, because
it comprehends the distinct regulations of many

---

* Written in 1850.

trades; and it is cheaply purchased by the beneficial results.

Where the decisions of these councils are uniform and acted on, no master can now undersell by beating down wages or exacting more work; for all the masters are then subject to the same decisions of their respective councils, regulating the rate of wages and the hours of labor.

Even in England, *experience is showing us,* in spite of theories, that the new phenomena of production on a large scale by steam power and complex machinery are inconsistent with the old and simple relations between master and workmen. The Factory Act, and the laws against the truck system, are the aurora of a constructive and beneficent legislation.

The poor, however, in order to obtain justice, must have some point of support, some fulcrum on which to rest the lever. In England they already have it in the public provision made for them. But it is now found by experience that a too severe and niggardly administration of the Poor Law, so far from raising wages (as was once confidently predicted), depresses them, as might have been expected. Yet more generous support on the present lazy system would aggravate a burthen already intolerable.

The SECOND measure, therefore, is this: The industrial discipline and productive employment of the able-bodied pauper, especially on the land, or in the production of food, directly or indirectly. This labor, as we have seen, might be so directed as not only not to supersede any other labor, but even to increase the demand for it, and thus doubly relieve the labor market, while it added to the permanent and most valuable wealth of the kingdom, and actually diminished the poor-rates.*

---

* See the Chapter on Pauperism.

10

The THIRD measure is the prohibition or discouragement of work by little children.

Not merely in our great textile manufactures of cotton, wool, linen, and silk, but in a vast number of other great manufactures, nay, even of mechanical and handicraft trades, the labor of little children has of late been introduced. Here is a modern but overwhelming eruption of cheap labor, flooding the labor market. "A child," says the master, "can do this work as well as you, at a fourth of what you demand : why should I pay you more than the child?" In many trades children assist their parents in piece-work at home. The ultimate consequence is, that the laborer gets no more for the week's work of his whole family than he would have done, or did, for his own work alone. Indeed, he often does not even get what his children earn ; for there has grown up of late a trade in little children. The middle-man hires little boys and girls of six or seven years old, and lets them out in gangs (to a button manufacturer, for example), at so much an hour. A portion only of what he receives he pays to their parents, the residue is his profit on his human live stock.

And what is the consequence to the wretched children? The joyous morning of life brings no joy to them. Their parents, no longer their affectionate protectors, are transformed into task-masters and slave-drivers. The state abandons and condemns the little boys and girls to ignorance, vice, and premature decay.

Yet that very state, with marvellous caprice and inconsistency, protects them in other things where they need protection infinitely less. A child contracts to pay a shilling. In steps the offended law and exclaims, "I will not allow a child to be bound by a contract, I will interfere and avoid it. Childhood and youth are vanity, and should be so : they require my extraordinary and special protection." Yet the same law sees with infinite complacency the life and health and morals of millions of children mortgaged. "Let a slave touch my soil," says the law, "and his fetters drop off." Yet the children of the land are now born to the worst and most destructive slavery.

Of such measures the consequence might be a general, inflexible, and permanent advance of wages.

But the masters are mistaken if they suppose that in such an event either the producing power of the country would suffer, or that they would themselves be losers, unless, indeed, they are exposed to the competition of worse-paid foreign labor. There is no increased cost of production in the proper sense of the expression. No more labor is necessary to produce an article than before. But the laborer gets his fair share. And under a system of protection from unlimited and unregulated foreign competition, the increased rate of wages does not fall on one producer or some producers only; it affects ALL alike. It would be more correct to say it benefits all alike. Commodities, it is true, rise in proportion; but the general ability to purchase rises in a greater proportion still. The wages of labor, no longer compressible, are no longer, as heretofore, fixed by the price of commodities; but the price of commodities (as they used to be and ought to be) by the necessary and just wages of labor; for the meat and drink of the workman can now no more be stinted, than the fuel and water of his indefatigable and hundred-handed fellow-laborer, the steam-engine.

Nor let employers fear a loss of markets. Their markets would not be diminished, but enormously augmented in extent; and, moreover, instead of precarious and fluctuating markets, they would have domestic and permanent ones.

Every increase of the rate in wages enormously increases the power of the BULK OF THE NATION to consume, and *pay for what they consume*. It creates a new and enormous demand. It creates a new and immense home market. An increase of but a shilling a day in the average wages of the working classes would amount to forty or fifty millions sterling a year, or more. It increases their effective demand to that extent. It creates a new market to such an extent as would almost compensate for the loss of our whole export trade. So, on the other hand, a decrease in the wages of labor, to the extent of a shilling a day, diminishes the market which the expenditure of the laboring classes creates, to the extent of forty or fifty millions a year or more.

What is wanting to increase production and augment capital? MARKETS—EXTENSIVE AND INSATIABLE MARKETS. These are the one thing needful. But extensive and insatiable markets are exactly what a better remuneration of the working classes will supply.

What! it will be said, are both to gain—masters and workpeople too? Yes! both are to gain. Infinitely more work will be done, and what is done will be better done. The secret is this. MORE INDUSTRY BEING EMPLOYED, MORE WEALTH WILL BE CREATED. THE PRODUCING FORCES OF THE NATION WILL BE EFFECTUALLY DEVELOPED. The annual produce of the land and labor of the kingdom will be prodigiously augmented. There will therefore be more to divide between profits and wages. Masters will have more as well as workmen. The funds which employ labor will be *augmented*, not *diminished*.

There will be at once more for all, and it will be better distributed amongst all.

And as did the old and vicious state of things, so will the new and better state of things tend to perpetuate, increase, and establish itself. Each increase of wages is an increase of markets; each increase of markets, a further increase of production; each increase of production, a further demand for labor.

But it will be said: "According to you, the more the laborer is paid, the richer and better able to pay him the country will be." No! you soon reach a limit. Pay him so that he can and must work hard, work well, and work constantly, and you need not fear. That is not only the JUST, but the only TRUE standard. Production will outstrip consumption. His wages, no less than his work, will augment the national wealth and the national markets. Pay him more, so that he can live in idleness or luxury, and the sources of wages are dried up.

Next it is said: "This will diminish exports."

It will not affect exports to foreign countries much. It will not affect exports to the Colonies at all.* And any trifling loss on the foreign trade will be compensated over and over again by the immense increase of the home market.

Then it is said: "Population will increase."

Those who fear it are referred to the remarks already made on the subject.

Lastly, it is objected; "All this is artificial." So is every really good measure.†

The laboring classes alone produce all the wealth of the kingdom. Under a proper system, they would enjoy their just share of that wealth, in the shape of fair and reasonable wages—a system, under which they

---

* This passage was written before colonial duties on imports existed.

† It has been truly said, that most of our recent legislation has been destructive. It is time to revert to a constructive policy.

do not enjoy it, is not only vicious and unnecessary, but, while unjust and cruel to them, is injurious and dangerous to all.

Deep wisdom lies in the sacred precept—THOU SHALT NOT MUZZLE THE OX THAT TREADETH OUT THE CORN.

CHAPTER XXVII.

" Don't tax the nation for the benefit of a producing class. Take care of the consumer, and let the producer take care of himself."

THE maxims of our ancient and successful policy were very different.

A nation, whether it consume its own products, or with them purchase from abroad, can have no more value than it produces. The supreme policy of every nation, therefore, is to develop the producing forces of its own country. What are they? The working men, the land, the mines, the machinery, the water-power, etc.

Our fathers said, "Whatsoever you do, be sure you take care to DEVELOP THE PRODUCING FORCES OF YOUR OWN COUNTRY. The gain of doing this will be so immense that it will present the nation with an ample fund, not only sufficient to pay the tax on consumers of which you complain, but after having paid it still super-abounding, and leaving in the hands of the nation for its own spending, a surplus ten times as great as that tax. Nay, the very tax itself will, in most cases, soon disappear; for the development of your own producing power will not only, at first and at once, bring plenty and riches, but in the end will bring a steady cheapness too, and along with that cheapness the powers of purchasing. It will add accessibility to cheapness."

So reasoned Cromwell, Lord Chatham, Sir Robert Walpole, Edmund Burke, Peter the Great, Colbert, Napoleon. So at this day reason France, Belgium, Russia, Germany, America, and, unfortunately for us, Canada and Australia too.

Our fathers, and we, the children, must, however, both cordially agree in this. The more a nation produces, the richer it is.

Indeed, this seems a self-evident proposition. Without production of value you can neither consume nor buy. *Ex nihilo nihil fit.* Every increase of domestic production is an addition of so much wealth and so much of the means of purchase: any diminution of domestic production is a subtraction of so much wealth and of so much of the means of purchase.

We, the children, however, now seem unconsciously to assume that the amount of production in a country (the land, the men, and the actual property remaining the same) is an unvarying quantity. But the fathers thought that (the land, the men, and the actual property of a country remaining the same) that country will produce infinitely more, or infinitely less, according as certain regulations, favorable to domestic production and internal exchange, are present or absent.

Produce within your own dominions what you formerly imported from abroad, and your land, labor, and capital produce what they otherwise would not have produced. They still produce the articles which might have been used to purchase the new domestic product, just as much as they did before. But over and above this, they now produce the whole value of the new domestic product. Tried by the rule that the more a nation produces the richer it is, you are now the richer. You have now developed a new producing power of the country, which otherwise, instead of being developed, would have been stifled and smothered by foreign imports, perhaps a little cheaper. By a sacrifice it may be of one per cent., not the producers, but the nation have gained the other ninety-nine. To pay your tax of one pound, you are presented with a new and additional net income of a hundred pounds. And what you have done, other nations may also do. The producing power of all the earth may thus be effectually developed, and yet, as we have seen, ample scope everywhere left for foreign trade and international exchanges. *

So far from the amount of production, in a country being an unvarying quantity (the land labor and property remaining the same), we have elsewhere seen what immense masses of capital and labor in Great Britain and Ireland, formerly active in the work of production, are now actually idle. Capable not so much of immediately augmenting the national wealth by a miserable gain of one or two per cent. on the price of commodities, as of augmenting the produce of the land labor and capital of the united kingdom by tens of millions annually. If it should cost the nation something in the price of commodities, to develop these, our own producing forces, those forces will present the nation with millions to pay it. The nation surely ought not to complain of being taxed by those who give it first money to pay the tax, and then fifty times as much for the nation itself.

But the children are not yet silent. They say, " It is the producers that gain, while the consumers lose."

Again the fathers rejoin, " You are wrong in marshalling the nation into two hostile camps of producers and consumers. Not only is every producer a consumer, but there is not a single consumer who is not

---

* See Chapters VI. and X.

10*

either a producer, or else living entirely out of the income of a producer—standing or falling with him."

Laborers, farmers, manufacturers, are all clearly producers. The landlords derive all their rent from the revenue of producers; so, of course, do the mortgagees to whom they pay interest. The professional man is ultimately paid by producers: so is the fund-holder himself, and the public servant too. Find, if you can, a living man who is not either a producer or maintained by a producer. Whatever, therefore, furthers the interest of producers, not only benefits them, but also augments the common fund from which every consumer derives his income; and on the other hand, whatever ruins or injures producers, ruins or injures the common fund on which all consumers depend.

But suppose, secondly, that instead of being wrong, you were right, and that consumers and producers were really two distinct and mutually independent classes, as you pretend. Yet they are still, at any rate, members of the same political community, and we are now discussing the effect of fiscal regulations on the wealth of the *whole country*. If you develop your producing power so as to produce at home (although 1 per cent. dearer) what you used to produce abroad, the aggregate of customers lose 1, where the aggregate of producers gain 100. The nation at large still gains 99.

So if you used to produce at home, but now prefer to import from abroad because you can save 1 per cent. in price, you (the nation) sacrifice 100 to gain 1. The nation at large loses 99. Supposing even consumers and producers to be distinct classes, the result would be this: you take a tax of 1 per cent. off one class, and lay a tax of 100 per cent. on another class.

Thirdly and lastly, you assume that the trifling tax

(under which you are so impatient that you would blindly change it for one of fifty or a hundred times as great) will continue for ever.   It is a gratuitous and unfounded assumption.   Develop your own industrial forces, and concentrate them on industries for which your climate, soil, and people are fit, and you will have at once plenty and riches, and very soon cheapness too.

Reflect, and you will find that the wise and really gainful policy is not that which prematurely grasps anyhow at cheapness, but that which develops the producing power of the country.

Our fathers, therefore, were right and we are wrong. They knew how to grow rich nationally as well as individually.   We have seen how their theory has everywhere been justified by experience in time past, here and elsewhere.   It is still justified in America, in France, in Germany, in Russia.

CHAPTER XXVIII.

" Individuals know their own interests, and may and should be left to take care of them in their own way; for the interest of individuals, and the interest of the public, which is but an aggregation of individuals, coincide."

It is to be feared that a rigorous analysis of these two propositions would raise very serious doubts of both.

Take the last of them first.

Thousands every year find it their interest to appropriate the goods of others to their own use, in the most direct way possible. The burglar employs his capital (which is a picklock and a bunch of skeleton keys) as he deems most conducive to his private interest. But the general opinion of mankind is, that the public interest is very much concerned in putting down such employment of labor and capital.

It is true that those marauders who have been found out mistook their own interest. But then the first part of the proposition is no truer than the second. Men do not, it appears, always know their own interest.

Adam Smith, when he promulgated this maxim of the let-alone school, had never seen a modern cotton-mill, and therefore had no conception of the necessity or utility of a Factory Act. Let any candid man have visited Manchester before it, and visited Manchester since—he, and not Adam Smith, is qualified to form a judgment.

Adam Smith had not witnessed the debasing and brutalising employment of women in collieries.

He had never seen a middle-man hiring a gang of little boys and girls of six or seven years old, and letting them out at so much an hour to Birmingham button manufacturers.

We have already passed in review* a multitude of instances in which individuals mistake their true interest, and in which the public interferes most beneficially for their guidance and protection.

We have seen many more instances, in which the interest of individuals, and the true interest of the public, are at open variance, and in which, again, the wisdom and power of the whole community is compelled to interpose.

So it may sometimes be for the interest of individuals to buy in one market; but it may at the same time be for the interest of the public at large, that they should buy in another.

We do not say that such *is* the interest of the public, but only that it may be. Whether it actually be so or not, and to what extent it is so, has been already discussed.†

---

* See ante, Chapter VIII.
† See Chapters IV., V., and XXVII.

CHAPTER XXIX.

" England may be made the workshop of the world."

SUPPOSING this consummation as possible as it is visionary, the next inquiry is, whether it be desirable.

An illustration of the nature of manufacturing industry had better be taken from our neighbors than ourselves. The old rule, which Terence lays down for individuals, is good for nations too.

> Inspicere tanquam in speculum in vitas omnium
> Jubeo, atque ex aliis sumere exemplum sibi.

We shall be less likely to be warped by party spirit; more likely to see facts in their true light; and instructed by observing how far the same causes produce the like effects under different circumstances.*

The department of the north boasts of the richest soil in France, and the greatest wealth.

It is the workshop of France. Cotton, linen, and iron are manufactured on a vast scale.

No Factory Acts there protect the poor.†　In this

---

* The materials for much of what is said below, on the subject of French manufacturing industry, are drawn from the report of M. Blanqui to the Academie des Sciences Morales et Politiques. His book is entitled *Des Classes ouvrières en France.* He is a friend of order, and, what is rare in France, a free-trader.

† There are laws touching the employment of young children in manufactories, but not enforced. Since the last revolution, the hours of labor for workmen of all ages have been limited by law throughout France.

respect things are, in many manufactories, left to their natural course. Ceaseless competition, not only between laborers, but between employers, drives down prices and wages to the lowest possible standard. Any new establishment, either on a larger scale, or furnished with improved machinery, at once imposes on all smaller establishments or inferior machinery, the necessity of yet greater and greater exertion, and yet lower and lower wages. Night and day, the indefatigable and ponderous piston stamps. Night and day, relays of human flesh struggle to keep up with its remorseless and unwearied march. The white slaves, in crowded apartments, breathe an atmosphere here loaded with dust, there charged with moisture. The liquid eye and bright complexion of childhood no longer shine. Health is stolen from children who know not its value. Their moral ruin is as complete as their physical ruin. The conscience, the moral sense, has never been developed by parental and domestic influence, or invigorated and fortified by the solemn services and sanctions of religion. Education is impracticable, virtue impossible, vice and disease triumphant. Here is the true modern martyrology! Here, the true massacre of the innocents.

Thousands of the manufacturing poor in Lisle are, even when employed, reduced to such a state of poverty in the midst of abounding and brilliant opulence, that they live, not in houses, but in underground cellars, lighted only by the entrance. Day-light comes to them an hour later than to other people, and leaves them an hour earlier. No chair, no bed is found in many of these subterraneous caverns. The wretched inmates huddle together without distinction of age or sex, sometimes on the broken straw of rape-seed, sometimes even on dry sand. The father of the family is at home only to sleep. He is obliged to sell his little ones to the Moloch of the place. You may see the shadow of a man gliding to the factory with a little boy or girl, in the grey twilight, sometimes of the morning, sometimes of the evening. The wretched but tender and vigilant mother in vain watches her helpless offspring. It is affirmed of these children in Lisle, that 20,700 out of 21,000 * die before they are five years old. And if you would know the condition of multitudes that survive, visit the quarter of Saint Sauveur, the Rue des Etaques, the Cour Gha, the Cour du Sauvage, the Place aux Oignons, and you are surrounded by clamorous demands for charity from a swarm of little human animals— ragged and nearly naked—pale, ill-favored, rickety, scrofulous, and deformed.

Such is the manufacturing industry of Lisle, even in the season of prosperity. But French manufacturing industry, like English, perpetually alternates between over-production and stoppage—between fever and ague. When trade languishes, cold, famine, and disease devour the population.

The masters are in a condition equally precarious and anxious, if not equally wretched. They are in continual danger from destruction by competition. They dare not stop, and hardly dare to proceed. They produce without any certain market, and are sailing without a compass, they know not whither.

The extremes of wealth and poverty meet in the department of the north. Every third person is said to be in hopeless indigence—or, in English phraseology, a pauper.

The bulk of the manufacturing population in Rouen is in a condition little better than that in Lisle.

The evils that afflict Lyons under a different system, and in a better climate, are of a somewhat different class. The workpeople are not there congregated into large factories working by machinery. But the struggle

---

* This proportion seems incredible. But M. Blanqui reports it on the authority of a medical man at Lisle.

for wages, between the life of the workman on one hand, and the necessities of the exporting master on the other, is as intense and infinitely more violent. The hot blood and exalted imagination of the South are engaged. Here rise and rage socialism, communism, fourrierism, phalansterianism, and all those other portentous and monstrous births, and grim but living abortions, engendered by half-knowledge on the intolerable miseries of the unregulated manufacturing system. Twice even during the reign of Louis Philippe was Lyons in full insurrection. Twice was this rebellion of the belly quelled by necessary severity. Twice did grape-shot rake the streets, and the kennels run with blood.

Who shall resolve the terrible problems that manufacturing industry produces? What exists in Lisle, Rouen, and Lyons exists more or less wherever unregulated manufacturing industry is to be found.

Surely experience teaches that manufacturing industry, if it is to promote the solid interest of a country, requires moderation and control; that its undue ascendancy over all other industries is attended with great evil and danger.

Even political economists, who have maturely reflected on the subject, and not only its social, but its political aspect, regard the unlimited extension of manufactures already existing, even in England, with alarm. "Perhaps," says Mr. M'Culloch, "it may in the end be found that it was unwise to allow the manufacturing system to gain so great an ascendancy as it has done in this country; *and that measures should have been early adopted to check and moderate its growth.*"*

The hostile tariffs, therefore, which do and will effectually prevent our becoming the work-shop of the world, are perhaps not altogether unmitigated evils.

---

* *Principles of Political Economy*, p. 185.

Surely the wisdom and the care of the whole community should be directed to making the basis on which manufactures repose as permanent and stable as possible.

Our greatest manufacture, in addition to the uncertainty incident to all manufacturing industry, has elements of instability and decay peculiarly its own. It rests at present on two foundations, equally insecure and precarious. It unnecessarily depends for its raw material on a distant and rival state,* and for many of its present markets on jealous and encroaching competitors.

They are its true friends who would persuade it to draw its materials as much as possible from British India and other British dependencies; and to find, in addition to its present vent, not only secure, but larger and unlimited markets in British possessions.

But there is another raw material of home growth adapted to our textile manufactures—FLAX.

The natural use and (if one may presume to say so) the design of this plant is the clothing of mankind.

The Egyptian men and women who walked about in the time of Moses or Cambyses, and whose mummies we now unrol, were clad in home-grown and home spun linen garments. Nearly all soils in England and Ireland are adapted to the growth of flax. So univer sal in old time was its use in this country, that the under-clothing, for the person, and the textures applied to domestic uses, are still always called *linen*, whatever the materials of which they are made. Unfortunately of late, having been superseded by cotton, it has become almost a luxury of the upper and middle classes..

The main obstacles which have hitherto prevented

---

* These observations were written and published long before the late interruption of the supply of cotton from America.

its successful rivalry with cotton are said to be these:—
The large bulk of the crop augmenting the expenses of
transport and limiting the market, and the exhaustion
of the soil, by removing so much produce from the
land. But it is affirmed, that instead of being pulled
before it is ripe, the flax may now be permitted to
mature its seed, with which the farmer may fatten his
bullocks and enrich his land. It may be stacked—and
at any time, by a simple machine, the fibre may be sepa-
rated from the straw. The fibre alone may be sent to
market, and the straw, being sixty or seventy per cent.
of the bulk, may be kept at home to be converted into
manure. Flax prepared in the method patented by M.
Claussen may, it is said, be woven either with cotton
or with wool. Under these improved conditions it is
affirmed to be now a more profitable crop than wheat,
even supposing the price of wheat be very much
higher than of late it has been.*

Without venturing to obtrude any opinion on matters which can only be decided by the experience of
practical men, but only as an illustration, let us see
what would be the consequences if home-grown flax
could be produced cheaper than American cotton, or
substituted for it.

Suppose that we now pay ten millions a year for
American cotton, and suppose we now export manufactured cotton, hardware, and other manufactures to pay
for it, to the same amount.†

Suppose that hereafter, instead of this, we pay our
own laborers, farmers, and landlords ten millions a
year for flax. It is now the English and the Irish that
have the spending of this ten millions—not the Americans. English markets are annually increased by the

---

* These passages were written twenty years ago.
† This passage was written in 1850.

expenditure of that amount, instead of American markets.

If it be said, Your exports of manufactures to America will fall off by ten millions. Suppose they should. The manufacturers are no losers by that. The English and Irish are now their customers instead of the Americans—that is all.

The whole value of the cotton was resolvable into American net gain. The whole value of the flax is now resolvable into English and Irish net gain.*

Moreover, your supply is always certain, and you enjoy immense advantages in that full and various employment of the people, which attends the mutual vicinity of growers and manufacturers.†

It is said that Mr. Warne's introduction of flax into the parish of Trimingham, has destroyed its pauperism. Suppose the substitution of home-grown flax for American cotton to be possible—it would in like manner diminish the pauperism of Great Britain and Ireland.

Again: The miseries springing from the want of a factory act in France, and its great success here, shew that manufacturing labor requires artificial regulation.

Lastly: The evils arising from an undue proportion of manufacturing industry are to be corrected, not by limiting its absolute but its *relative* amount; that is to say, by energetic and stubborn efforts to promote in every possible way the subjugation and improvement of British, Irish, and colonial soils.

Common sense, nature, reason, history, economy, experience, all unite in one loud and overwhelming cry:—Employ your people on the land; not only in

---

* See Chapters IV. and V.
† See Chapter VI.

your Colonies, but even at home—and in Ireland you have unoccupied and waste lands enough, and more than enough. No machinery, no factory, is like the land. Light, air and human hands are the elements of unexpected and unknown productiveness, even on soil that is now little better than mere horizontal surface.

"Replenish the earth, AND SUBDUE IT," is a command not yet superseded. But you cannot fulfil the first branch safely without the second.

CHAPTER XXX.

" War and invasion are but dangers of bygone ages."

THE authors of our new commercial policy do not deprecate war without very good reason.

It will wake up the nation to the stern reality that it has become dependent on a victory at sea for its bread and meat; that from a naval defeat flows at once an inundation of horrors, inevitable, universal, indescribable. No one can answer for the excesses of popular indignation and vengeance.

But in the meantime the nation is rocked to sleep with the comfortable assurance that there will never be any more war.*

Would to God it were so!

But human nature, and human passions and depravity, are ever the same. Those who, despising the authentic and unvarying record of three thousand years, legislate on the assumption that human nature is changed, and that there will now at last be no more war, are like those who build villas and towns on the slopes of Ætna or Vesuvius. Thirty or forty years of treacherous silence and serenity have obliterated the recollection and the dread of the subterraneous thunder, the mid-day darkness, and the glowing lava and cinders.

Famine, pestilence, and war are the three ministers by whom the Almighty has in all ages past chastised

---

* This passage was written in 1849.

the nations. Four short years ago our presumptuous security deemed itself inaccessible to any one of the three.

A mysterious and inexplicable disease in a single esculent root suddenly brings the first. Famine rages in our borders.

A new and awful malady, in the presence of which our precautions are vain, and our science, folly, seizes our human bodies. Pestilence is come, and mows down its thousands.*

Hitherto we have escaped the plague of war—or, rather, have had a longer respite than usual. But the interval is short, and, in the reckoning of history, nothing. We are but approaching the end of the first half of the century. How did even this short period begin? The first half of the nineteenth century found all Europe in a deadly struggle, and for one-third of its course waded through blood and war on a scale of unprecedented magnitude. The thunder of the cannon has scarce died on our ears. Men yet in middle life remember Waterloo.

And, during the precarious interval that remained, how many times, especially in late years, have we been on the very brink of war? It is in vain that we are bound (as Lord Brougham says) in heavy recognisances to keep the peace. It is in vain that this once high-spirited nation has tamely submitted to demands and slights which Lord Chatham would not have brooked. A reduction of our armaments does but increase the danger of war by emboldening those who, with the envy and jealousy natural to mankind, are watching for an opportunity to humble us.

To say nothing of our hair-breadth escapes in 1840, and again in 1844, from a war with the first military power on earth—nothing of the high, captious, and

---

* Written in 1849.

exacting tone assumed on more than one recent occasion by the new and great power of the West—look at what happened but the other day. A few weeks ago, when Russia and Austria threatened Turkey for affording an asylum to the Hungarian refugees, we ventured once more to listen to the dictates of honor, and, to use old English language, in behalf of an oppressed but faithful and magnanimous ally. The whole nation really meant what it said. Straightway peace or war hung suspended on the caprice of a single individual. A restless night, or an indigestion, might have been (as it often has been) the spark to fire the train. And what a mine was ready to explode! Five great powers at once engaged. The bright-harnessed hosts of Europe, in numbers innumerable, awaiting the signal. The original cause of war, as always happens, soon forgotten. Italy, Germany, Denmark, Belgium, Holland, embraced in an unextinguishable conflagration. The deadly conflict not confined to the narrow limits of Europe, but lighting up both hemispheres, and blazing on every sea, all round this terrestrial ball!

Nay, within the last five years actual war has raged in all four quarters of the globe. In the North and South of Africa; in South America; in North America, on a great scale, and followed by an immense and apparently durable conquest; in Asia, where we ourselves have, within that short period, been thrice actors. Here, as in America, conquest has been the result. In many parts of Europe—in Italy, in Denmark, and in Hungary. The recent military operations in Hungary alone were on a scale of enormous magnitude. Nearly six hundred thousand regular troops were, in the field.

We say nothing of the infinitely worse calamity of civil war. Paris, Vienna, Berlin, Milan, two years ago, little anticipated that the music of their balls, their Italian and German operas, were so soon to give place to the whistling of shells. What reason had the inoffensive and peaceable kingdom of Denmark to anticipate the bloody events of the past year? Only this—that, as in the natural, so in the political world, sunshine nowhere lasts always.

No degree of foresight, wisdom, or care, on our part, will or can preserve us from the contingency of war. Our solemn obligations, our national honor, must at all events be preserved. With nations, as with individuals, where honor is in question, interest is not to be heard. But our true, solid, and well understood interest speaks the same language. The certain consequence of disregarding national honor is a struggle a little procrastinated, but at greater disadvantage when it does come—a struggle, not with the help of allies, for they will have been deserted and disgusted, but alone and single-handed—a struggle, not for victory, but for existence.

Ours is not the only period in history, and very recent history too, when men have vainly flattered themselves that the world had grown too wise to engage in the work of mutual destruction. It has been well observed by a modern French writer,* that in 1791, Camille Desmoulins published a work entitled *La France Libre,* in which may be found these words: "L'esprit de conquête est perdu." But at that very hour came forth from the Military School of Brienne a sub-lieutenant of artillery, destined to be the greatest conqueror that the world had ever seen. There may be seen at the mint in Paris, a medal struck by Bonaparte when first consul, the motto of which is—"Paix de l'univers." In 1787 Mr. Pitt said, in one of his speeches, "The time is at hand when, conformably to the will of Provi-

---

* M. Chevalier, to whom we are indebted for some of the illustrations which follow.

11

dence, the two great nations of France and England will show the world that they were made to cherish relations of mutual beneficence and friendship." Little did the speaker imagine that these two nations were then crossing the threshold to long years of carnage, in comparison of which all former wars were mere skirmishes.

Do we look to history for encouragement? She offers very little. The "rich and solemn pencil" of Tacitus portrays men as they were in the time of the Roman Empire. The most recent experience evinces that men are the same now.

Do we look to the influence of religion? It has again been observed that she has for ages come to an understanding with war. She has greatly mitigated its horrors. Some of her most eminent and exemplary professors have defined its province and traced its laws. Search Christendom—only one small sect condemns all war. Accordingly we saw the other day a dignitary of the English Church consecrating the flags of a regiment; and the friends and patrons of the Protestant Christian missionaries in Tahiti, if not preaching the necessity of war, at least taunting the government of the day for its forbearing and pacific conduct.

Shall we turn to modern philosophy? Who has ever inveighed more eloquently against war than Voltaire? Yet it has again been truly said that his disciples, his successors, as it were his executors, saturated the earth with blood.

Shall we look to education? At the first sound of the trumpet, mark the educated English youth. Cressy and Poictiers are part of his English nature. Modern accomplishments are straw to the fire in the blood.

Railways and steam-ships may do much to promote peace among nations. But to the thoughtful mind, the

new power of nature, subjugated to human uses since
the last general war, has other but sinister and portentous aspects. It affords such means of offence by land
and sea, such facility of concentrating aggressive as well
as defensive forces, of over-leaping ancient boundaries,
and holding new conquests, that its effects, in remodel-
ling the earth, may turn out to be as unexpected and
marvellous in war as in peace. The very possession of
a novel and untried means of offence, will add a double
intensity to the passions of cupidity, vengeance, and
fear. What living flesh can foresee either the venture
or the stakes, when the awful game of war comes to be
played again with the power of steam! What terri
torial changes may a convulsion among the nations, by
the help of that new agency, permanently effect! In
the meantime the principles of human nature, which
from the commencement of authentic history, have
periodically and invariably produced wars, remain the
same. National pride and resentment, the scrupulosity
of national honor, the love of novelty and excitement
in the public, the domestic difficulties of statesmen, the
undue preponderance in other nations of the demo-
cratic element, knowing little and acting intemperately,
are a dormant but fulminating compound, which may
at any moment explode in an unexpected and universal war.

War is of all calamities the greatest. But seeing
that it has been so long and so often permitted, we
may reverently suppose that it is not without its permanent uses in the economy of Divine Providence,
and therefore may be permitted again. It does not,
after all, cause a single death that would not otherwise
have happened. Which, on an average, is the worst—
death in the field, or the dying strife of the natural
death-bed? War is the theatre of great talents and
great virtues. The vain theories, the epicurean principles, the luxurious and enervating habits of peace,

perish together. The storm clears the atmosphere, and the moral health of nations is renovated.

But if war be the greatest of calamities even to a nation well prepared, what will it be when the storm bursts suddenly on a nation unprepared, and dependent for its existence on the arrangements of peace?

"Cuique creditur in arte suâ," is a maxim no less of common prudence, than of common law. Address, then, the question to your military and naval authorities. They tell you that steam has now thrown a bridge across the English channel. The greatest military authority now living, if not the greatest that ever lived, tells you that an undisciplined multitude, even of Englishmen, in the presence of modern military science, is just so much gun-carrion. *

One of your greatest naval authorities, Lord Dundonald, tells you, that supposed dangers of landing, and even fortified coasts, are no defence at all; that your true and only external defence is the old-fashioned one—the overwhelming and ubiquitous offensive efficacy of a military marine, which shall again sweep, as it has before swept, your enemies off the seas.†

---

* The Duke of Wellington was living when these observations were written.

† Since this Chapter was written, twenty years ago, events have happened which may test the soundness of its views.

First, the Crimean war between four Great Powers—England, France, Russia, and Turkey.

Next the Italian war between France and Austria.

Then a war of the first magnitude, not between ambitious sovereigns, but between two divisions of the United Republics of America.

Next a war between two of the greatest military powers on earth—Austria and Prussia—changing the constitution of Germany.

Lastly, at this moment, a scale of military preparations in existence such as was never witnessed before.

These are the solemn warnings of England's most illustrious sons. But we prefer prophets that prophesy smooth things. On military and naval affairs we have the happiness to possess much greater authorities than naval or military men.

CHAPTER XXXI.

" The Navigation Laws were useless and injurious."

To appreciate the real magnitude of the Andes or the Cordilleras, you must view them from a distance. Near their base the eye is obstructed by meaner elevations, but seen from a distance of fifty miles, Chimborazo pierces the sky.

So, as we fall down the stream of time, and recede from the Administration of Oliver Cromwell, its real grandeur gradually breaks upon the mental vision. Cromwell and the Long Parliament devised the Navigation Laws, and founded the British Empire.

From that hour the maritime greatness of England dates. From that hour it steadily and uninterruptedly advanced for more than a hundred and fifty years, till at the close of the last war England's meteor flag floated in every clime, and rode on every sea, undisputed and universal victor.

This splendid success did not flow from the let-alone policy, but from a wise and highly artificial system of law. The great and original legislators of the day, proposed to themselves as a national object, the increase of British shipping. They saw that sailors and ships were the true army and omnipresent artillery of the British Islands. Their sagacity prefigured at once the safest and cheapest defence, and the most irresistible means of aggression and aggrandisement. They thought that the high seas might be able to compensate England for the narrow extent of her ploughed lands—

might be made to yield wealth as great, sons as warlike and hardy, and power much greater. This sure instinct taught them that a great national object like this was not to be trusted to the natural course of events—to the chapter of accidents. They did not hesitate at once to realise their grand conceptions in direct and stringent legislation.

They confined the whole coasting trade, and the whole trade with the British colonies and plantations, to British subjects.

They secured the importation of most articles, the produce of Asia, Africa, and America, to British ships. And foreseeing that this wholesome provision might be evaded by a previous importation into other parts of Europe in foreign bottoms, they prohibited the importation of Asiatic, African, and American produce from Europe, not only in foreign, but even in British ships. In a word, they took the most effectual measures that British ships should supply the British markets.

But with the descrimination which distinguishes the legislation of true wisdom from the headlong legislation of mere theory, they were not unmindful of the foreign trade of the country. They allowed foreign ships to import the produce of their own respective countries. Any foreign vessels infringing these regulations were with their whole cargoes at once confiscated.

Having given the British shipowner these advantages, our fathers took good care that they should not be merely private, but truly national advantages. They obliged the shipowner to use a British built ship. They would not allow him to navigate with an underpaid foreign crew, but secured the maritime employment of their own countrymen, by insisting that the owners, masters and three-fourths of the crew should

be British subjects, of whom they took care to insure
a never-failing supply by the system of compulsory
apprenticeship. This is what they would have done
with the poor little boys now playing in the gutter,
and making every man's heart ache that sees them.
No matter how suddenly a war might break out, while
the raw maritime levies of other countries were helpless and sea-sick, thousands, and tens of thousands of
skilful, well-fed, lion-hearted British seamen of all ages
were thus, even in profound peace, and without the
least expense, or danger to liberty, kept ready for the
defence of the country.

Let us hear what Adam Smith says of this maritime
code, so adverse to our modern notions.

After remarking that some of its regulations may
have proceeded from national animosity, he adds,
"They are as wise, however, as if they had all been dic-
tated by the most deliberate wisdom." And again:
"As defence is of much more importance than opu-
lence, THE ACT OF NAVIGATION IS PERHAPS THE
WISEST OF ALL THE COMMERCIAL REGULATIONS OF
ENGLAND." *

The eminent success of this policy vindicated it in
Adam Smith's time: its yet more triumphant success
has more fully justified it since. Through the muta-
tions of nearly two centuries it steadily upheld our
maritime power, and the inviolability of our native
land.

But we are not to be satisfied of the wisdom of a
course of action by its success. We must make trial
of its opposite. We must eat of the tree of the knowledge of good and evil. "Eat," says the tempter, "ye
shall not surely die."

---

* *Wealth of Nations*, book 4, chap. 2.

We are now told that, as in everything else, so in ships, sailors, and freights, we are to go to the cheapest market. If the Norwegians can carry coals from New-castle or Sunderland to London, cheaper than the English, the trade should on principle be surrendered to them. If the Americans can find it profitable to invade our British commerce with India, Jamaica, the Cape of Good Hope, Australia, or China, the trade should be at once opened to them. If half-starved Swedes, or Norwegians, or Lascars, can man our own vessels cheaper than the beef-eating, ruddy English tar, our countryman's proper place is not the night-watch, or the top-mast, but some other employment (nobody knows what)—and failing that, the workhouse. If it should happen that ships can be built cheaper in the ports of the Baltic than at Sunderland, the English ship-building trade should migrate thither. The strong will of our fathers controlled circumstances : we sur-render ourselves to circumstances and theories, to be carried—we know not whither.

In the last Session of Parliament, the Navigation Laws were repealed.

Precious in the sight of posterity will be the names that resisted with all their might, at all hazards, this suicidal measure. In the meantime, whatever betide, they have won the noblest of all possessions—the con-sciousness of duty faithfully discharged amidst mis-representation and obloquy.

But the dark view of what we have done remains to be considered.

The blackest horrors of war are seen in a populous and blockaded city. Incomparably more awful would be the famine of an island swarming with people, dependent on foreign supplies of food, but beleaguered by superior naval forces.

11*

Such a catastrophe has hitherto been impossible, for three reasons.

First: We were not dependent on foreign supplies of food. Till very recent times we could produce enough for our own consumption, and, in the last century, a great superfluity.

Secondly: Our military and commercial marine (owing chiefly to the navigation laws) has been so large, as at all times not only to supply a cheap and effectual defence, but to sweep the seas.

Thirdly: No other power, either separately or combined, possessed any naval strength comparable to ours.

All these three things are now changed.

First: We have become (and in a great measure suddenly, if not necessarily) dependent on foreign countries for large supplies of corn, to say nothing of sugar and cotton. It has been said that we draw, or shall soon draw, nearly a fourth of our supply of food from abroad.* The sudden and forcible withdrawal of that proportion would instantly cause famine prices—prices ten times, twenty times, as high as at present. Such prices, frightful as they are, are yet but the heralds of actual famine.

Secondly: We have now, at the very crisis when we have begun to require this increased supply, repealed our navigation laws, and reduced our military marine. The effect of the repeal will be (there is too much reason to fear) highly injurious to British seamen. Steamboats may increase, but will British sailors? The best that can be said of the experiment is, that its results are untried and unknown. We are calling out for still further reductions in our Royal Navy. Already it is no longer such an effectual defence as our altered circumstances and vast possessions might suddenly require.

---

* Written in 1850.

Thirdly: The marine of France, of Russia, and of the United States are now, each of them, formidable rivals. Combined they are already our actual superiors.

It is said that it would be as inconvenient to the exporting countries to withhold their supplies as it would be for us to forego them. Alas! these are the dreams of men of peace. The answer is, first—It would not. Which is the greatest evil—famine, or a temporary superfluity? One is death—the other, but transient inconvenience. The animosity and evil passions of war have often and joyfully endured a temporary and partial inconvenience to consummate the final ruin of an ancient and haughty enemy. Next the attacking and beleaguering powers may be those who have the least interest in the commercial question, but who in intercepting supplies of food from neutral parties may have not only superior force, but, in some conjunctures, public law on their side.*

---

* We ourselves have treated corn and flour as contraband of war.

CHAPTER XXXII.

" Labor should be left to flow in its own natural channels."

OF all the idols worshipped by the *let-alone* superstition, this is perhaps the Moloch. Never before were human sacrifices offered up on so vast a scale.

We have already seen that the channels in which both capital and labor, when left to themselves, may chance by accident to flow, are not necessarily the most advantageous. That both capital and labor may be (and often have been) artificially diverted into channels ten times, twenty times, a hundred times, as advantageous to the whole nation. Just as many a river, which, left to itself, spreads and stagnates in shallow and pestilential marshes and lagoons, may have its course or its levels artificially altered and improved, so as to irrigate whole countries, and feed great nations, or bear their commerce on its deep and ample bosom.

But what we propose here to consider is the *distribution of the population itself.* Will it naturally distribute itself in the most advantageous manner?

Reader! have you ever seen a map of England shaded according to the density of the population? Middlesex, Lancashire, and West Riding of Yorkshire, a portion of South Wales, and a few other places are almost black. But the residue of the kingdom is either slightly shaded, or almost white. This map shews the English population to be, not so much large as congested.

Let things alone, and the fatal congestion is aggravated. The recent returns shew that the population of our largest towns grows rapidly, but the rural population does not. Men are more and more driven from their natural, virtuous, and healthy calling in the open air—the subjugation, fertilisation, and culture of the soil. They encourage foreigners to cultivate foreign soils, but are themselves driven to herd promiscuously, like brutes, in the cellars of Liverpool, the garrets of St. Giles's, the wynds of Glasgow, the victims and parent of idleness, disease, want, filth, vice, and irreligion.

No sanitary measures, no education, no schools, no churches, will ever stop the progress of evils like these. You might as well attempt to stop a hundred-and-twenty gun ship in full sail with a bit of pack-thread. There is but one remedy. Restore these really exiled children of the land to their natural condition and occupation. Plant them on the soil. This is the only true and solid sanitary improvement. Then, indeed, and not till then, will what is now the refuse and sewerage of your cities really fertilise the land. In the United Kingdom alone, the room is more ample than is supposed. There are millions of British and Irish acres waste and sterile for want of the fertilising human animal, far more promising than Egypt or Holland were by nature ; there are hundreds of thousands of men gasping for their natural element. There is a system of railways ready to bring together man and the land, so useless apart, so fruitful together—a union which is the aim and end of all true political economy. Not only might the rights of landed property be religiously respected, but the value of it in many cases quadrupled. Public power is already there, but public wisdom stands by, manacled and handcuffed by the let-alone superstition. Seven or eight years ago the densest rural population was to be found in Ireland. Yet some of the most

intelligent and best-informed witnesses examined under
Lord Devon's Commission, were no advocates for
emigration, proclaiming their opinion even then to be,
that there was not a man too many, even in Ireland.
We have seen that practical men declare, that Ireland
might with ease, feed and employ two and a half times
her late population. And if the producing forces of
Great Britain and Ireland were properly developed,
the number of the really unemployed anywhere, would
be very small. To employ or plant the small surplus
on the land, would be a work of less difficulty than is
supposed—many times more advantageous both to the
poor and to the country, than to export them, even to
the Colonies. They would still further develop the
producing power of the kingdom, as much as if they
augmented its surface. Then, indeed, education and
religion might have their perfect work. But the fertilising stream will never, of itself, reach the waste.
Emancipated public wisdom must direct it. Government must stretch out its arm to save. And we have
here precedent to guide us. A government that we
look down on as blind and despotic, has done it already
—and done it with a scrupulous regard to the rights
of property. The Prussian government already has
actually planted the pauper over its soil, and transformed him into the most industrious and happy of
mankind.

But some think there is a real excess of population
in the British Isles.

Perhaps the truth may be, that there is now an
actual excess as compared with present means of employment; but not one pair of hands, or one mouth too
many, compared with those means of employment and
support, which a few years would present, both in Great
Britain and Ireland, when both nations, abandoning
barren, cosmopolitan theories, shall seriously address

themselves to the development of their own producing forces.

But suppose the fact to be that there is a real and not a mere apparent excess. Then imagine a population map, such as we have above described, of the British *Empire*. What does it present?—a few spots of population in a boundless field, white, not only with unoccupied, but with fertile land.

But for this fatal *let-alone* delusion, public wisdom might long ago have vigorously availed itself of these unparalleled resources. Instead of the human hash rotting and fermenting in London, Liverpool, and Glasgow, why should not those natural helpmates, man and the land, have been brought together on a grand scale? Why not plant the first of races, on the best and amplest of soils? A new and peaceful conquest entailing no ultimate expense, but bringing infinite gain, exhibiting to all nations a new sort of subjugation.

But how has our population gone forth?

Helter-skelter, the government cares not who, nor why, nor how, nor whence, nor whither.*

Those we can least spare are gone, leaving behind those that ought to go. It has been asserted by some that from Ireland alone, small farmers have gone, who have taken out more property with them than would pay for the estates hitherto sold under the Encumbered Estates Act. From England and Scotland it is the industrious and enterprising that go. Why are such multitudes from all parts of the United Kingdom going? Emigration should at all events be voluntary. It is not so. The furies of want, misery, and despair scourge the emigrants from our shores. How do they go?— huddled together in improper or ill-found vessels; during the voyage exposed to the merciless cupidity of

---

* This passage was written in 1850.

private enterprise; on landing, cruelly abandoned to their fate. The very proportion of the sexes, which nature so sedulously watches, is disturbed. The last census shows a sad disproportionate increase of women at home, while we have Colonies depraved and depopulated for want of them. Amidst all this, the dregs of population, the vicious and wretched outcasts of our great cities remain behind.

And whither do our countrymen go? Except a comparatively few, not to our Colonies at all.

Such is colonisation under the let-alone system. What might it be?

CHAPTER XXXIII.

*" The value of everything must now be settled by universal
competition."*

So say the modern free-traders.

"No!" say the socialists, "Competition is all wrong:
look at the miseries it produces. Co-operation is to be
the panacea."

Both these new sects, however, would fain persuade
us, that the world and human life are henceforth to be
something different, and very superior to what they have
always been. Both seem to forget that we have been in
a high state of civilisation for three or four hundred
years. Neither bear in mind that a large portion of
evil, private and social, is the inseparable and perpetual
accompaniment of our imperfect nature. Both liken
the beneficent and universal Parent to a capricious and
unnatural father, who, having neglected his first-born
children, should unjustly favor his younger offspring.
Both represent human life as a feast at which there is a
succession of guests; but the generations that sat down
first found a scanty and miserable board, while plenty
of substantial and invigorating viands were kept back
for those who should sit down last.

Many think Paley's view much nearer the truth:
that human life and the world form a system of com-
pensations; that if we are better off than our fathers
in some things, they were better off than we in others
—or if some of us are better off than they, others of
us are worse off. Take this vast metropolis. The

inhabitants, indeed, of Belgravia or Grosvenor Square may perhaps enjoy life more than the Saxons, who lived on the banks of the Thames, under King Harold. But, after surveying their sumptuous tables and gilded ceilings, you must make a huge deduction for the cares, the ambition, the restlessness, the dyspepsia, the insupportable ennui, the gloomy scepticism even of these spoilt children of fortune. What say you, how-ever, to the imperfect physical development, and wan faces, that issue in multitudinous but filthy and ragged swarms from the human styes of St. Giles's, Spital-fields, Whitechapel, Bethnal Green, and even West-minster? Which drank in most joy from "the com-mon air, the earth, the skies"—they, or their Saxon predecessors?

Nobody denies, or doubts the progress of physical science. But the question is—Are the masses of man-kind certainly better or happier, or (all things con-sidered) much about the same?

There are gloomy people who are apt to conclude that while human nature remains what it is, the distribution of good and evil will remain pretty much what it has been. All men of sense agree, at least, in this, that the motives and incentives of human action are ever the same.

And here the free-traders have the advantage of the socialists. Private property, individual interest, and competition have been the only adequate incentives to voluntary labor, from the first page of recorded time. No other can be substituted. Mankind at large will never submit to hard work from mere patriotism of benevolence, or even a sense of moral duty. These are not, with the masses, the actual springs of severe and incessant toil, though they are, or ought to be, the regu-lators of the motive force.

In a large association of a thousand, or five hundred

families of working-men, you dilute self-interest till it is no stimulus at all. Another danger is, that the complicated affairs of such a partnership may soon become a fruitful source of dispute. Idleness and dissensions, ultimate failure and dissolution, are to be feared. These associations may succeed, on a large and universal scale, when they have a new human nature to work with.*

But though the socialists have no solid reply to these objections of the free-traders, the socialists can nevertheless retort with terrible effect.

"Look," says the disciple of Louis Blanc—"look at the resplendent gold and silver tissue, which I am weaving; and then look at my rags. Your fierce competition is doing the same everywhere. The cheapest and worst-paid workmen in the whole world must beat all the rest. That is the standard at which your system aims. You establish a deadly struggle who shall descend first to the lowest level. You will deteriorate and brutalise the masses of mankind."

Here the socialist has the free-trader on the hip.

But the practical man sees that the objections of the socialists to that wild and unregulated competition which the free-traders introduce, are no objections at all to a competition duly regulated. Competition, like the great physical forces of nature, is, when left to itself, destructive and devastating; but guided and restrained by human art, it is an instrument of human happiness as mighty, but as harmless and docile, as the steam-engine itself.

But there will be misery still! Freely granted. It is, as we all know too well, the sad condition of human

---

* This remark does not apply to ready money associations for the sale of finished articles, competing with the extravagant prices of retail dealers.

nature. But whatever our speculative opinions as to the past or future progress of mankind, one thing is plain. Knowledge and progress are not for those who sit still and leave things to take their own course. Wherever they are vouchsafed, they are the reward of humble labor and diligence to attain them—of anxious thought and foresight—of repeated trials, and indefatigable perseverance.

The true mode of using, guiding, and restraining competition, is a new field of knowledge which will well repay the labor of exploring and cultivating.

CHAPTER XXXIV.

" Farming should be carried on like any other trade."

YEOMEN living on their own small properties were
formerly the principal cultivators in England and
Wales. With no outgoing for rent, and none for wages
(except to a farm laborer or two, living in the farm-
house, on the farm-produce), the well-grown, robust
and ruddy English yeoman, was the most independent
of mankind. Such was the English subject of Charles
the First. Stupendous revolutions, and changes of all
sorts, mattered little to him.

Unhappily the race is now almost extinct—large
estates and large farms have absorbed them. We are
now told that farming must be carried on like every
other trade; that large farms, like large cotton mills,
large ironworks, or blast furnaces, can produce cheaper
than small ones, and, therefore, very properly supersede
and obliterate them.

Let us assume that to produce cheap is the chief end
of man. Let us concede at once, that virtue, health,
happiness, domestic plenty and content, are not to be
measured against one degree in the descending scale of
cheapness.

Can the large farmer produce more or cheaper than
the small one? A question on which the learned in
these matters are not agreed. *La petite culture* has its
well-instructed partisans, as well as *la grande culture*,
not only in England, but many more in France, Prus-

sia, Belgium, Holland, Norway, Denmark, Switzerland, Northern Italy, and the Tyrol.

We do not pretend to knowledge sufficient to form an opinion where Mr. Mill decides one way, and Mr. M'Culloch the other. We only venture to remind the reader of some considerations which may induce him to pause before he makes up his mind against Mr. Mill.*

Suppose a farm of a thousand acres in the hands of a single occupier. There is one occupying resident family, one homestead and farm-yard, one garden, one set of cows and oxen, one team of horses, one flock of sheep, one set of pigs, one yard of poultry, one manufactory of manure. Most of these, doubtless, on a larger scale than in a small farm. But suppose that same farm of a thousand acres divided into twenty farms of fifty acres each.†

You have now twenty occupying resident families, twenty homesteads and farm-yards, twenty gardens, twenty sets of cows and oxen, twenty smaller teams of horses, twenty smaller flocks of sheep, twenty sets of pigs, twenty yards of poultry, twenty manufactories of manure. If a proper tenure exist, so as to secure to the occupier what he ought to have, the full and exclusive reward of his own industry, you have every square yard of land under the eye of practical skill, unwearied vigilance, intense thrift, and unremitting labor. The wife, the sons, even the daughters, of the farmer, uncorrupted by the expensive habits and vicious pursuits of the town, find their pleasure in rustic toil. The daughters assist the mother in the care of the cows, the dairy, the poultry, the garden, and even the lighter but heal-

---

* And we refer to his far abler arguments.
† Or perhaps in many cases fifty farms of twenty acres, or even a greater number of less average.

thy and agreeable labor of the field. The sons help
their father in digging, ploughing, ditching, draining,
sowing, weeding, irrigating, clearing away and picking
up stones and rubbish, repairing the farm buildings.
The land has become the true, safe, and liberal SAV-
INGS BANK, where every half-hour of voluntary and
gratuitous labor is put out at large interest. Cheap but
effectual contrivances retain every particle and drop of
manure. Carefully mixed and preserved, it is used
and spread with a special reference to the wants and
capabilities of every square foot of ground. The gratuitous labor lavished on the farm can, either alone
or in concert with neighbors, undertake permanent
improvements ruinous and impossible to the farmer who
has to hire his workmen. The peasant proprietors of
Languedoc push cultivation to the mountain-top by
carrying up the earth in baskets on their shoulders.
In our damp northern climate the land wants drainage: in the sunny south, it wants irrigation. See the
concerted system of irrigation and the miles of water-
meadows created by the combined labors of peasant proprietors in the French departments of the Vaucluse and
Bouches du Rhone, in Lombardy, Tuscany, Piedmont,
Sienna, Lucca, and Bergamo—nay, even in the plain
of Valencia, in the west of Spain. So extensive practical systems of thorough drainage, inspired by the same
energetic motives, and using the same cheap but invincible means, would not only improve the best lands,
but reclaim bogs and morasses in England, Scotland,
and Ireland.

"A mere picture of the imagination!" cries the practical man. He never was more mistaken. Every
lineament of the peasant proprietor here is sketched
from the life.* You will find him at this hour just as

---

* As a synopsis of authorities on this subject and for the

we have described him all over Holland, Belgium, Norway, Denmark, Switzerland, the Tyrol, in Northern Italy, and in many parts of Germany and France. Take, for example, the banks of the Rhine. Forty years ago these lands were half cultivated, by very poor and wretched farmers at very low rents. Stein and Hardenberg, the great Prussian ministers, planted the peasant on the soil. Now, the banks of the Rhine are cultivated like a garden: the value of property there has wonderfully risen: the number of horses, cows, and oxen, sheep and pigs is greatly increased.

Nor need you fear the exhaustion of the land. The more you cultivate it in this way, the richer and more grateful it is found to be. In Belgium and the Low Countries, fertile and inexhaustible soils have thus been *created*. The residence and labor of man have transmuted sand into gold.

Suppose the whole of England, Scotland, and Ire-

---

result of personal observation, the reader is referred to a valuable book recently published, *The Social Condition and Education of the People in England and Europe*, by Joseph Kaye, Esq., London, 1850. But however just Mr. Kaye's views of the advantages of the continental tenures, and the mischief of the English ones, may be, he seems to expect far too much from a mere abolition of the law of primogeniture in England. Neither is he correct in assuming that continental titles are always so simple. The fact in France at least is far otherwise. Indeed, the introduction of the Code Napoleon, advantageous as it has been in making the law uniform throughout France, has had very little effect in simplifying the French law. There are arising continually legal questions, which require three different states of the French law to be examined and understood: the ancient, the intermediate, and the existing legislation, not to mention the new questions of construction that arise on the code. Such is the imperfection of human language, and such the subtilty of human affairs, that you cannot pen a document of five lines without raising questions of construction. Mr. Mill's observations on Peasant Proprietors are eminently deserving of attention. (Note of 1850.)

land, thus cultivated, the plenty of wheat, barley, oats, beans, peas, rye, hay, flax, oxen, cows, sheep, wool, poultry, eggs, garden stuff and fruit, would, we are assured, nourish more than the present population. The main producing forces of a country are man and the land: bring them together, and you develop an all-sufficing, superabounding plenty.

And might not food be cheap when most of the labor would be gratuitous?

Hitherto we have looked merely at cheapness. But not only is the earth changed and improved by man's residence and labor upon it: man himself is regenerated and saved by being restored to his original and natural occupation.

Many of the wan, sickly, degraded, restless, dangerous population of the towns are transformed into the well-grown, healthy, virtuous, and industrious cultivators of land. We are assured that it is the general diffusion of property in land that has mitigated the horrors of the late political convulsions on the Continent.

But then, it is said, granting that small farms should *produce* more than large ones, yet they *consume* more. Such multitudes live on the land. Granted. But this is exactly what is politically, as well as economically desirable, that consumers as well as producers, should be less congregated in large cities and more diffused over the country.

Without venturing to assert, therefore, that cultivation by small farms is *always* more advantageous than by large ones, we may safely conclude that it is *often* as advantageous and sometimes more so. We may safely affirm that it ought at least to have its place. Why should not both systems of cultivation exist? Why should not their mutual emulation and rivalry, side by side, enable us satisfactorily to solve the pro-

12

blem, which of the two is the most productive?   And
when the eye wanders over the extent of uncultivated
land in the United Kingdom, and the vast multitudes
of unemployed people, we cannot be wrong in holding
that there is here an opportunity of introducing cultivation by the occupying owner himself, though not
perhaps so great as Stein and Hardenburg found in
Prussia.

But how is it to be done?   How are small occupying
or peasant proprietors to be introduced with a scrupulous regard to the rights of property; for if you once
violate property, there is an end of all stimulus to
labor, and of all plenty and prosperity.

How is the tendency of landed property to accumu-
late in few hands to be met?

Persons unacquainted with the law spend their lives
from infancy to age, crying, "Abolish the law of entail
and primogeniture."

This remedy is no remedy at all.   It would not have
any appreciable effect.   As primogeniture and entail are
not the causes of the aggregation of property in a few
hands, so the abolition of these laws to-morrow would
leave the evil intact.   Much more efficacious and immediate remedies are demanded.

Let us examine these obnoxious laws of entail and
primogeniture, throwing aside as much as possible all
technical terms.   And first, of the law of entail.

An estate is said in popular language to be entailed
when it is settled by deed or will on a man and his
lineal descendants.   According to the ancient common
law, the course of descent prescribed by the donor
could not be interrupted, and the estate became in-
alienable.   But now for several centuries it has been
in the power of every tenant in tail, by certain as-
surances called fines and recoveries, to destroy the

entail, and expand the estate into a fee-simple, alienable, like any other fee-simple. Of late years these antiquated and circuitous modes of destroying entails, have been superseded by the statutory introduction of a more simple form of conveyance. Any tenant in tail may now destroy the estate-tail, and convert it into a common fee-simple by a disentailing deed merely. It is in vain that you settle on a man an estate-tail: he can destroy it to-morrow. All you can effectually do is to give him an estate for his own life, or the life of some other person now living.

Estates are kept in families, not by the law of entail, but by the power which exists of creating life estates.

A nobleman or wealthy commoner has an estate-tail. He could bar it—nothing prevents him. But what he does in practice, and what he would equally do (though in a different form), were there no such estate known to the law as an estate-tail, is this: On his marriage he limits to himself an estate for life, with remainders in tail to the children of the marriage successively. He becomes tenant for life, his son tenant in remainder. As soon as the eldest son becomes of age, he can make away with his interest, just as his father could before him; or father and son may join, and sometimes do join, in aliening the estate together. But in practice the more usual course is this: The son is about to marry, and is advised or chooses to settle a life-estate on himself, and to provide, after his death, for his wife and the issue of the marriage. He re-settles the estate. Perhaps the son wants a maintenance during his father's life; the father grants it out of his estate in possession; the father on his part wants to raise money on the estate, as he could have done had he retained the fee-tail or fee-simple, and the son in return for his previous maintenance allows the father to charge the estate. And so, in fact, estates are kept together and re-settled every generation, by the voluntary act, or, if you please, the family pride of their owners, and not by the law of entail. Suppose the law of entail abolished to-morrow, the very same arrangements substantially might be, and would be, made, although the machinery would be somewhat different.

Indeed, personal property may be settled by means of life-estates as effectually as landed property, and the fund may be, and often is, tied up just as long; although such a thing as an estate-tail in personal property never existed at any period of our law.

It is clear, therefore, that the law of entail does not cause the accumulation of landed property in few hands, and that it would exist, and exist to the same extent, were the law of entail abolished.

Is it the law of primogeniture?

As a general rule, freehold or copyhold land, in the absence of a will or settlement, descends to the eldest son. But it may be devised by will among all the children, or to any stranger, or it may be settled or charged in the life-time of the owner. It is only where there is the accident of intestacy that the law of primogeniture operates at all. In one county of England, Kent, and in some other places, land, in the event of intestacy, by the custom of Gavelkind there prevailing, goes to all the children equally. Yet the aggregation of landed property in few hands is not, that I am aware of, materially less in Kent than elsewhere.

The tenure of large masses of very valuable property is leasehold. In the event of intestacy, beneficial leasehold property is distributed amongst the next of kin. But when it is the subject of devise and settlement, it is rarely left to be so distributed.

So that where the law of primogeniture does not exist, the distribution of property is much the same as where it does. Practically, therefore, the law of primo-

geniture has little or no operation in producing an
aggregation of landed property in few hands.

The real sources of the existence of large landed
proprietors are these four: First, the natural aristocratic feelings of the English nation, prompting every
successful man to endeavor to found a family, and
every head of an old family to do his utmost to perpetuate and preserve it. Secondly and chiefly, the
liberty which the law allows of creating life-estates.
Thirdly, the unlimited power of devising. Fourthly,
the unlimited power of settling and charging. A bit
of land once drawn within the charmed circle of a settled estate, is practically taken out of the market.

Whether the aristocratic tendency of the English
nation be an evil or not, is a question on which men
will think differently, according to their political bias—
and this is not the place to discuss it. But those who
have maturely reflected on the immense stimulus which
it supplies for exertion, and on the materials which it
affords for stable and prescriptive government (on which
all prosperity, and public and private credit depend)
will be very slow to pronounce that it is an unmitigated evil. But evil or no evil, the aristocratic element exists everywhere in England—not in the House
of Peers only, but is latent in the bosom of the humble
peasant. It is universal and ineradicable.

This feeling avails itself of the power to create life-
estates, and of the power to devise and settle.

Will you have the law, then, interfere further than it
has already done, and prohibit life-estates? Is a man
not to be allowed to settle an estate or an income on his
wife or child for life, or to retain an estate for his own
life? Is he not to *bequeath* his property as he pleases?
Such an intermeddling with the disposition of private
property, would in this country be considered vexatious
and intolerable.

It is not uncommon to hear persons abusing the law, as if by some artificial arrangement it created and perpetuated large hereditary estates. Thoughtless but ill-informed partisans of the *let-alone* system, cry, Why does an artificial system of law raise up such abuses? Whereas the abuse, if such it be, is the act of an individual doing as he will with his own—it is the result of the let-alone system ; and the accomplishment of their wishes, so far from requiring *less,* would require *more* interference on the part of the law.

The law has already actively interfered to a considerable extent, to keep land in the market.

It has imposed great restraints on the acquisition of property by corporate bodies.

It has prohibited the tying-up of any property by natural persons, and the keeping the fee-simple out of the market, for a period beyond a life or lives in being. It adds twenty one years after, to allow for the possible incapacity of infancy. So jealous is the law of suffering a perpetuity, that every provision in a deed or will attempting to infringe or evade this salutary rule; is absolutely void. In effect the law is, that you cannot do more than create a life-estate. You cannot tie up your property, real or personal, beyond a life or lives in being, and twenty-one years after.

The law has even prohibited trusts for accumulation beyond certain limits.

But with these exceptions, all directed against accumulations, it has allowed the most perfect liberty of dealing with property of every description, real and personal.

This perfect liberty, coinciding with a minute subdivision of interests, necessarily existing in a highly-advanced state of society, has, like every other human good, its attendant evils. Titles are complex—alienation, difficult and expensive.

The true remedies for these evils, so far as they are

remediable, are very different from the abolition of the laws of primogeniture and entail.

Let us see, however, whether such remedies are not possible; remedies that would not only be ultimately effectual, but immediate in their operation.

But if these measures are to bear any really good fruit, several cautions are to be observed.

First: It must be borne in mind what a complicated system the law of real property in England actually, and to a great extent necessarily, is. Four or five years' hard study will enable a good head to acquire far more knowledge in pure and mixed mathematics than ever Sir Isaac Newton possessed; but four or five years' study of this single branch of the law of England will only produce a novice. A proprietor or purchaser who should act on the advice of such a tyro, would run an imminent risk of losing his estate or his money. But if the aid of profound learning and experience be essential when you are going to settle or purchase, much more essential is it when you are going to alter the law. Hasty and passionate alterations only make confusion worse confounded. Disappointment disgusts a whole generation, and in despair they bequeath the evil in an aggravated shape to their successors. We have been amending and symplifying the law of real property for twenty years. An experienced practitioner may perhaps tell you that it is now more complex and less certain than before the simplification began. When, therefore, you have made up your mind definitely as to what it is you really want, you must carefully avoid all quacks. You must go to men who have spent their lives in the study—such men as Sir Edward Sugden and Mr. Brodie.* They will tell you whether, and by what practical measures, you can attain your wishes.

---

* Written in 1850.

Next: The rights of property must be scrupulously and religiously respected. Once take liberties with property, and its value is gone; the stimulus to exertion, the great end of civilised society, is destroyed.

Yet, thirdly, the evil is pressing. A remedy is required that will operate, not merely in the time of our children or grandchildren, but NOW and WITH US. Depend on it, the aggregation of real property in too few hands not only obstructs the due cultivation of the soil, but greatly detracts from the present value of land, and is not unattended with imminent political danger.

Once more, there is a remedy which would undoubtedly be ultimately effectual, but which ought not to be adopted.

Merely to abolish primogeniture would (as we have seen) be doing nothing.

But to abolish the power of devising or settling lands after a man's death on his eldest son, and to make, as in France, the division of every man's land among all his children, or collateral relations in the same degree of consanguinity, *compulsory*—this, indeed, would, in a few generations, break up and break to pieces every estate large or small.

But the objections are obvious. The disintegration goes on to an extreme subdivision, or, rather, pulverisation of every estate, inconsistent with the residence of the cultivating occupier on the land, and therefore with effectual cultivation. Who will construct a house or homestead fit for the small estate, when on the death of the proprietor to-morrow, the tyrant law may sever the house from the land, or mince up the land into little bits? Accordingly we find that the little French proprietors do not generally live on their little estates (as they ought to do), but in villages. Nay, even the tendency of the land to re-unite is not without its evils. You often find the lands of a single small French proprietor lying not together, but dispersedly, in little patches at a great distance from each other.   It is moreover a common complaint that immense quantities of land are wasted, and infinite litigation and expense created by rights of way.   Again, liberty of disposition taken away, property loses one of its attractions. Children rendered independent of their parents are less subject to parental control.   Lastly, such a measure would utterly destroy the aristocratical branch of our mixed government, and that stability of political institutions which is indispensable to the development of national prosperity.

But violent and destructive as the ultimate operation of this potent medicine would be, it would in our time lie dormant in the system.   It is not, therefore, that instant and immediately efficacious remedy that we so urgently need.

Another inapplicable remedy which has been proposed is this—to limit the interests which a man may carve out of land, in order that every owner above the occupying tenant should have a fee-simple, which fee-simple he may sell, and do as he pleases with.

Some restraint on the interests which a man may now carve out of land, and on the capricious and unintelligible conditions, on which he may make the enjoyment of his property hinge, would probably be good.   But the owner of land would think it very hard that he should not be able to leave his wife a life-estate, or to provide out of it portions for his daughters or younger children, or to mortgage it a first and second time if he will, and a third and fourth time if he can.

Yet, if he is to be allowed to do these things, huge masses of property are at once by settlements and encumbrances kept out of the market.*   Nor is even

---

* Since these observations were written in 1850, statutes have been passed remedying the evil in some small degree.

this all. Men like to round their estates. They buy up and engross the little neighboring properties, and charge the whole estate with money to pay for the new purchase. Thus the complication of settlements and charges embraces and corrupts even the sound parts, like the hideous roots of a cancer.

Where are you to turn amidst these practical and apparently insuperable difficulties, which superficial observers never consider, but which present themselves at once to those who will condescend to look narrowly and steadily into the real facts?

Why do you want every owner to have an estate in fee-simple? Not for his sake, but for the sake of the public. It is because you want to enable him to SELL, and to enable an eager purchaser and certain and great improver to BUY. You want, moreover, to simplify the title.

In a word, you want an adequate POWER OF SALE. Now you have the true clue. Follow it, and it may lead you out of the labyrinth.

The first remedy, therefore, would seem to be this. You may enact that there shall always (notwithstanding all settlements and incumbrances, present or future) be some person (*e.g.*, the protector of the settlement), where there is one, some single will, that can, under proper guards, exercise a power of sale, not only over the fee-simple of the whole of the land, but over the fee-simple of every part of it. Then give the purchaser under that power of sale a new parliamentary title, in fee-simple, such as he has under the Irish Encumbered Estates Act, leaving the purchase-money to be invested at interest, under the sanction of public authority, for the benefit of those who had particular interests in the land; *so that the purchase-money instead of the land may hereafter be the subject of settlement and of claims and litigation*, should any arise.

A mode of investing the purchase-money on government security so as immediately and certainly to bring interest for every day, and so as that the *whole principal* (without increase or decrease, from an alteration in the value of money or otherwise) shall, when necessary, be forthcoming, for the benefit of the parties interested, is practicable without loss to the public.* Renewable government bonds would secure the whole principal from that decline in price to which investments in the funds are exposed; and if principal and interest were both made payable according to the tithe-rent charge tables, then neither principal nor interest could suffer by a decline in the value of money. In the mean time, the property, in its new shape, remains subject to all the interests, all the incumbrances, and all the claims to which it was subject when it was in the shape of land. But that land itself is now as effectually discharged from all these estates, interests, incumbrances, and claims, as if it were a portion of the virgin soil of a new colony. The purchaser of any portion of it takes a new, clear, unassailable title.

By such measures all the estates in England and Ireland, every field and bit of ground—not at some remote and uncertain period, but *now, immediately*— would be endued (wherever and whenever desirable) with a vital power of shuffling off the coil of complicated settlements and charges, without expense—and not only without injury to any one, but with great augmentation of value, and great benefit to all parties as well as to the public.

The law would say to every proprietor, "Settle or incumber your property as you please, within the same

---

* This security against decline in the value of the purchase-money was here proposed in 1850.

limits as now restrain you; but if you do choose to settle and incumber, the public interest requires that no land should be thereby taken out of the market. Without this provision experience shews that you will create a *mortmain* as bad as the *mortmain* of the middle ages. There must be no obstacle to the sale of land. There must be free-trade in land."

Such a state of things once existing, wherever a man is willing to give a good price for an estate, or a portion of it—for a field or a house—there is a vendor who can, for the mutual advantage of all concerned, sell, and make a new, indisputable, inexpensive title. No claimant is injured, for there are the renewable government bonds securing effectually principal and interest. Government makes no advances, but receives the purchase-money in trust for those to whom it belongs, and makes and pays fair interest.

Incumbrances on landed property would thus at once cease to prejudice the public; and facilities would everywhere be afforded for the creation of new freehold estates of moderate size, fit for the residence of proprietors. Titles would everywhere grow more simple, instead of growing more complex.

You do more violence to property than this, when you want land for a railway, a new street or dock, or any other public improvement. You take the land at a fair price, vendor or no vendor, in spite of the opposition of all concerned. Here the greatest of all public improvers, a resident and cultivating occupier, wants land: here, also, the vendor wants to sell; but as things now are, the law, disregarding the interests and wishes of the vendor, the purchaser, and the public, in effect forbids the sale.

Another measure is this—Applying the scheme of association to the purchase of estates.*

---

* Written in 1850.

A large English, Irish, or Scotch estate is brought into the market. The size and price is such that the number of competitors for it is very limited. The estate does not fetch its fair value. And the purchaser after all cannot pay for it. He lets a large portion of the purchase-money remain on mortgage. It is an incumbered estate still. But if it could be sold in smaller portions, it would be bid for by hundreds of anxious purchasers, who have small property to invest. Yet, to put it up, and sell, and convey it in lots, is sometimes impossible, often inconvenient, always highly and disproportionately expensive to every small purchaser, for every one has to investigate the title, and to obtain numerous conveyances from all the parties interested in the property. And after all you cannot say of the title of any of these purchasers that it is certainly safe.

Why should not a joint-stock company purchase such a large estate, especially where such a power of sale exists as we have described? The company acquires a large tract of good, or at least improvable, land in fee, with a new and clear title. It can divide it into convenient allotments of different sizes, for which, if resold, there would be a hot competition. The principle is this. A number of individuals combine to buy in undivided shares, and they afterwards divide their purchase.

But sad experience of building societies, and other societies on the same principle, has shown that, left to themselves, such companies *may* become the very hotbeds of jobbery and malversation. One reason is that the sub-purchases are on far too small a scale. The extent of the lands allotted in severalty is not enough to form a small farm. Possibly, when they are in the hands of persons of more substance and intelligence, these evils may be abated. But if not, then there is a clear case for legislative interference and regulation for the benefit of the public.

At all events, pecuniary liability beyond the amount of a man's subscription must be entirely taken away, and the object of the society must be restricted to the mere purchase of land and its subsequent division among the shareholders. As soon as this is accomplished, the society must be at an end, and its affairs wound up. The simplicity, both of the object and of the means, and the shortness of the society's duration, would alone be a great security against misconduct.

It is most respectfully suggested that this is the very crisis, when the great landed interest should favor and forward every safe and practicable scheme, to diffuse the ownership of land extensively and immediately among the nation at large.

Freehold land societies have been instituted to purchase 40s. freeholds, and so weaken the landed interest yet more in the House of Commons. But they are a doubled-edged weapon. Freehold land societies on a larger scale, which shall enable people in England or Ireland to purchase land in quantities varying from thirty to fifty acres, will be infinitely more popular than a society merely to purchase county votes, about which most people really care very little. These new proprietors will all be conservative in the best sense of the word. More than all this, if a safe but effectual reform in this matter is procrastinated, there is at hand danger of a very different and much more serious nature.

A third measure is this.

A power conferred on the *public* of taking, at its fair existing value, all unimproved and really waste land.*

The public, we have seen, has the deepest interest in developing the producing forces of a nation. The

---

* Written in 1850. But see the recent speech of Mr. Gladstone on Irish land tenure—one of the ablest ever delivered in parliament.

greatest of these is the land.   Millions of acres in England, Scotland, and Ireland are lying waste, while the public is maintaining at vast expense in idleness and vice thousands of paupers.   All that is wanting is to bring together man and the land.

If the owner will do it himself, let him ; but if he cannot or will not, the public must do it for him.

The public would not continue a landed proprietor. It would embark in no untried scheme.   It would only do what the Prussian government has actually done already.

It would sell and allot the land in portions large enough to enable a family by its own labor to maintain itself, but not smaller, prohibiting subdivision.   For the first two or three years with little rent.   Then at a very moderate rent.   The purchase-money of each lot to the occupying tenant should be fixed beforehand.   It ought to be no more than sufficient to save the public from loss, and it would then be very low.   The land remains as a security to the public.   The rent paid should go to the credit of the purchase-money, and (the state being resolved not to lose a farthing) of the interest on this purchase-money also.   The occupier would thus become a purchaser.

We have seen that superhuman industry, and concerted but gratuitous labor would immediately, certainly and profitably, subjugate, drain, and utterly change the most unpromising tracts.   This, as we have seen, is not theory, but constant and universal experience.

The state not only need lose nothing ; perhaps, it need not even advance anything.   The land itself would be ample and improving security for the purchase-money.

Can the owner complain ?   What does he say to the case of hundreds of other owners, whose valuable and improved land, perhaps building or ornamental land, is taken at its fair existing value, for railways, streets, or docks, the best of which improvements are of far less public utility? By this greatest of improvements, not only the land taken, but all the adjoining land whether it belong to him or anybody else, is augmented in value.

Much preliminary work in draining, levelling, clearing, would doubtless have to be done.

But here stand the idle laborers, spade in hand, beseeching for employment.

The influence of the scheme would be felt even by distant parishes. Railways could bring the preliminary laborer, as well as the cultivating occupier, from any distance.

What stands in the way? Once more, the wretched *let-alone* superstition.

CHAPTER XXXV.

" Repeal the Bubble Act."

So cried the experimentalists of 1825. And it was done. Here and there a warning voice was raised. Many a high-spirited but ruined and broken-hearted man knows now but too well how wise that warning was.

The plague, the cholera, the black death, the sweating sickness, are epidemics that have periodically devastated the earth. But mankind are subject to moral as well as physical epidemics. Ever and anon there stalk abroad palpable delusions that attack and prostrate the reason of whole nations. The wisest are sometimes the first victims. Such epidemics have been seen in our own time, both political and economical. They were no novelties, and as they were not the first, will doubtless not be the last.*

The tulipomania broke out in Holland about 1634, and before 1637 had spread over a large part of Europe. The cultivation of the tulip had been carried

---

* It is to be feared that the passionate and almost universal cry, some years ago, for the indiscriminate abolition of all import duties, under the specious but inappropriate name of FREE-TRADE, will turn out to have been one of these popular delusions.

Some future Chancellor of the Exchequer, however, wiser and more sagacious than his predecessors, will hereafter find in customs duties a great harvest for the financial sickle. Taxes, in the shape of import duties, will be imposed, at once eminently popular, very productive, and generally beneficial.

to great perfection in Holland. Many of the roots were valuable. People found that by buying up particular sorts they could sell them again at very high prices. Then came the fever of speculation. Tulips rose to such a price, that for a single root of a sort called the Viceroy were given, we are told, 2 lasts of wheat, 4 lasts of rye, 4 fat oxen, 3 fat swine, 12 fat sheep, 2 hogsheads of wine, 4 tuns of beer, 2 tuns of butter, 1000 pounds of cheese, a complete bed, a suit of clothes, and a silver beaker. Nay, joint-stock companies were formed, holding undivided shares in one root. People bought and sold tulips that never existed ; and were known by both buyer and seller not to exist. As now, on the stock exchange, there are the different manœuvres of putting on stock, differences, continuations, backwardations ; so it was then with tulip roots. It is said, that in three years ten millions of Dutch money thus changed hands in a single town in Holland. At length the bubble broke, and all the dealers were ruined. No, not all. In every delusion of this kind, long-headed knaves stand by, urge on the game, sell out in time, sweep the stakes into their pouch, and leave the swindled public to stare at one another.

After the lapse of a little more than eighty years, the Mississippi and South Sea schemes broke out in France and England. South Sea stock was bought and sold till the price was driven up to 1000. Bubble companies of the most absurd description were eagerly embraced as lucrative speculations or profitable investments. Plodding industry was despised by a nation of gamblers. Sages of the law, dignitaries of church, the principal nobility, male and female—nay, the Royal family and the Prince of Wales himself—were swept into the devouring whirlpool of Capel Court. Besides losing their venture, it was found that by becoming partners, many had risked their all. When at last the crash came, multitudes were ruined in fortune and character, and public credit itself was shaken.

This was the very crisis for wise legislation. Events had developed a mischief. Experience had demonstrated, amongst other things, that the unlicensed power to create joint-stock companies, not only nourished a spirit of gambling, but involved unwary purchasers and their innocent families in the awful liabilities of partnership.

Accordingly, parliament legislated by the light of experience, and in 1719 the Bubble Act* was passed, putting a stop to joint-stock companies without the licence of parliament or the Crown.

The mischief was kept under for little more than a century. But in 1825 parliament was persuaded by the disciples of the let-alone system (which superstition was then even more accredited than it is now) to repeal the Bubble Act. In 1826 an inundation of joint-stock schemes exceeded anything that had been ever before known. A fearful revulsion again involved multitudes in ruin.

In 1845, the same gambling returned, and the same destruction.†

And ever since 1825, how many instances have been continually occurring of men of property unwarily purchasing, or accepting as a gift or bequest, or taking for the sake of encouraging a useful enterprise, a share or two in an unincorporated joint-stock bank, or other trading or manufacturing company! A lawyer, indeed,

---

* This Act of Parliament is known as Sir John Barnard's Act. Sir John Barnard, for sagacity, integrity, and experience, was one of the most eminent persons who have ever represented the city of London since its foundation. His statue was placed in the Royal Exchange during his life, and after his death his fellow-citizens inscribed on the pedestal the words, "HUMANI GENERIS DECUS."

† This passage was written in 1850. Unhappily the sad experience of 1866 confirms and illustrates the truth of the remarks in this chapter.

would have told them that they ought not to touch such a thing with a pair of tongs. But mankind are not, and cannot be skilled in the law, and hate those that are. Suddenly they find themselves brought in as partners, and stript of their last acre and last shilling. Indeed, it is in vain that men abstain. An executor, far too prudent to hold shares in an unincorporated, joint-stock company, administers an estate and pays the legacies. He afterwards finds that a share which his testator once held in a joint-stock undertaking brings on the estate large liabilities. He has committed a *devastavit* by paying legacies, and has to that extent become himself personally liable for the debts of a company, of whose very existence he was ignorant.

"Oh," say the partisans of the let-alone system, "men will learn wisdom by experience." * Alas! suppose they did—wisdom comes too late, when a man is ruined. And what say you to his children? Up rises another and another generation to be, like their fathers, ruined first, and taught afterwards. You might, on the same principle, repeal all the laws against gaming. Indeed, the Bubble Act was directed against the most ruinous sort of gaming.

"What!" it will be said, "are there to be no joint-stock companies?" Quite the contrary. There are to be more than there are now, and safer and better. Association is a powerful engine for increasing national wealth, but, like all other human institutions, it requires regulation and control.

These observations do not touch companies incorporated by act of parliament or royal charter. Such companies have a public sanction, which is *some·security* that their objects are good, and of such magnitude or public interest as to justify the association of many capi-

---

* We have already observed on this fallacy (page 80).

tals. A person subscribing to incorporated companies where the capital is paid up is safe.

But they are levelled at unincorporated joint-stock companies.* Every man that holds even a fractional part of a small share, an interest to the value of a shilling (though he has no control over the entrance of partners into the firm, and very little over the management) is here personally liable to every creditor of the concern down to his last farthing. Many of such companies really are, what the Bubble Act in terms made them, public nuisances—and all of them are subject to become so.

Unincorporated joint-stock companies are of two sorts—those that really answer, and those that do not.

Those that really answer would answer just as well with a limited liability in the shareholders—perhaps much better, for more men of capital and judgment would then belong to them. Those that do not answer are silently involving and swamping all their shareholders in unlimited liabilities: they are really nuisances, and the sooner they are again put an end to by law the better.

All manufacturing and trading concerns of moderate size are best carried on, as they usually are, by the care, experience, and undivided interest of a single individual. No manager of a joint-stock concern can ever display the judgment and vigilance of a man grown grey in the conduct of his own business. When such a concern is too large for the means of a single individual, or other motives prompt to association, a common partnership, with the unlimited responsibility of each partner to his co-partner, and to the world, meets the necessities of the case, and provides security for the public. But in such a private partnership each partner

---

* This Chapter was written in 1850.

has a veto on the introduction of every new partner. He can take care that none but a man of integrity, property, activity, ability, and experience enters the firm. He may therefore with propriety, and comparative safety, be made responsible for the acts of co-partners of his own selection.

You next ascend to enterprises of a public nature, or too great for private means—to railways, canals, harbors, gas companies, water companies, steam navigation companies. These are properly undertaken by joint-stock companies, with transferable shares. But wherever they exist without legislative interference, this is their condition. Anybody may purchase a share. Anybody's executors, or specific legatees, or assignees in bankruptcy or insolvency, may become partners. Nobody can tell into what hands the concern may fall. Unlimited liability is so dangerous that if men of property duly appreciated their position, no man of property would belong to companies where it exists. Who would even hold a share in a railway company if he were personally responsible for the debts and liabilites of the concern ? *

Accordingly, many of these companies, like all railway companies, are incorporated either by act of parliament or royal charter.

But many unincorporated joint-stock companies remain, the liability of whose members is unlimited. And many more which might be formed for the most useful public objects, are nipped in the bud, because there are no means of effectually limiting the liability of subscribers without a charter or act of parliament.†

---

* These obsevations were written before the statutes introducing limited liability.

† Since these observations were written parliament has adopted the principle of limited liability, but with very imperfect regulations. Such companies should not exist without licence from competent authority, and the margin between the

Experience has shewn that shareholders, even in incorporated companies, need infinitely more control than they at present possess over directors and accounts.

And why should they not possess it? If the members of a private partnership fall out, any one of them may by law compel the accounts to be taken in the Court of Chancery.*

Why should not the members of a joint-stock company have a power more easily, quickly, and cheaply exercisable?

Why should not a cheaper and more effectual tribunal be established for supervising the accounts of every railway, and every joint-stock company? Most manifestly the interest of every shareholder requires it. The majority of shareholders are themselves no more capable of understanding or checking the accounts furnished by directors than of deciphering the hieroglyphics on Cleopatra's obelisk; nor have they the means of properly delegating the power. No directors ought to be trusted with such licence in dealing with large sums. What stands in the way of an effectual system of supervision? The wretched let-alone superstition.

When the limits within which joint-stock companies should exist are defined—when a really limited liability of shareholders, and an easy and effectual control over directors and their expenditure is introduced—then, and not till then, will be seen what association can achieve.

How many men of ample property, grown grey in business, but retired from active life, now waste the

---

subscribed and paid up capital, if it exist, should be greatly reduced.

* It has been said "that partnership accounts go into that court, but do not come out."

maturity of their judgment and experience, and shorten their lives in doing nothing? What a field might be opened to their practical wisdom, for the public benefit at home and abroad, on land and sea, by a safe system of association.

INDEX.

CATALOGUE

OF

PRACTICAL AND SCIENTIFIC BOOKS,

PUBLISHED BY

HENRY CAREY BAIRD,

INDUSTRIAL PUBLISHER,

No. 406 WALNUT STREET,

PHILADELPHIA.

☞ Any of the Books comprised in this Catalogue will be sent by mail, free of postage, at the publication price.

☞ My NEW AND ENLARGED CATALOGUE, 95 pages 8vo., with full descriptions of Books, will be sent, free of postage, to any one who will favor me with his address.

ARMENGAUD, AMOUROUX, AND JOHNSON.—THE PRACTICAL DRAUGHTSMAN'S BOOK OF INDUSTRIAL DESIGN, AND MACHINIST'S AND ENGINEER'S DRAWING COMPANION: Forming a complete course of Mechanical Engineering and Architectural Drawing. From the French of M. Armengaud the elder, Prof. of Design in the Conservatoire of Arts and Industry, Paris, and MM. Armengaud the younger and Amouroux, Civil Engineers. Rewritten and arranged, with additional matter and plates, selections from and examples of the most useful and generally employed mechanism of the day. By WILLIAM JOHNSON, Assoc. Inst. C. E., Editor of "The Practical Mechanic's Journal." Illustrated by 50 folio steel plates and 50 wood-cuts. A new edition, 4to.   . $10 00

ARLOT.—A COMPLETE GUIDE FOR COACH PAINTERS. Translated from the French of M. ARLOT, Coach Painter; late Master Painter for eleven years with M. Ehrler, Coach Manufacturer, Paris. With important American additions .   . $1 25

ARROWSMITH.—PAPER-HANGER'S COMPANION: A Treatise in which the Practical Operations of the Trade are Systematically laid down: with Copious Directions Preparatory to Papering; Preventives against the Effect of Damp on Walls; the Various Cements and Pastes adapted to the Several Purposes of the Trade; Observations and Directions for the Panelling and Ornamenting of Rooms, &c. By JAMES ARROWSMITH. 12mo., cloth $1 25

BAIRD.—THE AMERICAN COTTON SPINNER, AND MANA-
GER'S AND CARDER'S GUIDE:

A Practical Treatise on Cotton Spinning; giving the Dimensions and Speed of Machinery, Draught and Twist Calculations, etc.; with notices of recent Improvements: together
with Rules and Examples for making changes in the sizes and
numbers of Roving and Yarn. Compiled from the papers of
the late ROBERT H. BAIRD. 12mo.   .   .   . $1 50

BAKER.—LONG-SPAN RAILWAY BRIDGES:

Comprising Investigations of the Comparative Theoretical and
Practical Advantages of the various Adopted or Proposed Type
Systems of Construction; with numerous Formulæ and Ta-
bles. By B. Baker. 12mo. $2 00

BAKEWELL.—A MANUAL OF ELECTRICITY—PRACTICAL AND
THEORETICAL:

By F. C. BAKEWELL, Inventor of the Copying Telegraph. Second Edition. Revised and enlarged. Illustrated by numerous engravings. . 12mo. Cloth   .   .   .   .

BEANS—A TREATISE ON RAILROAD CURVES AND THE LO-
CATION OF RAILROADS:

By E. W. BEANS, C. E. 12mo.   .   .   . $2 00

BLENKARN.—PRACTICAL SPECIFICATIONS OF WORKS EXE-
CUTED IN ARCHITECTURE, CIVIL AND MECHANICAL
ENGINEERING, AND IN ROAD MAKING AND SEWER-
ING:

To which are added a series of practically useful Agreements
and Reports. By JOHN BLENKARN. Illustrated by fifteen
large folding plates. 8vo. $9 00

BLINN.—A PRACTICAL WORKSHOP COMPANION FOR TIN,
SHEET-IRON, AND COPPER-PLATE WORKERS:

Containing Rules for Describing various kinds of Patterns
used by Tin, Sheet-iron, and Copper-plate Workers; Practical
Geometry; Mensuration of Surfaces and Solids; Tables of the
Weight of Metals, Lead Pipe, etc.; Tables of Areas and Cir-
cumferences of Circles; Japans, Varnishes, Lackers, Cements,
Compositions, etc. etc. By LEROY J. BLINN, Master Mechanic. With over One Hundred Illustrations. 12mo. $2 50

BOOTH.—MARBLE WORKER'S MANUAL:

Containing Practical Information respecting Marbles in general, their Cutting, Working, and Polishing; Veneering of Marble; Mosaics; Composition and Use of Artificial Marble, Stuccos, Cements, Receipts, Secrets, etc. etc. Translated from the French by M. L. Booth. With an Appendix concerning American Marbles. 12mo., cloth   .   . $1 50

BOOTH AND MORFIT.—THE ENCYCLOPEDIA OF CHEMISTRY, PRACTICAL AND THEORETICAL:

Embracing its application to the Arts, Metallurgy, Mineralogy, Geology, Medicine, and Pharmacy. By JAMES C. BOOTH, Melter and Refiner in the United States Mint, Professor of Applied Chemistry in the Franklin Institute, etc., assisted by CAMPBELL MORFIT, author of "Chemical Manipulations," etc. Seventh edition. Complete in one volume, royal 8vo., 978 pages, with numerous wood-cuts and other illustrations. $5 00

BOWDITCH.—ANALYSIS, TECHNICAL VALUATION, PURIFICATION, AND USE OF COAL GAS:

By Rev. W. R. Bowditch. Illustrated with wood engravings. 8vo. $6 50

BOX.—PRACTICAL HYDRAULICS:

A Series of Rules and Tables for the use of Engineers, etc. By Thomas Box. 12mo. $2 50

BUCKMASTER.—THE ELEMENTS OF MECHANICAL PHYSICS:

By J. C. Buckmaster, late Student in the Government School of Mines; Certified Teacher of Science by the Department of Science and Art; Examiner in Chemistry and Physics in the Royal College of Preceptors; and late Lecturer in Chemistry and Physics of the Royal Polytechnic Institute. Illustrated with numerous engravings. In one vol. 12mo.   . $1 50

BULLOCK.—THE AMERICAN COTTAGE BUILDER:

A Series of Designs, Plans, and Specifications, from $200 to to $20,000 for Homes for the People; together with Warming, Ventilation, Drainage, Painting, and Landscape Gardening. By John Bullock, Architect, Civil Engineer, Mechanician, and Editor of "The Rudiments of Architecture and Building," etc. Illustrated by 75 engravings. In one vol. 8vo. $3 50

BULLOCK.—THE RUDIMENTS OF ARCHITECTURE AND BUILDING:

For the use of Architects, Builders, Draughtsmen, Machinists, Engineers, and Mechanics. Edited by JOHN BULLOCK, author of "The American Cottage Builder." Illustrated by 250 engravings. In one volume 8vo. . . . $3 50

BURGH.—PRACTICAL ILLUSTRATIONS OF LAND AND MARINE ENGINES:

Showing in detail the Modern Improvements of High and Low Pressure, Surface Condensation, and Super-heating, together with Land and Marine Boilers. By N. P. BURGH, Engineer. Illustrated by twenty plates, double elephant folio, with text. $21 00

BURGH.—PRACTICAL RULES FOR THE PROPORTIONS OF MODERN ENGINES AND BOILERS FOR LAND AND MARINE PURPOSES.

By N. P. Burgh, Engineer. 12mo. . . . $2 00

BURGH.—THE SLIDE-VALVE PRACTICALLY CONSIDERED:

By N. P. BURGH, author of "A Treatise on Sugar Machinery," "Practical Illustrations of Land and Marine Engines," "A Pocket-Book of Practical Rules for Designing Land and Marine Engines, Boilers," etc. etc. etc. Completely illustrated. 12mo. $2 00

BYRN.—THE COMPLETE PRACTICAL BREWER:

Or, Plain, Accurate, and Thorough Instructions in the Art of Brewing Beer, Ale, Porter, including the Process of making Bavarian Beer, all the Small Beers, such as Root-beer, Ginger-pop, Sarsaparilla-beer, Mead, Spruce beer, etc. etc. Adapted to the use of Public Brewers and Private Families. By M. LA FAYETTE BYRN, M. D. With illustrations. 12mo. $1 25

BYRN.—THE COMPLETE PRACTICAL DISTILLER:

Comprising the most perfect and exact Theoretical and Practical Description of the Art of Distillation and Rectification; including all of the most recent improvements in distilling apparatus; instructions for preparing spirits from the numerous vegetables, fruits, etc.; directions for the distillation and preparation of all kinds of brandies and other spirits, spirituous and other compounds, etc. etc.; all of which is so simplified that it is adapted not only to the use of extensive distillers, but for every farmer, or others who may wish to engage in the art of distilling. By M. LA FAYETTE BYRN, M. D. With numerous engravings. In one volume, 12mo. $1 50

BYRNE.—POCKET BOOK FOR RAILROAD AND CIVIL ENGI-
NEERS:

Containing New, Exact, and Concise Methods for Laying out
Railroad Curves, Switches, Frog Angles and Crossings: the
Staking out of work; Levelling; the Calculation of Cut-
tings; Embankments; Earth-work, etc. By OLIVER BYRNE.
Illustrated, 18mo., full bound $1 75

BYRNE.—THE HANDBOOK FOR THE ARTISAN, MECHANIC,
AND ENGINEER:

By OLIVER BYRNE. Illustrated by 185 Wood Engravings. 8vo.
$5 00

BYRNE.—THE ESSENTIAL ELEMENTS OF PRACTICAL ME-
CHANICS:

For Engineering Students, based on the Principle of Work.
By OLIVER BYRNE. Illustrated by Numerous Wood Engravings, 12mo. $3 63

BYRNE.—THE PRACTICAL METAL-WORKER'S ASSISTANT:

Comprising Metallurgic Chemistry; the Arts of Working all
Metals and Alloys; Forging of Iron and Steel; Hardening and
Tempering; Melting and Mixing; Casting and Founding;
Works in Sheet Metal; the Processes Dependent on the
Ductility of the Metals; Soldering; and the most Improved
Processes and Tools employed by Metal-Workers. With the
Application of the Art of Electro-Metallurgy to Manufactu-
ring Processes; collected from Original Sources, and from the
Works of Holtzapffel, Bergeron, Leupold, Plumier, Napier, and
others. By OLIVER BYRNE. A New, Revised, and improved
Edition, with Additions by John Scoffern, M. B , William Clay,
Wm. Fairbairn, F. R. S., and James Napier. With Five Hun-
dred and Ninety-two Engravings; Illustrating every Branch
of the Subject. In one volume, 8vo. 652 pages . $7 00

BYRNE.—THE PRACTICAL MODEL CALCULATOR:

For the Engineer, Mechanic, Manufacturer of Engine Work,
Naval Architect, Miner, and Millwright. By OLIVER BYRNE.
1 volume, 8vo., nearly 600 pages $4 50

BEMROSE.—MANUAL OF WOOD CARVING: With Practical Illustrations for Learners of the Art, and Original and Selected designs. By WILLIAM BEMROSE, Jr. With an Introduction by
LLEWELLYN JEWITT, F. S. A., etc. With 128 Illustrations. 4to.,
cloth $3 00

BAIRD.—PROTECTION OF HOME LABOR AND HOME PRO-
DUCTIONS NECESSARY TO THE PROSPERITY OF THE
AMERICAN FARMER:
By HENRY CAREY BAIRD. 8vo., paper 10

BAIRD.—THE RIGHTS OF AMERICAN PRODUCERS, AND THE
WRONGS OF BRITISH FREE TRADE REVENUE REFORM.
By HENRY CAREY BAIRD. (1870) 5

BAIRD.—SOME OF THE FALLACIES OF BRITISH-FREE-TRADE
REVENUE-REFORM.
Two Letters to Prof. A. L. Perry, of Williams College, Mass. By
HENRY CAREY BAIRD. (1871.) Paper 5

BAIRD.—STANDARD WAGES COMPUTING TABLES:
An Improvement in all former Methods of Computation, so arranged that wages for days, hours, or fractions of hours, at a spe-
cified rate per day or hour, may be ascertained at a glance. By
T. SPANGLER BAIRD. Oblong folio $5 00

BAUERMAN.—TREATISE ON THE METALLURGY OF IRON.
Illustrated. 12mo. $2 50

BICKNELL'S VILLAGE BUILDER.
55 large plates. 4to. $10 00

BISHOP.—A HISTORY OF AMERICAN MANUFACTURES:
From 1608 to 1866; exhibiting the Origin and Growth of the Prin-
cipal Mechanic Arts and Manufactures, from the Earliest Colonial
Period to the Present Time; By J. LEANDER BISHOP, M. D., ED-
WARD YOUNG, and EDWIN T. FREEDLEY. Three vols. 8vo.,
$10 00

BOX.—A PRACTICAL TREATISE ON HEAT AS APPLIED TO
THE USEFUL ARTS:
For the use of Engineers, Architects, etc. By THOMAS BOX, author of "Practical Hydraulics." Illustrated by 14 plates, containing 114 figures. 12mo. $4 25

CABINET MAKER'S ALBUM OF FURNITURE:
Comprising a Collection of Designs for the Newest and Most
Elegant Styles of Furniture. Illustrated by Forty-eight Large
and Beautifully Engraved Plates. In one volume, oblong
$5 00

CHAPMAN.—A TREATISE ON ROPE-MAKING:
As practised in private and public Rope-yards, with a Description
of the Manufacture, Rules, Tables of Weights, etc., adapted to the
Trade; Shipping, Mining, Railways, Builders, etc. By ROBERT
CHAPMAN. 24mo. $1 50

CRAIK.—THE PRACTICAL AMERICAN MILLWRIGHT AND MILLER.

Comprising the Elementary Principles of Mechanics, Mechanism, and Motive Power, Hydraulics and Hydraulic Motors, Mill-dams, Saw Mills, Grist Mills, the Oat Meal Mill, the Barley Mill, Wool Carding, and Cloth Fulling and Dressing, Wind Mills, Steam Power, &c. By DAVID CRAIK, Millwright. Illustrated by numerous wood engravings, and five folding plates. 1 vol. 8vo. $5 00

CAMPIN.—A PRACTICAL TREATISE ON MECHANICAL ENGINEERING:

Comprising Metallurgy, Moulding, Casting, Forging, Tools, Workshop Machinery, Mechanical Manipulation, Manufacture of Steam-engines, etc. etc. With an Appendix on the Analysis of Iron and Iron Ores. By FRANCIS CAMPIN, C. E. To which are added, Observations on the Construction of Steam Boilers, and Remarks upon Furnaces used for Smoke Prevention; with a Chapter on Explosions. By R. Armstrong, C. E., and John Bourne. Rules for Calculating the Change Wheels for Screws on a Turning Lathe, and for a Wheel-cutting Machine. By J. LA NICCA. Management of Steel, including Forging, Hardening, Tempering, Annealing, Shrinking, and Expansion. And the Case-hardening of Iron. By G. EDE. 8vo. Illustrated with 29 plates and 100 wood engravings.

$6 00

CAMPIN.—THE PRACTICE OF HAND-TURNING IN WOOD, IVORY, SHELL, ETC.:

With Instructions for Turning such works in Metal as may be required in the Practice of Turning Wood, Ivory, etc. Also an Appendix on Ornamental Turning. By FRANCIS CAMPIN, with Numerous Illustrations, 12mo., cloth . . $3 00

CAPRON DE DOLE.—DUSSAUCE.—BLUES AND CARMINES OF INDIGO.

A Practical Treatise on the Fabrication of every Commercial Product derived from Indigo. By FELICIEN CAPRON DE DOLE. Translated, with important additions, by Professor H. DUSSAUCE. 12mo.

CAREY.—THE WORKS OF HENRY C. CAREY:

CONTRACTION OR EXPANSION? REPUDIATION OR RE-
SUMPTION? Letters to Hon. Hugh McCulloch. 8vo.   38

FINANCIAL CRISES, their Causes and Effects. 8vo. paper
                                                   25

HARMONY OF INTERESTS; Agricultural, Manufacturing,
and Commercial. 8vo., paper $1 00
        Do.   do.   cloth   .   .   . $1 50

LETTERS TO THE PRESIDENT OF THE UNITED STATES.
Paper $1 00

MANUAL OF SOCIAL SCIENCE. Condensed from Carey's
"Principles of Social Science." By KATE McKEAN. 1 vol.
12mo. $2 25

MISCELLANEOUS WORKS: comprising "Harmony of Interests," "Money," "Letters to the President," "French and
American Tariffs," "Financial Crises," "The Way to Outdo
England without Fighting Her," "Resources of the Union,"
"The Public Debt," "Contraction or Expansion," "Review
of the Decade 1857—'67," "Reconstruction," etc. etc. 1 vol.
8vo., cloth $4 50

MONEY: A LECTURE before the N. Y. Geographical and Statistical Society. 8vo., paper 25

PAST, PRESENT, AND FUTURE. 8vo. .   .   . $2 50

PRINCIPLES OF SOCIAL SCIENCE. 3 volumes 8vo., cloth
                                                $10 00

REVIEW OF THE DECADE 1857—'67. 8vo., paper   50

RECONSTRUCTION: INDUSTRIAL, FINANCIAL, AND PO-
LITICAL. Letters to the Hon. Henry Wilson, U. S. S. 8vo
paper   50

THE PUBLIC DEBT, LOCAL AND NATIONAL. How to
provide for its discharge while lessening the burden of Taxation. Letter to David A. Wells, Esq., U. S. Revenue Commission. 8vo., paper 25

THE RESOURCES OF THE UNION. A Lecture read, Dec.
1865, before the American Geographical and Statistical Society, N. Y., and before the American Association for the Advancement of Social Science, Boston   .   .   . 50

THE SLAVE TRADE, DOMESTIC AND FOREIGN; Why it
Exists, and How it may be Extinguished. 12mo., cloth $1 50

LETTERS ON INTERNATIONAL COPYRIGHT. (1867.)
Paper 50

REVIEW OF THE FARMERS' QUESTION. (1870.) Paper 25

RESUMPTION! HOW IT MAY PROFITABLY BE BROUGHT
ABOUT. (1869.) 8vo., paper 50

REVIEW OF THE REPORT OF HON. D. A. WELLS, Special
Commissioner of the Revenue. (1869.) 8vo., paper 50

SHALL WE HAVE PEACE? Peace Financial and Peace Political. Letters to the President Elect. (1868.) 8vo., paper 50

THE FINANCE MINISTER AND THE CURRENCY, AND
THE PUBLIC DEBT. (1868.) 8vo., paper . . 50

THE WAY TO OUTDO ENGLAND WITHOUT FIGHTING
HER. Letters to Hon. Schuyler Colfax. (1865.) 8vo., paper
$1 00

WEALTH! OF WHAT DOES IT CONSIST? (1870.) Paper 25

CAMUS.—A TREATISE ON THE TEETH OF WHEELS:
Demonstrating the best forms which can be given to them for the
purposes of Machinery, such as Mill-work and Clock-work. Translated from the French of M. CAMUS. By JOHN I. HAWKINS.
Illustrated by 40 plates. 8vo. $3 00

COXE.—MINING LEGISLATION.
A paper read before the Am. Social Science Association. By
ECKLEY B. COXE. Paper 20

COLBURN.—THE GAS-WORKS OF LONDON:
Comprising a sketch of the Gas-works of the city, Process of
Manufacture, Quantity Produced, Cost, Profit, etc. By ZERAH
COLBURN. 8vo., cloth 75

COLBURN.—THE LOCOMOTIVE ENGINE:
Including a Description of its Structure, Rules for Estimating its Capabilities, and Practical Observations on its Construction and Management. By ZERAH COLBURN. Illustrated. A
new edition. 12mo. $1 25

COLBURN AND MAW.—THE WATER-WORKS OF LONDON:
Together with a Series of Articles on various other Water-
works. By ZERAH COLBURN and W. MAW. Reprinted from
"Engineering." In one volume, 8vo. . . $4 00

DAGUERREOTYPIST AND PHOTOGRAPHER'S COMPANION:
12mo., cloth $1 25

DIRCKS.—PERPETUAL MOTION:
> Or Search for Self-Motive Power during the 17th, 18th, and
> 19th centuries. Illustrated from various authentic sources in
> Papers, Essays, Letters, Paragraphs, and numerous Patent
> Specifications, with an Introductory Essay by HENRY DIRCKS,
> C. E. Illustrated by numerous engravings of machines.
> 12mo., cloth $3 50

DIXON.—THE PRACTICAL MILLWRIGHT'S AND ENGINEER'S
GUIDE:
> Or Tables for Finding the Diameter and Power of Cogwheels;
> Diameter, Weight, and Power of Shafts; Diameter and Strength
> of Bolts, etc. etc. By THOMAS DIXON. 12mo., cloth. $1 50

DUNCAN.—PRACTICAL SURVEYOR'S GUIDE:
> Containing the necessary information to make any person, of
> common capacity, a finished land surveyor without the aid of
> a teacher. By ANDREW DUNCAN. Illustrated. 12mo., cloth.
> $1 25

DUSSAUCE.—A NEW AND COMPLETE TREATISE ON THE
ARTS OF TANNING, CURRYING, AND LEATHER DRESS-
ING:
> Comprising all the Discoveries and Improvements made in
> France, Great Britain, and the United States. Edited from
> Notes and Documents of Messrs. Sallerou, Grouvelle, Duval,
> Dessables, Labarraque, Payen, René, De Fontenelle, Mala-
> peyre, etc. etc. By Prof. H. DUSSAUCE, Chemist. Illustrated
> by 212 wood engravings. 8vo. $10 00

DUSSAUCE.—A GENERAL TREATISE ON THE MANUFACTURE
OF SOAP, THEORETICAL AND PRACTICAL:
> Comprising the Chemistry of the Art, a Description of all the Raw
> Materials and their Uses. Directions for the Establishment of a
> Soap Factory, with the necessary Apparatus, Instructions in the
> Manufacture of every variety of Soap, the Assay and Determination
> of the Value of Alkalies, Fatty Substances, Soaps, etc. etc. By
> PROFESSOR H. DUSSAUCE. With an Appendix, containing Ex-
> tracts from the Reports of the International Jury on Soaps, as
> exhibited in the Paris Universal Exposition, 1867, numerous
> Tables, etc. etc. Illustrated by engravings. In one volume 8vo.
> of over 800 pages $10 00

DUSSAUCE.—PRACTICAL TREATISE ON THE FABRICATION
OF MATCHES, GUN COTTON, AND FULMINATING POW-
DERS.
> By Professor H. DUSSAUCE. 12mo. . . . $3 00

DUSSAUCE.—A PRACTICAL GUIDE FOR THE PERFUMER:
Being a New Treatise on Perfumery the most favorable to the
Beauty without being injurious to the Health, comprising a
Description of the substances used in Perfumery, the Formu-
læ of more than one thousand Preparations, such as Cosme-
tics, Perfumed Oils, Tooth Powders, Waters, Extracts, Tinc-
tures, Infusions, Vinaigres, Essential Oils, Pastels, Creams,
Soaps, and many new Hygienic Products not hitherto described.
Edited from Notes and Documents of Messrs. Debay, Lunel,
etc. With additions by Professor H. DUSSAUCE, Chemist. 12mo.
$3 00

DUSSAUCE.—A GENERAL TREATISE ON THE MANUFACTURE
OF VINEGAR, THEORETICAL AND PRACTICAL.
Comprising the various methods, by the slow and the quick processes, with Alcohol, Wine, Grain, Cider, and Molasses, as well
as the Fabrication of Wood Vinegar, etc. By Prof. H. DUSSAUCE.
12mo. $5 00

DUPLAIS.—A COMPLETE TREATISE ON THE DISTILLATION
AND MANUFACTURE OF ALCOHOLIC LIQUORS:
From the French of M. DUPLAIS. Translated and Edited by M.
McKENNIE, M D. Illustrated by numerous large plates and wood
engravings of the best apparatus calculated for producing the
finest products. In one vol. royal 8vo. $10 00
☞ This is a treatise of the highest scientific merit and of the
greatest practical value, surpassing in these respects, as well as
in the variety of its contents, any similar volume in the English
language.

DE GRAFF.—THE GEOMETRICAL STAIR-BUILDERS' GUIDE:
Being a Plain Practical System of Hand-Railing, embracing all
its necessary Details, and Geometrically Illustrated by 22 Steel
Engravings: together with the use of the most approved principles of Practical Geometry. By SIMON DE GRAFF, Architect.
4to. $5 00

DYER AND COLOR-MAKER'S COMPANION:
Containing upwards of two hundred Receipts for making Colors, on the most approved principles, for all the various styles
and fabrics now in existence; with the Scouring Process, and
plain Directions for Preparing, Washing-off, and Finishing the
Goods. In one vol. 12mo. $1 25

EASTON.—A PRACTICAL TREATISE ON STREET OR HORSE-POWER RAILWAYS:

Their Location, Construction, and Management; with General Plans and Rules for their Organization and Operation; together with Examinations as to their Comparative Advantages over the Omnibus System, and Inquiries as to their Value for Investment; including Copies of Municipal Ordinances relating thereto. By ALEXANDER EASTON, C. E. Illustrated by 23 plates, 8vo., cloth $2 00

FORSYTH.—BOOK OF DESIGNS FOR HEAD-STONES, MURAL, AND OTHER MONUMENTS:

Containing 78 Elaborate and Exquisite Designs. By FORSYTH. 4to., cloth $5 00

*** This volume, for the beauty and variety of its designs, has never been surpassed by any publication of the kind, and should be in the hands of every marble-worker who does fine monumental work.

FAIRBAIRN.—THE PRINCIPLES OF MECHANISM AND MACHINERY OF TRANSMISSION:

Comprising the Principles of Mechanism, Wheels, and Pulleys, Strength and Proportions of Shafts, Couplings of Shafts, and Engaging and Disengaging Gear. By WILLIAM FAIRBAIRN, Esq., C. E., LL. D , F. R. S., F. G. S., Corresponding Member of the National Institute of France, and of the Royal Academy of Turin; Chevalier of the Legion of Honor, etc. etc. Beautifully illustrated by over 150 wood-cuts. In one volume 12mo. $2 50

FAIRBAIRN.—PRIME-MOVERS:

Comprising the Accumulation of Water-power: the Construction of Water-wheels and Turbines; the Properties of Steam; the Varieties of Steam-engines and Boilers and Wind-mills. By WILLIAM FAIRBAIRN, C. E , LL. D., F. R. S., F. G. S. Author of "Principles of Mechanism and the Machinery of Transmission." With Numerous Illustrations. In one volume. (In press.)

GILBART.—A PRACTICAL TREATISE ON BANKING:

By JAMES WILLIAM GILBART. To which is added: THE NATIONAL BANK ACT AS NOW IN FORCE. 8vo. . . $4 50

GESNER.—A PRACTICAL TREATISE ON COAL, PETROLEUM, AND OTHER DISTILLED OILS.

By ABRAHAM GESNER, M. D., F. G. S. Second edition, revised and enlarged. By GEORGE WELTDEN GESNER, Consulting Chemist and Engineer. Illustrated. 8vo. . . $3 50

GOTHIC ALBUM FOR CABINET MAKERS:

Comprising a Collection of Designs for Gothic Furniture. Illustrated by twenty-three large and beautifully engraved plates. Oblong $3 00

GRANT.—BEET-ROOT SUGAR AND CULTIVATION OF THE BEET:

By E. B. Grant. 12mo. $1 25

GREGORY.—MATHEMATICS FOR PRACTICAL MEN:

Adapted to the Pursuits of Surveyors, Architects, Mechanics, and Civil Engineers. By Olinthus Gregory. 8vo., plates, cloth $3 00

GRISWOLD.—RAILROAD ENGINEER'S POCKET COMPANION.

Comprising Rules for Calculating Deflection Distances and Angles, Tangential Distances and Angles, and all Necessary Tables for Engineers; also the art of Levelling from Preliminary Survey to the Construction of Railroads, intended Expressly for the Young Engineer, together with Numerous Valuable Rules and Examples. By W. Griswold. 12mo., tucks. $1 75

GUETTIER.—METALLIC ALLOYS:

Being a Practical Guide to their Chemical and Physical Properties, their Preparation, Composition, and Uses. Translated from the French of A. Guettier, Engineer and Director of Founderies, author of "La Fonderie en France," etc. etc. By A. A. Fesquet, Chemist and Engineer. In one volume, 12mo. $3 00

HATS AND FELTING:

A Practical Treatise on their Manufacture. By a Practical Hatter. Illustrated by Drawings of Machinery, &c., 8vo. $1 25

HAY.—THE INTERIOR DECORATOR:

The Laws of Harmonious Coloring adapted to Interior Decorations: with a Practical Treatise on House-Painting. By D. R. Hay, House-Painter and Decorator. Illustrated by a Diagram of the Primary, Secondary, and Tertiary Colors. 12mo. $2 25

HUGHES.—AMERICAN MILLER AND MILLWRIGHT'S ASSISTANT:

By Wm. Carter Hughes. A new edition. In one volume, 12mo. $1 50

HUNT.—THE PRACTICE OF PHOTOGRAPHY.

By ROBERT HUNT, Vice-President of the Photographic Society, London. With numerous illustrations. 12mo., cloth .   75

HURST.—A HAND-BOOK FOR ARCHITECTURAL SURVEYORS:

Comprising Formulæ useful in Designing Builders' work, Table of Weights, of the materials used in Building, Memoranda connected with Builders' work, Mensuration, the Practice of Builders' Measurement, Contracts of Labor, Valuation of Property, Summary of the Practice in Dilapidation, etc. etc. By J. F. HURST, C. E. 2d edition, pocket-book form, full bound
$2 50

JERVIS.—RAILWAY PROPERTY:

A Treatise on the Construction and Management of Railways; designed to afford useful knowledge, in the popular style, to the holders of this class of property; as well as Railway Managers, Officers, and Agents. By JOHN B. JERVIS, late Chief Engineer of the Hudson River Railroad, Croton Aqueduct, &c. One vol. 12mo., cloth $2 00

JOHNSON.—A REPORT TO THE NAVY DEPARTMENT OF THE UNITED STATES ON AMERICAN COALS:

Applicable to Steam Navigation and to other purposes. By WALTER R. JOHNSON. With numerous illustrations. 607 pp. 8vo., ... $10 00

JOHNSTON.—INSTRUCTIONS FOR THE ANALYSIS OF SOILS, LIMESTONES, AND MANURES

By J. W. F. JOHNSTON. 12mo.   35

KEENE.—A HAND-BOOK OF PRACTICAL GAUGING,

For the Use of Beginners, to which is added a Chapter on Distillation, describing the process in operation at the Custom House for ascertaining the strength of wines. By JAMES B. KEENE, of H. M. Customs. 8vo.   .   .   . $1 25

KENTISH.—A TREATISE ON A BOX OF INSTRUMENTS,

And the Slide Rule; with the Theory of Trigonometry and Logarithms, including Practical Geometry, Surveying, Measuring of Timber, Cask and Malt Gauging, Heights, and Distances. By THOMAS KENTISH. In one volume. 12mo. . . $1 25

KOBELL.—ERNI.—MINERALOGY SIMPLIFIED:

A short method of Determining and Classifying Minerals, by means of simple Chemical Experiments in the Wet Way. Translated from the last German Edition of F. VON KOBELL, with an Introduction to Blowpipe Analysis and other additions. By HENRI ERNI, M. D., Chief Chemist, Department of Agriculture, author of "Coal Oil and Petroleum." In one volume. 12mo. $2 50

LANDRIN.—A TREATISE ON STEEL:

Comprising its Theory, Metallurgy, Properties, Practical Working, and Use. By M. H. C. LANDRIN, Jr., Civil Engineer. Translated from the French, with Notes, by A. A. FESQUET, Chemist and Engineer. With an Appendix on the Bessemer and the Martin Processes for Manufacturing Steel, from the Report of ABRAM S. HEWITT, United States Commissioner to the Universal Exposition, Paris, 1867. 12mo. . . . $3 00

LARKIN.—THE PRACTICAL BRASS AND IRON FOUNDER'S GUIDE.

A Concise Treatise on Brass Founding, Moulding, the Metals and their Alloys, etc.; to which are added Recent Improvements in the Manufacture of Iron, Steel by the Bessemer Process, etc. etc. By JAMES LARKIN, late Conductor of the Brass Foundry Department in Reany, Neafie & Co.'s Penn Works, Philadelphia. Fifth edition, revised, with extensive Additions. In one volume. 12mo. $2 25

LEAVITT.—FACTS ABOUT PEAT AS AN ARTICLE OF FUEL:
With Remarks upon its Origin and Composition, the Localities in which it is found, the Methods of Preparation and Manufacture, and the various Uses to which it is applicable; together with many other matters of Practical and Scientific Interest. To which is added a chapter on the Utilization of Coal Dust with Peat for the Production of an Excellent Fuel at Moderate Cost, especially adapted for Steam Service. By H. T. LEAVITT. Third edition. 12mo. . . . $1 75

LEROUX—A PRACTICAL TREATISE ON THE MANUFACTURE OF WORSTEDS AND CARDED YARNS:
Translated from the French of CHARLES LEROUX, Mechanical Engineer, and Superintendent of a Spinning Mill. By Dr H. PAINE, and A. A. FESQUET. Illustrated by 12 large plates. In one volume 8vo. $5 00

LESLIE (MISS).—COMPLETE COOKERY:
Directions for Cookery in its Various Branches. By Miss LESLIE. 60th edition. Thoroughly revised, with the addition of New Receipts. In 1 vol. 12mo., cloth . . $1 50

LESLIE (MISS). LADIES' HOUSE BOOK:
a Manual of Domestic Economy. 20th revised edition. 12mo., cloth $1 25

LESLIE (MISS).—TWO HUNDRED RECEIPTS IN FRENCH COOKERY.
12mo. 50

LIEBER.—ASSAYER'S GUIDE:
Or, Practical Directions to Assayers, Miners, and Smelters, for the Tests and Assays, by Heat and by Wet Processes, for the Ores of all the principal Metals, of Gold and Silver Coins and Alloys, and of Coal, etc. By OSCAR M. LIEBER. 12mo., cloth
$1 25

LOVE.—THE ART OF DYEING, CLEANING, SCOURING, AND FINISHING:
On the most approved English and French methods; being Practical Instructions in Dyeing Silks, Woollens, and Cottons, Feathers, Chips, Straw, etc.; Scouring and Cleaning Bed and Window Curtains, Carpets, Rugs, etc.; French and English Cleaning, etc. By THOMAS LOVE. Second American Edition, to which are added General Instructions for the Use of Aniline Colors. 8vo. 5 00

MAIN AND BROWN.—QUESTIONS ON SUBJECTS CONNECTED WITH THE MARINE STEAM-ENGINE:
And Examination Papers; with Hints for their Solution. By THOMAS J. MAIN, Professor of Mathematics, Royal Naval College, and THOMAS BROWN, Chief Engineer, R. N. 12mo., cloth $1 50

MAIN AND BROWN.—THE INDICATOR AND DYNAMOMETER:
With their Practical Applications to the Steam-Engine. By THOMAS J. MAIN, M. A. F. R., Ass't Prof. Royal Naval College, Portsmouth, and THOMAS BROWN, Assoc. Inst. C. E., Chief Engineer, R. N., attached to the R. N. College. Illustrated. From the Fourth London Edition. 8vo. $1 50

MAIN AND BROWN.—THE MARINE STEAM-ENGINE.
By THOMAS J. MAIN, F. R. Ass't S. Mathematical Professor at Royal Naval College, and THOMAS BROWN, Assoc. Inst. C. E. Chief Engineer, R. N. Attached to the Royal Naval College. Authors of "Questions Connected with the Marine Steam-Engine," and the "Indicator and Dynamometer." With numerous Illustrations. In one volume 8vo. $5 00

MARTIN.—SCREW-CUTTING TABLES, FOR THE USE OF MECHANICAL ENGINEERS:
Showing the Proper Arrangement of Wheels for Cutting the Threads of Screws of any required Pitch; with a Table for Making the Universal Gas-Pipe Thread and Taps. By W. A. MARTIN, Engineer. 8vo. 50

MILES—A PLAIN TREATISE ON HORSE-SHOEING.
With Illustrations. By WILLIAM MILES, author of "The Horse's Foot"

MOLESWORTH.—POCKET-BOOK OF USEFUL FORMULÆ AND MEMORANDA FOR CIVIL AND MECHANICAL ENGINEERS.
By GUILFORD L. MOLESWORTH, Member of the Institution of Civil Engineers, Chief Resident Engineer of the Ceylon Railway. Second American from the Tenth London Edition. In one volume, full bound in pocket-book form $2 00

MOORE.—THE INVENTOR'S GUIDE:
Patent Office and Patent Laws: or, a Guide to Inventors, and a Book of Reference for Judges, Lawyers, Magistrates, and others. By J G. MOORE. 12mo., cloth $1 25

NAPIER.—A MANUAL OF ELECTRO-METALLURGY:
Including the Application of the Art to Manufacturing Processes. By JAMES NAPIER. Fourth American, from the Fourth London edition, revised and enlarged. Illustrated by engravings. In one volume, 8vo. $2 00

NAPIER.—A SYSTEM OF CHEMISTRY APPLIED TO DYEING:
By JAMES NAPIER, F. C. S. A New and Thoroughly Revised
Edition, completely brought up to the present state of the
Science, including the Chemistry of Coal Tar Colors. By A. A.
FESQUET, Chemist and Engineer. With an Appendix on Dyeing
and Calico Printing, as shown at the Paris Universal Exposition
of 1867, from the Reports of the International Jury, etc. Illus-
trated. In one volume 8vo., 400 pages $5 00

**NEWBERY.— GLEANINGS FROM ORNAMENTAL ART OF
EVERY STYLE;**
Drawn from Examples in the British, South Kensington, Indian,
Crystal Palace, and other Museums, the Exhibitions of 1851 and
1862, and the best English and Foreign works. In a series of one
hundred exquisitely drawn Plates, containing many hundred examples. By ROBERT NEWBERY. 4to. $15 00

NICHOLSON.—A MANUAL OF THE ART OF BOOK-BINDING:
Containing full instructions in the different Branches of Forward-
ing, Gilding, and Finishing. Also, the Art of Marbling Book-
edges and Paper. By JAMES B. NICHOLSON. Illustrated. 12mo.
cloth $2 25

**NORRIS.—A HAND-BOOK FOR LOCOMOTIVE ENGINEERS AND
MACHINISTS:**
Comprising the Proportions and Calculations for Constructing
Locomotives; Manner of Setting Valves; Tables of Squares,
Cubes, Areas, etc. etc. By SEPTIMUS NORRIS, Civil and Me-
chanical Engineer. New edition. Illustrated, 12mo., cloth
$2 00

**NYSTROM.— ON TECHNOLOGICAL EDUCATION AND THE
CONSTRUCTION OF SHIPS AND SCREW PROPELLERS:**
For Naval and Marine Engineers. By JOHN W. NYSTROM, late
Acting Chief Engineer U. S. N. Second edition, revised with
additional matter. Illustrated by seven engravings. 12mo.
$2 50

**O'NEILL.—A DICTIONARY OF DYEING AND CALICO PRINT-
ING:**
Containing a brief account of all the Substances and Processes in
use in the Art of Dyeing and Printing Textile Fabrics: with Prac-
tical Receipts and Scientific Information. By CHARLES O'NEILL,
Analytical Chemist; Fellow of the Chemical Society of London;
Member of the Literary and Philosophical Society of Manchester;
Author of "Chemistry of Calico Printing and Dyeing." To which
is added An Essay on Coal Tar Colors and their Application to

Dyeing and Calico Printing. By A. A. FESQUET, Chemist and Engineer. With an Appendix on Dyeing and Calico Printing, as shown at the Exposition of 1867, from the Reports of the International Jury, etc. In one volume 8vo., 491 pages . . $6 00

OSBORN.—THE METALLURGY OF IRON AND STEEL:
Theoretical and Practical : In all its Branches ; With Special Reference to American Materials and Processes. By H. S. OSBORN, LL. D., Professor of Mining and Metallurgy in Lafayette College, Easton, Pa. Illustrated by 230 Engravings on Wood, and 6 Folding Plates. 8vo., 972 pages $10 00

OSBORN.—AMERICAN MINES AND MINING :
Theoretically and Practically Considered. By Prof. H. S. OSBORN, Illustrated by numerous engravings. 8vo. (*In preparation.*)

PAINTER, GILDER, AND VARNISHER'S COMPANION :
Containing Rules and Regulations in everything relating to the Arts of Painting, Gilding, Varnishing, and Glass Staining, with numerous useful and valuable Receipts; Tests for the Detection of Adulterations in Oils and Colors, and a statement of the Diseases and Accidents to which Painters, Gilders, and Varnishers are particularly liable, with the simplest methods of Prevention and Remedy. With Directions for Graining, Marbling, Sign Writing, and Gilding on Glass. To which are added COMPLETE INSTRUCTIONS FOR COACH PAINTING AND VARNISHING. 12mo., cloth, $1 50

PALLETT.—THE MILLER'S, MILLWRIGHT'S, AND ENGINEER'S GUIDE.
By HENRY PALLETT. Illustrated. In one vol. 12mo. . $3 00

PERKINS.—GAS AND VENTILATION.
Practical Treatise on Gas and Ventilation. With Special Relation to Illuminating, Heating, and Cooking by Gas. Including Scientific Helps to Engineer-students and others. With illustrated Diagrams. By E. E. PERKINS. 12mo., cloth . . . $1 25

PERKINS AND STOWE.—A NEW GUIDE TO THE SHEET-IRON AND BOILER PLATE ROLLER :
Containing a Series of Tables showing the Weight of Slabs and Piles to Produce Boiler Plates, and of the Weight of Piles and the Sizes of Bars to Produce Sheet-iron; the Thickness of the Bar Gauge in Decimals; the Weight per foot, and the Thickness on the Bar or Wire Gauge of the fractional parts of an inch; the Weight per sheet, and the Thickness on the Wire Gauge of Sheet-iron of various dimensions to weigh 112 lbs. per bundle; and the conversion of Short Weight into Long Weight, and Long Weight into Short. Estimated and collected by G. H. PERKINS and J. G. STOWE $2 50

PHILLIPS AND DARLINGTON.—RECORDS OF MINING AND METALLURGY:

Or, Facts and Memoranda for the use of the Mine Agent and Smelter. By J. Arthur Phillips, Mining Engineer, Graduate of the Imperial School of Mines, France, etc., and John Darlington. Illustrated by numerous engravings. In one vol. 12mo. . $2 00

PRADAL, MALEPEYRE, AND DUSSAUCE.—A COMPLETE TREATISE ON PERFUMERY:

Containing notices of the Raw Material used in the Art, and the Best Formulæ. According to the most approved Methods followed in France, England, and the United States. By M. P. Pradal, Perfumer-Chemist, and M. F. Malepeyre. Translated from the French, with extensive additions, by Prof. H. Dussauce. 8vo. $10

PROTEAUX.—PRACTICAL GUIDE FOR THE MANUFACTURE OF PAPER AND BOARDS.

By A. Proteaux, Civil Engineer, and Graduate of the School of Arts and Manufactures, Director of Thiers's Paper Mill, 'Puy-de-Dôme. With additions, by L. S. Le Normand. Translated from the French, with Notes, by Horatio Paine, A. B., M. D. To which is added a Chapter on the Manufacture of Paper from Wood in the United States, by Henry T. Brown, of the "American Artisan." Illustrated by six plates, containing Drawings of Raw Materials, Machinery, Plans of Paper-Mills, etc. etc. 8vo. $5 00

REGNAULT.—ELEMENTS OF CHEMISTRY.

By M. V. Regnault. Translated from the French by T. Forrest Benton, M. B., and edited, with notes, by James C. Booth, Melter and Refiner U. S. Mint, and Wm. L. Faber, Metallurgist and Mining Engineer. Illustrated by nearly 700 wood engravings. Comprising nearly 1500 pages. In two vols. 8vo., cloth $10 00

REID.—A PRACTICAL TREATISE ON THE MANUFACTURE OF PORTLAND CEMENT:

By Henry Reid, C. E. To which is added a Translation of M. A. Lipowitz's Work, describing a new method adopted in Germany of Manufacturing that Cement. By W. F. Reid. Illustrated by plates and wood engravings. 8vo. $7 00

RIFFAULT, VERGNAUD, AND TOUSSAINT.—A PRACTICAL TREATISE ON THE MANUFACTURE OF COLORS FOR PAINTING:

Containing the best Formulæ and the Processes the Newest and in most General Use. By MM. Riffault, Vergnaud, and Toussaint. Revised and Edited by M. F. Malepeyre and Dr. Emil Winckler. Illustrated by Engravings. In one vol. 8vo. (*In preparation.*)

RIFFAULT, VERGNAUD, AND TOUSSAINT.—A PRACTICAL
TREATISE ON THE MANUFACTURE OF VARNISHES:
By MM. RIFFAULT, VERGNAUD, and TOUSSAINT. Revised and
Edited by M. F. MALEPEYRE and Dr. EMIL WINCKLER. Illus-
trated. In one vol. 8vo. (*In preparation.*)

SHUNK.—A PRACTICAL TREATISE ON RAILWAY CURVES
AND LOCATION, FOR YOUNG ENGINEERS.
By WM. F. SHUNK, Civil Engineer. 12mo., tucks . . $2 00

SMEATON.—BUILDER'S POCKET COMPANION:
Containing the Elements of Building, Surveying, and Architecture ; with Practical Rules and Instructions connected with the subject. By A. C. SMEATON, Civil Engineer, etc. In one volume,
12mo. $1 50

SMITH.—THE DYER'S INSTRUCTOR:
Comprising Practical Instructions in the Art of Dyeing Silk, Cotton, Wool, and Worsted, and Woollen Goods : containing nearly
800 Receipts. To which is added a Treatise on the Art of Padding ; and the Printing of Silk Warps, Skeins, and Handkerchiefs,
and the various Mordants and Colors for the different styles of
such work. By DAVID SMITH, Pattern Dyer, 12mo., cloth
$3 00

SMITH.—THE PRACTICAL DYER'S GUIDE:
Comprising Practical Instructions in the Dyeing of Shot Cobourgs,
Silk Striped Orleans, Colored Orleans from Black Warps, ditto
from White Warps, Colored Cobourgs from White Warps, Merinos,
Yarns, Woollen Cloths, etc. Containing nearly 300 Receipts, to
most of which a Dyed Pattern is annexed. Also, a Treatise on
the Art of Padding. By DAVID SMITH. In one vol. 8vo. $25 00

SHAW.—CIVIL ARCHITECTURE:
Being a Complete Theoretical and Practical System of Building,
containing the Fundamental Principles of the Art. By EDWARD
SHAW, Architect. To which is added a Treatise on Gothic Architecture, &c. By THOMAS W. SILLOWAY and GEORGE M. HARD-
ING, Architects. The whole illustrated by 102 quarto plates finely
engraved on copper. Eleventh Edition. 4to. Cloth. $10 00

SLOAN.—AMERICAN HOUSES:
A variety of Original Designs for Rural Buildings. Illustrated by
26 colored Engravings, with Descriptive References. By SAMUEL
SLOAN, Architect, author of the " Model Architect," etc. etc. 8vo.
$2 50

SCHINZ.—RESEARCHES ON THE ACTION OF THE BLAST-
FURNACE.
By CHAS. SCHINZ. Seven plates. 12mo. . . . $4 25

SMITH.—PARKS AND PLEASURE GROUNDS:

Or, Practical Notes on Country Residences, Villas, Public Parks, and Gardens. By CHARLES H. J. SMITH, Landscape Gardener and Garden Architect, etc. etc. 12mo. $2 25

STOKES.—CABINET-MAKER'S AND UPHOLSTERER'S COMPANION:

Comprising the Rudiments and Principles of Cabinet-making and Upholstery, with Familiar Instructions, Illustrated by Examples for attaining a Proficiency in the Art of Drawing, as applicable to Cabinet-work; The Processes of Veneering, Inlaying, and Buhl-work; the Art of Dyeing and Staining Wood, Bone, Tortoise Shell, etc. Directions for Lackering, Japanning, and Varnishing; to make French Polish; to prepare the Best Glues, Cements, and Compositions, and a number of Receipts, particularly for workmen generally. By J. STOKES. In one vol. 12mo. With illustrations
$1 25

STRENGTH AND OTHER PROPERTIES OF METALS.

Reports of Experiments on the Strength and other Properties of Metals for Cannon. With a Description of the Machines for Testing Metals, and of the Classification of Cannon in service. By Officers of the Ordnance Department U. S. Army. By authority of the Secretary of War. Illustrated by 25 large steel plates. In 1 vol. quarto $10 00

SULLIVAN.—PROTECTION TO NATIVE INDUSTRY.

By Sir EDWARD SULLIVAN, Baronet. (1870.) 8vo.   . $1 50

TABLES SHOWING THE WEIGHT OF ROUND, SQUARE, AND FLAT BAR IRON, STEEL, ETC.

By Measurement. Cloth   63

TAYLOR.—STATISTICS OF COAL:

Including Mineral Bituminous Substances employed in Arts and Manufactures; with their Geographical, Geological, and Commercial Distribution and amount of Production and Consumption on the American Continent. With Incidental Statistics of the Iron Manufacture. By R. C. TAYLOR. Second edition, revised by S. S. HALDEMAN. Illustrated by five Maps and many wood engravings. 8vo., cloth $6 00

TEMPLETON.—THE PRACTICAL EXAMINATOR ON STEAM AND THE STEAM-ENGINE:

With Instructive References relative thereto, for the Use of Engineers, Students, and others. By WM. TEMPLETON, Engineer 12mo.
$1 25

THOMAS.—THE MODERN PRACTICE OF PHOTOGRAPHY.
By R. W. Thomas, F. C. S. 8vo., cloth   75

THOMSON.—FREIGHT CHARGES CALCULATOR.
By Andrew Thomson, Freight Agent $1 25

TURNING: SPECIMENS OF FANCY TURNING EXECUTED ON THE HAND OR FOOT LATHE:
With Geometric, Oval, and Eccentric Chucks, and Elliptical Cutting Frame. By an Amateur. Illustrated by 30 exquisite Photographs. 4to. $3 00

TURNER'S (THE) COMPANION:
Containing Instructions in Concentric, Elliptic, and Eccentric Turning; also various Plates of Chucks, Tools, and Instruments; and Directions for using the Eccentric Cutter, Drill, Vertical Cutter, and Circular Rest; with Patterns and Instructions for working them. A new edition in 1 vol. 12mo. $1 50

URBIN—BRULL.—A PRACTICAL GUIDE FOR PUDDLING IRON AND STEEL.
By Ed. Urbin, Engineer of Arts and Manufactures. A Prize Essay read before the Association of Engineers, Graduate of the School of Mines, of Liege, Belgium, at the Meeting of 1865-6. To which is added a Comparison of the Resisting Properties of Iron and Steel. By A. Brull. Translated from the French by A. A. Fesquet, Chemist and Engineer. In one volume, 8vo.
$1 00

VOGDES.—THE ARCHITECT'S AND BUILDER'S POCKET COMPANION AND PRICE BOOK.
By F. W. Vogdes, Architect. Illustrated. Full bound in pocketbook form. $2 00
In book form, 18mo., muslin 1 50

WARN.—THE SHEET METAL WORKER'S INSTRUCTOR, FOR ZINC, SHEET-IRON, COPPER AND TIN PLATE WORKERS, &c.
By Reuben Henry Warn, Practical Tin Plate Worker. Illustrated by 32 plates and 37 wood engravings. 8vo. . . $3 00

WATSON.—A MANUAL OF THE HAND-LATHE.
By Egbert P. Watson, Late of the "Scientific American," Author of "Modern Practice of American Machinists and Engineers," In one volume, 12mo. $1 50

WATSON.—THE MODERN PRACTICE OF AMERICAN MA-CHINISTS AND ENGINEERS:

Including the Construction, Application, and Use of Drills, Lathe Tools, Cutters for Boring Cylinders, and Hollow Work Generally, with the most Economical Speed of the same, the Results verified by Actual Practice at the Lathe, the Vice, and on the Floor. Together with Workshop management, Economy of Manufacture, the Steam-Engine, Boilers, Gears, Belting, etc. etc. By EGBERT P. WATSON, late of the "Scientific American." Illustrated by eighty-six engravings. 12mo. $2 50

WATSON.—THE THEORY AND PRACTICE OF THE ART OF WEAVING BY HAND AND POWER:

With Calculations and Tables for the use of those connected with the Trade. By JOHN WATSON, Manufacturer and Practical Machine Maker. Illustrated by large drawings of the best Power-Looms. 8vo. $10 00

WEATHERLY.—TREATISE ON THE ART OF BOILING SU-GAR, CRYSTALLIZING, LOZENGE-MAKING, COMFITS, GUM GOODS,

And other processes for Confectionery, &c. In which are explained, in an easy and familiar manner, the various Methods of Manufacturing every description of Raw and Refined Sugar Goods, as sold by Confectioners and others . . . $2 00

WILL.—TABLES FOR QUALITATIVE CHEMICAL ANALYSIS.

By Prof. HEINRICH WILL, of Giessen, Germany. Seventh edition. Translated by CHARLES F. HIMES, Ph. D., Professor of Natural Science, Dickinson College, Carlisle, Pa. . . $1 25

WILLIAMS.—ON HEAT AND STEAM:

Embracing New Views of Vaporization, Condensation, and Expansion. By CHARLES WYE WILLIAMS, A. I. C. E. Illustrated. 8vo.
$3 50

WORSSAM.—ON MECHANICAL SAWS:

From the Transactions of the Society of Engineers, 1867. By S. W. WORSSAM, Jr. Illustrated by 18 large folding plates. 8vo.
$5 00

WÖHLER.—A HAND-BOOK OF MINERAL ANALYSIS.

By F. WÖHLER. Edited by H. B. NASON, Professor of Chemistry, Rensselaer Institute, Troy, N. Y. With numerous Illustrations. 12mo. $3 00